Leaves from a prison diary, or, Lectures to a "solitary" audience. Volume 2 of 2

Michael Davitt

The Making of Modern Law collection of legal archives constitutes a genuine revolution in historical legal research because it opens up a wealth of rare and previously inaccessible sources in legal, constitutional, administrative, political, cultural, intellectual, and social history. This unique collection consists of three extensive archives that provide insight into more than 300 years of American and British history. These collections include:

Legal Treatises, 1800-1926: over 20,000 legal treatises provide a comprehensive collection in legal history, business and economics, politics and government.

Trials, 1600-1926: nearly 10,000 titles reveal the drama of famous, infamous, and obscure courtroom cases in America and the British Empire across three centuries.

Primary Sources, 1620-1926: includes reports, statutes and regulations in American history, including early state codes, municipal ordinances, constitutional conventions and compilations, and law dictionaries.

These archives provide a unique research tool for tracking the development of our modern legal system and how it has affected our culture, government, business – nearly every aspect of our everyday life. For the first time, these high-quality digital scans of original works are available via print-on-demand, making them readily accessible to libraries, students, independent scholars, and readers of all ages.

The BiblioLife Network

This project was made possible in part by the BiblioLife Network (BLN), a project aimed at addressing some of the huge challenges facing book preservationists around the world. The BLN includes libraries, library networks, archives, subject matter experts, online communities and library service providers. We believe every book ever published should be available as a high-quality print reproduction; printed on-demand anywhere in the world. This insures the ongoing accessibility of the content and helps generate sustainable revenue for the libraries and organizations that work to preserve these important materials.

The following book is in the "public domain" and represents an authentic reproduction of the text as printed by the original publisher. While we have attempted to accurately maintain the integrity of the original work, there are sometimes problems with the original work or the micro-film from which the books were digitized. This can result in minor errors in reproduction. Possible imperfections include missing and blurred pages, poor pictures, markings and other reproduction issues beyond our control. Because this work is culturally important, we have made it available as part of our commitment to protecting, preserving, and promoting the world's literature.

GUIDE TO FOLD-OUTS MAPS and OVERSIZED IMAGES

The book you are reading was digitized from microfilm captured over the past thirty to forty years. Years after the creation of the original microfilm, the book was converted to digital files and made available in an online database.

In an online database, page images do not need to conform to the size restrictions found in a printed book. When converting these images back into a printed bound book, the page sizes are standardized in ways that maintain the detail of the original. For large images, such as fold-out maps, the original page image is split into two or more pages

Guidelines used to determine how to split the page image follows:

• Some images are split vertically; large images require vertical and horizontal splits.
• For horizontal splits, the content is split left to right.
• For vertical splits, the content is split from top to bottom.
• For both vertical and horizontal splits, the image is processed from top left to bottom right.

LEAVES FROM A PRISON DIARY;

OR,

LECTURES TO A "SOLITARY" AUDIENCE.

LEAVES

FROM

PRISON DIARY.

Or, Lectures to a "Solitary" Audience

BY

MICHAEL DAVITT,

FOUNDER OF THE LAND LEAGUE.

IN TWO VOLUMES.

VOLUME II.

LONDON. CHAPMAN AND HALL,

LIMITED

1885.

LONDON·
R. CLAY SONS, AND TAYLOR,
BREAD STREET HILL.

CONTENTS.

PART II. (*continued*).

SOCIAL EVILS AND SUGGESTED REMEDIES.

LECTURE XXII

EDUCATION AS A PREVENTIVE OF CRIME

LECTURE XXV

CAUSE OF POVERTY.

LECTURE XXVI.

REMEDIAL PROPOSALS.

LECTURE XXVII

RIVAL REMEDIAL PROPOSALS.

LECTURE XXVIII

THE ORGANIZATION OF LABOUR.

LECTURE XXIX.

STATE SOCIALISM.

LECTURE XXX

STATE OWNERSHIP OF RAILWAYS.

LECTURE XXXI

GOVERNMENT BY PRIVILEGE AND WEALTH.

LECTURE XXXII

POLITICAL CRIME

LECTURE XXXIII

POLITICAL CRIME (CONTINUED)

LECTURE XXXIV.

POLITICAL JUSTICE: HOW THE ANGLO IRISH PROBLEM COULD BE SOLVED.

LEAVES FROM A PRISON DIARY;

or,

Lectures to a "Solitary" Audience.

LECTURE XXII.

EDUCATION AS A PREVENTIVE OF CRIME.

Imaginary Flight from Prison—A Scene *en route*—Confines of London—Crime Germination—Children in Slums and Workhouses—The Remedy—Reformatory Institutions—Combination of the Kindergarten, Elementary Schools, and Manual Instruction—Their Management—The Class of Children to be Rescued—Evidence of the Efficacy of the Kindergarten—An Appalling Fact—Twelve Hundred Paupers, Vagabonds, and Criminals traced for origin to the Children of one Abandoned Woman—The Shelter Schools of France—The Higher Work of Reformatory Institutions.

FIGURATIVELY speaking, we are now about to quit this our involuntary "hermitage." In fancy, we shall breathe the air of liberty and commingle with the busy outside world, as if stone walls did not a prison make, for me, nor iron bars a cage, for you. As yet, you are a complete stranger to civilised life beyond

this cell, excepting what little has been revealed of it
in the course of our previous lectures. The scenes
which we shall witness in our imaginary excursion, will
not therefore have that interest for you which they
will possess for me.

In our flight of fancy towards the confines of the
nearest large city, we shall pass many objects, animate
and inanimate, which would point the moral for our
lectures; but we shall leave them for a more close
observation later on.

But stay, for a moment! Do you see that field in
which men and women are bent down working? This
is Dorsetshire. These labourers are but earning a few
shillings a week for the maintenance of themselves and
families. Yonder wretched-looking huts, which you
see disfiguring the landscape, are their homes. Comfort
or cleanliness within there is little or none. They are
the residences of human beings but little removed from
the condition of chattel slavery—men who plod on from
year to year in sluggish misery, seemingly indifferent to
those causes which tie them down to this animal-like
existence——

"Do they own this land?"

Bless you, no. They are the wage servants of the
farmers, who are the rent-payers to the landlord, who
is the monopolist of this portion of the soil of England.

"Does *he* work?"

Why, yes—in a way. He collects, or causes to be collected, the rent once or twice a year; he hunts, shoots, and fishes over these lands, and, as Justice of the Peace for this locality, he occasionally sends some of these workers whom you see in the fields to the county prison for daring to catch a hare for a Sunday dinner, or lift a trout from that running stream at our feet. He probably goes to Parliament, also, to represent the interests of his class and to defend and perpetuate those laws which enable him and his like to make others do all the work while he and his kind do all the enjoyment of life. Away in that stately residence, whose turrets you see peeping above the trees of that distant demesne, you perceive his country seat, or the place where he spends a few weeks each year when tired of city pleasures

Look upon that picture and then upon these huts and those toilers in the fields, and say whether the workers and the idler should not, in justice, change residences?

But I am delaying our journey to the nearest large city. Here we are at last! You perceive that we have exchanged the bracing air, the varied landscape and the calm repose of country life, for the smoky atmosphere, the lines of narrow streets and the noise and jostle of this crowded place. Poverty associated with green fields and fragrant hawthorn is bad enough, in all truth; but when cooped up in those small and ill-ventilated tenements, which you see rising up on each side of these narrow, dirty slums around us, it is truly a condition of social wretchedness which may well cause you to wonder why life is worth living to the creatures whom you see prowling about.

Look at that group of little children, making mud pies in yonder gutter! You can easily picture what their training will be from the character of these surroundings. This morning, some of them were probably hawked round the outskirts of the city on the arms of professional beggars, for the purpose of exciting the charity of benevolent people. A similar plan will be put into operation to-night, among the drink-shops. If the parents of the children do not themselves resort to this practice, they lend their offspring to other vagabonds who will pay them interest on those human loans out of the alms that will be gathered by their aid.

What will the future of these children be? What can it be but the life of sin and wretchedness which begets those strange beings whose crimes and characters we have been portraying in our previous discourses? They are the criminal seedlings for the next generation of thieves and desperadoes who will people the convict prisons of England.

Let us visit another nursery of poverty and depravity.

You see that long, prison-like building, away to the left? That is the workhouse. A workhouse is an institution of licensed idleness for broken-down drunkards and "ne'er-do-weels," and a prison for such honest poverty as will not starve or steal in the midst of abundant but unjustly distributed wealth. It is the symbol of the Community's obligation towards providing its destitute members with that sustenance which will prevent the crime of starvation. It is a just and Christian idea; but like many more beneficent ideas in our social economy, it is vitiated in the application.

There are two classes of inmates here. One is an idle and immoral class, which occupies a mid position between known criminals and the labouring masses in the economy of society; the other comprises the aged, the wrecked, and the unfortunate belonging to the working orders. Both classes are placed on a footing of equality—they are all paupers. The professional loafer is as well-fed and cared for as the aged or over-worked artisan or labourer. This is not as it ought to be. The man who by years of industry in his native land, no matter how humble the occupation at which he has been employed, has contributed alike to the wealth of the nation and the riches of landlord or capitalist employer, is justly entitled in his old age to be taken care of by the State, without the association

of quasi-criminals or the stigma of degrading pauperism.
He it is who should really be the pensioner of the
nation, at least to the extent of being maintained
respectably when he is incapacitated by age or infirmity
from providing for himself.

As for the other class, they should be dealt with in
the way John Ruskin prescribes·

" Since for every idle person some one else must be
working somewhere to provide him with food and
clothes, and doing, therefore, double the quantity of
work that would be enough for his own needs, it is only
a matter of pure justice to compel the idle person to
work for his maintenance himself. The conscription
has been used in many countries, to take away labourers
who supported their families from their useful work,
and maintain them for purposes chiefly of military
display at the public expense Since this has been
long endured by the most civilized nations, let it not be
thought that they would not much more gladly endure
a conscription which would seize only the vicious and
idle, already living by criminal procedures at the public
expense; and which should discipline and educate them
to labour which would not only maintain themselves,
but be serviceable to the commonwealth. The question
is simply this: We must feed the drunkard, vagabond,
and thief; but shall we do so by letting them steal their
food, and do no work for it? or shall we give them their

food in appointed quantity, and enforce their doing work which shall be worth it; and which, in process of time, will redeem their own characters, and make them happy and serviceable members of society? Your idle people, as they are now, are not merely waste coal-beds. They are explosive coal-beds, which you pay a high annual rent for. You are keeping all these idle persons, remember, at a far greater cost than if they were busy. Do you think a vicious person eats less than an honest one? or that it is cheaper to keep a bad man drunk than a good man sober?"

But we have come to this place to look after the children. Our object is to point out how the pauper and criminal classes can be reduced in society; and we must, therefore, keep the children, rather than the parents, in view. There are probably two or three hundred children of both sexes inside of this one workhouse. A large portion of these are of criminal parentage and have criminal natures. They should be kept apart from those who are not thus inoculated with criminal propensities; but no such classification is adopted here, and thus we see how crime-breeding is ignorantly fostered at the very stage of life when it is most important, both for the good of 'the child and the welfare of society, to begin the work of reformation. Well, now, it is only natural that I should be asked to submit proposals, such as, in my judgment, would remedy the evils of which I have been speaking ↳ admit the fairness of the demand, and I gladly respond to it. I entertain very emphatic opinions as to what ought to be done with a view, at least, to minimise the evils of the existing social system. Whether or not these opinions are likely to be considered "practical," remains to be seen. I only affirm that they are sincerely held, and that they have been reached after much earnest thought.

I would take the children of both hardened and casual criminals from their parents, and unprotected or neglected children from wherever found, and place them in kindergarten, industrial, or reformatory schools, placing all such institutions directly under State supervision and control, aided by ladies and gentlemen resident within reasonable distance. My acquaintance with institutions of this character is not extensive; but it is sufficient to enable me to bear testimony to the nobleness of private efforts in the direction I speak of. I would have the State avail itself of this laudable devotion to the regeneration of the unfortunate, so unstintingly shown by philanthropic citizens throughout Great Britain and Ireland, and largely extend its opportunity of application. I am satisfied that the State could not make too heavy a demand upon the benevolent energies of sympathetic men and women in a work of this kind;

and I am equally convinced that the demand, however heavy, ought to be made. If we placed such institutions exclusively under the control of officials, we should but aggravate the admitted evil of officialism, pure and simple. But if to the official element we added the voluntary element, we should, in my judgment, obtain a control of the most prudent, and yet earnest and enlightened, character. I am well aware that the combination of which I speak already exists to a considerable extent in regard to many public institutions, but it is capable of much improvement and very wide extension.

In all great centres of population, then, I would establish reformatory institutions which should be a combination of the kindergarten, the elementary, the industrial, and the reformatory schools; the aim of these institutions should be both preventive and curative. Beginning with the children of the criminal population, who as yet are too young to be criminal, I would take them away from their present surroundings, and place them in the kindergarten of a reformatory institution. In the next place, I would take the boys and girls who are just entering upon careers of crime, and place these in the higher departments of the reformatory institutions. To the work of these several departments I will refer later on, after having indicated how I would have them governed. In this matter I would follow the same principle, viz. that of combination. Indeed, I doubt if I have any more brilliant suggestion to make in this connection than this—that I would organise the various agencies for the prevention and cure of crime into one grand national enterprise.

The reformatory institutions—I can at this moment think of no better name—should be, I say, a combination of the methods of government pursued in the institutions whose place they are to take. There should be a Board of Management for each institution, composed of one paid Inspector, ranking with the Chief Inspectors of schools or factories, and appointed by the Home Office, and say twenty or thirty ordinary members of both sexes, nominated by the governing authorities of the towns, cities, or counties interested in any given institution.

The Inspector should be the official member of the Board of Management of perhaps four or five such institutions. His wide experience would be invaluable, and his position would command the respect and consideration of every ordinary member of the Boards with which he would be connected. Let us suppose him the direct representative of the Secretary of State for the Home Department, and then let us suppose the action of every Board liable to revision at the hands of that functionary, and we see at once that the official element would be sufficiently represented on all Boards of Management. The business of such Boards, in connection with any institution under their control, would be purely administrative. The Board would appoint the necessary superintendents and subordinate officers of both sexes, who should be responsible to the Board for the proper carrying out of all duties, regulations, and work of the institutions. It would receive all children committed to its charge, and have them watched over with a tenderer care and a more moral solicitude than would be extended to them if left to breathe the pestilential atmosphere of habitual criminality, or follow in the footsteps of drunken and depraved vagabondage.

What children should be taken into such institutions? and how would you avoid interfering with parental authority in cases where proof of criminal pursuits or evidence of criminal neglect on the part of the parents would not be very clear?

The following conditions, laid down in the Neglected and Criminal Children's Act of the colony of Victoria (Australia), ought, in my opinion, to determine the character of children that should be rescued from crime and vagabondage, and trained in the reformatory institutions:

1. Any child found begging or receiving alms, or being in any street or public place for the purpose of begging or receiving.

2. Any child who shall be found wandering about or frequenting any street, thoroughfare, tavern or place of public resort, or sleeping in the open air, and who shall not have any home or settled place of abode, or any visible means of subsistence.

3 Any child who shall reside in any brothel or associate or dwell with any person known or reputed to be a thief, prostitute or habitual drunkard, or with any person convicted of vagrancy under any Act now or hereafter to be in force.

4. Any child who, having committed an offence punishable by imprisonment, or some less punishment, ought, nevertheless, in the opinion of the Justices, regard being had to his age and the circumstances of his case, to be sent to an industrial school.

5 Any child whose parent represents that he is unable to control such child, and that he wishes him to be sent to an industrial school, and gives security to the satisfaction of the Justices, before whom such child may be brought for payment of the maintenance of such child in such school.

A special department in the police force could be created to seek out such children for removal, and it should be sufficient to secure their committal to a reformatory institution, that a stipendiary magistrate or a Judge should be satisfied that their committal was desirable. About the children of an old offender there need of course be no hesitation. But there is no doubt that some discretion would be required in the case of children under the control of persons who might be well known to the police as habitual criminals. It might be required of such persons that they should satisfy the proper authorities that the children were receiving due care. It is possible that here and there a case would arise of this kind Some man who had been an habitual offender, but had turned from his criminal career, quite unknown to the police, might be liable to be unjustly treated, but such cases would be comparatively rare, and while I would have all care taken to avoid injustice in such cases, I would act rigorously on the general principle that habitual criminals are unfit to have charge of children.

I would begin, then, with the children of such criminals, and I would place them in the kindergarten of a reformatory institution, but for the reasons given at the commencement of this lecture, the children of criminal parents should be kept in a special department of such a school apart from those who are not of such origin. The theory of Froebel's system is, that the exercise of the physical and mental faculties, when that exercise is not accompanied by the appearance of compulsion, is both healthy and enjoyable. The limbs of the body are developed by marching and gymnastic exercise, and such games as children delight in; and all the tastes that depend upon the senses may be culti-vated by drawing, singing, and modelling.

Wherever the kindergarten has had a fair trial,

its beneficial effects have been abundantly manifest.
The little pupils, under this delightful system of training, show a lively enjoyment of the teaching that is
imparted, and a readiness to receive with real pleasure
the knowledge which, under other systems of tuition,
would be distasteful to the child mind.

Mrs Cooper, a benevolent San Francisco lady, read a
paper a short time ago before the Prison Convention of
the Pacific Coast on "The Kindergarten as a Preventive of Crime," and in the course of this able contribution to reformatory literature, mentioned this appalling
fact: "It appears that from a single neglected child in
a wealthy county in New York State, there has come a
notorious stock of criminals, vagabonds, and paupers,
imperilling every dollar's worth of property and every
individual in the community. Not less than 1200
persons have been traced as the lineage of six children
who were born of this one perverted and depraved
woman."

But appalling as this one fact truly is, it is by no
means novel. It is, in short, an inevitable and natural
result of things as they are, and accordingly I agree
with Mrs. Cooper when she says, "We must get hold
of the little waifs, who grow up to form the criminal
element just as early in life as possible. Hunt up the
children of pauperism, of crime, of brutality, just as
soon as they can be reached; the children that flock in

the tenement houses, or the narrow dirty streets, the children who have no one to call them by dear names; children that are buffeted hither and thither, 'flotsam and jetsam on the wild, mad sea of life.' This is the element out of which criminals are made." The unanimous testimony of those who have given any attention to this subject is, that the kindergartens, wherever they have been established, have given abundant proof of their humanising influence. I would have the State hesitate no longer, then, but establish kindergartens as departments of reformatory institutions in all the large centres of population, and snatch the little children from those corrupting influences which breed misery for their future lives, and beget trained enemies to war against society.

Other departments of these reformatory institutions should take up the education of the children at say seven years of age. I would have first an elementary school, next a combination of elementary education and rudimentary technical instruction, and finally a finishing department in which technical instruction should predominate, and in which the "school" should be workshops. Imagine a boy three years of age taken from criminal surroundings and placed in such an institution as I have thus roughly outlined. The first four years of his life he would spend in what has not been inaptly called "the paradise of children"

—the kindergarten. The next four years he would spend in the elementary school The succeeding two years he would be receiving further elementary education combined with rudimentary technical instruction. The last two years he would be occupied in acquiring knowledge of handicrafts. He would then be fifteen years of age, and at that age I would have him make his entry upon the life of a free citizen.

I am well aware that this would be a period of supreme difficulty, but I am convinced that any obstacle that might present itself would be easily surmounted, in the vast majority of instances, if the work of the preceding twelve years should have been attended with even a moderate amount of success I am informed by those who have been for many years intimately associated with the management of industrial schools, that though difficulties occasionally present themselves in finding situations for boys and girls after they have finished their terms at the school, they are no greater than those of the ordinary applicants for labour. Employers of labour are generally found to be willing to take into their employment boys and girls who have gained such knowledge and experience as are imparted to children in industrial schools, and I see no reason to doubt that children brought up in the reformatory institutions of the kind I have indicated would find ample opportunity afforded

them of pursuing an honourable career. If their training had been attended with a fair measure of success,
I am satisfied that the chances of them making
their way in the world and of developing into intelligent
and useful citizens would be vastly superior to what
they are now. Certainly if we would minimize crime
we must reduce to a minimum those who are brought
up in an atmosphere of criminality. Oliver Wendell
Holmes, in his own pungent way, says, that at the first
indication of lying in a child he would have it gently
chloroformed into a better state of existence. I would
begin sooner. I would take it for granted that children
of habitual criminals and children brought up in criminal
surroundings have a tendency to become criminal, and
I would not wait for any manifestations of that tendency.
I would take the children away from their present
associations and purge them of the tendency to crime
through the agency of the reformatory institutions.

It is unnecessary that I should dwell upon the
character of the kindergarten and elementary departments of these institutions. These departments should
resemble kindergartens and elementary schools such
as we are already thoroughly familiar with.

In regard to the former, however, it may not be
out of place to mention here that hints in regard to
their management as well as arguments in favour
of their establishment might be obtained by an

inspection of the ' shelter schools" of France referred
to in the first Reports of the Royal Commission on
technical instruction. The Commissioners say : "The
number of children in the shelter schools in 1866-7
was 432,000, of whom three-fourths were received
without payment. In 1879-80, the shelter-schools
contained 606,000 children, of whom five-sixths were
received without payment. These institutions can
scarcely be styled 'infant schools' in the sense in
which we ordinarily use the term. Their aim, besides
affording shelter to children too young to attend the
primary school, is principally to train the senses
according to what is known as the *kindergarten* system.
Much importance is attached to the training in these
schools by those who are advocating the further
development of manual work in elementary schools."

It is necessary, perhaps, that I should dwell more
particularly upon the character of the higher departments of these reformatory institutions. Suppose a
boy to have passed through the kindergarten and
elementary departments, he would be, say, ten years
of age. He should now enter upon an important
stage of his education Instruction in the ordinary
subjects should be accompanied by a moderate amount
of instruction in the rudiments of a trade. After
spending three years in this department, I would have
him enter the finishing or technical department, in

which the technical instruction should be specialised, and with reference to girls, the same course should be followed. There should be a careful attention to the development of the faculties in the primary departments, and an equally careful direction of manifest individual capacity into its proper channel in the secondary departments. The end to be kept carefully in view, throughout the whole course in these institutions, should be to turn out, at the age of, say fifteen or sixteen years, boys and girls fitted in every way to become useful and honourable men and women. The work to be carried on in the secondary department would much resemble that already done in industrial and reformatory schools. But I am of the opinion that it might be carried to a much higher degree of perfection in institutions of the character here proposed.

One consideration of some importance here arises: The question will be asked what would you do with boys and girls such as are now frequently remitted to industrial and reformatory schools? My answer is, that I would have them remitted to these reformatory institutions, subject to the necessity for proper classification already insisted upon. I would throw upon the Boards of Management of these establishments all the responsibility I possibly could in the directions I have indicated, while taking care that the institutions, as departments of the public service, were lacking in nothing that was essential to their efficiency. In a word, I would organise the benevolent forces in the country in connection with State supported institutions for removing from evil influences all unfortunate and neglected children (such as have been specified at pages 11 and 12), and especially those of habitual criminals. Or to put this matter in another way, I would have the State say to the noble-minded men and women, everywhere to be found, who devote a great portion of their lives to a haphazard and often blind and little rewarded struggle to rescue the perishing: "Come, here are schools, amply furnished. Take under your charge these unfortunates whom you are seeking to save, from their earliest years until they arrive at an age to keep and guard themselves. Watch over them with a sympathetic care as they grow from childhood to youth, and then befriend them when they shall have to commence to fight the battle of life among the throngs of men."

LECTURE XXIII.

THE EDUCATION OF THE WORKING CLASSES.

Some Consequences of Defective Education—Contrary Result of various Public Educational Media—Waste of Capacity—Shelter Schools—Reforms of Elementary Schools—The Royal Commission's Report on Technical Instruction in France—Specification of Instruction given—Length of School Hours—The Defective Education of Girls—Reforms required—Higher Elementary Schools required—Free Meals for School Children—Specialisation of Technical Instruction—Enlargement of the Scholarship Incentive—Creation of Popular Universities—Double Character of Work—Day and Evening Classes—Scholarships open to Day and Evening Pupils alike—Provisions for Orphan Scholars—The Item of Cost—Note.

In my previous lecture I dealt solely with the education of the children connected with the pauper and criminal classes. In the present lecture I propose to make some observations upon education generally, and I shall venture to enter into greater detail regarding the combination of manual and technical instruction with the ordinary branches of education. Experience has convinced me that many youths fall into bad habits and contract evil associations mainly in consequence of their education having been of a deplorably limited character. The efforts of social reformers should be directed to the mitigation of this calamity, and I am satisfied that the system of popular education in these three countries is easily capable of improvement in such a direction that the number of young people of both sexes who can be seen wandering aimlessly about the streets of all large towns in the evenings, and contracting habits that to say the least do not contribute to their own well-being or the welfare of the State, might be enormously lessened. On the other hand, upon various occasions it has been my privilege and delight to witness the thronged public libraries, reading-rooms, art galleries, and museums, of cities and large towns in England, Scotland, and America, and, to a less extent, in Ireland, as well as to read the reports of public libraries and educational institutions, all showing that increasing numbers of young people are availing themselves of existing educational facilities. But, then again, how far has one to go from the Birmingham Free Library and Midland Institute, or the Manchester Mechanics' Institution, now a technical school ; or how far has one to go from the various splendid educational establishments in the vicinity of St. George's Hall, Liverpool, or from Cooper Union, New York, or the Mechanics' Institute in Dublin, to discover that, after all, the crowds to be seen in most of these places so engaged as to make one's heart rejoice, are but as a drop in a bucket compared with the crowds to be seen elsewhere, in each and all of these towns and cities, so engaged as to make one's heart ache ? Now the question is, how can we multiply the number of those who hunger and thirst after mental improvement, and the higher life which follows as "knowledge grows from more to more ?" The waste of capacity is the most appalling of all wastes. I have known people argue profoundly about "waste in nature," and I have a hazy idea that the conclusion of the whole matter was that this waste was providentially ordained.

The argument, however, always appeared to me to be lacking in conclusiveness when applied to the appalling waste of human—may I not, indeed, say Divine—capacity going on around us every day. The question is not whether we can account for this waste, but whether we can do anything to prevent it. It appears to me that we can, with comparative ease, multiply the seekers after knowledge, and minimise this waste of capacity of which I speak; and I shall venture to indicate two directions in which efforts should immediately be made with a view to the achievement of these desirable ends.

Our efforts should be directed in the first place to the improvement of the system both of elementary and higher education. And in the second place, to the better organisation of the educational forces already in existence in the large centres of population, particularly with reference to higher education, and the creation of such forces where they do not already exist.

To begin with, then, I would establish in all towns and villages shelter schools to which children from four to seven years of age might be sent for the whole day; and, as far as possible, I would have similar schools established in country districts. These shelter schools should be really kindergartens, for I am convinced that the principles of Froebel are those which ought to underlie all enlightened educational efforts. I have already briefly indicated those principles, and it is unnecessary that I should enlarge upon them, for they are familiar to all interested in education. The shelter schools or kindergartens might be attached to existing infant schools, but I would have them much more plentifully scattered through the population I have seen single streets in some of the large towns in which kindergartens in my judgment ought to exist Of course parents are naturally unwilling to allow any young children to pass unprotected through busy thoroughfares, but this difficulty would be largely over-come if the necessity of crossing such thoroughfares were reduced to a minimum And for the rest, if kindergartens were established in sufficient numbers, the elder children could take the younger ones to the kindergartens before proceeding to their own more advanced schools, and call for them again on returning.

Then I would have elementary schools more plentiful than they now are. I think our aim should be to have numerous schools of this character rather than a few large ones. The character of these elementary schools I would change somewhat. They should be a combination of the kindergarten and the ordinary elementary school. But the work of the kindergarten should be of a more advanced nature. It should consist of manual instruction in the rudiments of a trade or an art similar to what is now given in many of the elementary schools of France. This manual instruction, however, should not push the literary instruction to the wall, for it appears that it is in this respect that such schools have been considered defective even in France. The Royal Commissioners on technical instruction in their first report drew attention to this matter, and it is very gratifying to find that what has been the desire of many earnest educational reformers in these countries has actually been tried in France. We learn from this report that manual work has in recent years been introduced into many primary schools in the city of Paris. In some the children are taught the rudiments of a trade; in others they are simply accustomed to the use of tools commonly employed in working wood and iron. The primary communal school of the Rue Tournefort seems to have attracted the special attention of the commissioners. This school was established as far back as 1873 it appears The commissioners say, "Until the beginning of last year trade instruction was commenced at the age of ten years and continued for three years. During the first two years every child was taught drawing, modelling, carving, joiner's work and smith's and fitter's work. In the third year the work was specialised : some of the children being taught modelling and carving, others joiner's work and cabinet-making, others again forging and fitting. Since the beginning of last year the same plan has been continued, but in addition, the children in the lowest classes, beginning even at six years of age, have three courses of one hour each per week of the instruction in handicrafts, which, until then, did not begin until they had attained the age of ten years."

To complete the picture of this remarkable school the commissioners add . "Although, as has been said, the work is specialised in the last year, the pupils engaged in modelling and carving return one day in each week of that year to the joiner's bench and the forge; the joiners and turners return to the forge and modelling, and the smiths to modelling and joiner's work. The school hours are from eight in the morning till six at night, with a half holiday on

Thursdays. In the highest class they have eighteen hours per week in the 'shops,' besides instruction in drawing, geometry, and natural science There are 360 children in the school. The children on leaving this school are generally able to earn from two shillings and sixpence to four shillings per week."

Now I quote the observations of the Royal Commissioners on this school because I am thus enabled to say how far the primary communal school of the Rue Tournefort corresponds with my idea of what ought to be established in these three countries. I should say, however, that the school hours are too long for general application to primary schools in England, Ireland, and Scotland; while from the age of seven to the age of ten simple manual instruction, taking an interesting and even an amusing form, would in my judgment be preferable, but the plan of the school of the Rue Tournefort might be copied with advantage in the higher elementary schools which should be established in all great industrial centres. The children in the school here mentioned are under the charge of the masters from eight in the morning until six in the evening—ten hours; and of that time about two hours appear to be occupied with technical instruction. I apprehend the people of these three countries would be unanimous in refusing to allow children of ten years of age to be under pedagogic rule for quite so many hours. From nine o'clock until five, or eight hours in all, would be as long a time as parents could be expected to tolerate the confinement of their children. Long hours at anything are intolerable. Working men in France and other countries work too many hours, and they send their children to school for too many hours also. In Great Britain and Ireland a school-day of eight hours might be permitted, but two hours would have to be devoted to meals and recreation. Boys and girls from ten to thirteen years of age might fairly be expected to work six hours per day at school lessons, provided the lessons were sufficiently varied. At the Rue Tournefort there appear to be about two hours per day devoted to technical instruction. I consider that period of time sufficient, at all events, for the first two years, though it might be extended for children in their thirteenth year. The four hours remaining ought to be ample for purely literary instruction and music and drawing.

Of course the advanced manual or technical instruction which for children of from ten to thirteen years of age should succeed to the simple manual instruction given from the age of seven to the age of ten, should be adapted to the sex of the children. Girls should be taught the rudiments of such trades as women can conveniently engage in, though instruction in these should be subordinate to a much more careful training in the domestic arts than is common in England, Ireland, or Scotland at present   There is hardly any more glaring defect in the education system of these countries than the miserable provision made for the education of girls. It is gratifying to observe that the early education of boys is being gradually adapted to what are regarded as likely to be his necessities in after-life; but when we compare this with what is being done for girls with the same view, we must surely blush for shame. In the near future, we may depend upon it, women will be a far more important factor in both the industrial and political mechanism of society than they are now, and it would be well that this should be the case.   ·

For, however generally superior to women men may flatter themselves they are, there cannot be a doubt that there are many things beyond the domestic sphere which women are as well fitted for as men. Anyhow, we have no moral right to refuse to women the opportunity of achieving their independence of men in the struggle for existence. It is incumbent upon us to afford to girls as well as to boys in our elementary schools the opportunity of acquiring a rudimentary knowledge of such trades or occupations as they might subsequently find employment in if thrown upon their own resources for a livelihood. The number of such trades or occupations is constantly increasing, and it is impossible to do more than lay down a general rule applicable to both boys and girls, viz., that in all elementary schools containing pupils from ten to fifteen years of age, this technical education imparted should have a general reference to the future of the pupils of both sexes, and a particular reference to the trades or occupations of the part of the country in which any school is situated.

I speak of "fifteen years," for that is the age which, in my judgment, should be reached by children before leaving school. I am satisfied that many of the evils of our social system arise from sending children too early to work. I know well the dire necessity that compels, but I hope to be able to point a remedy for that ere I have done.

In the mean time, let me complete my idea of industrial education so far as it relates to primary schools.

I am now to deal with children of both sexes who have completed their thirteenth year. During that year they have been spending eight hours per day in school: four in literary instruction, two in technical instruction, and two in recreation, including meals. I would now extend the school hours and double the time allotted to technical instruction.

But the work now to be done should be carried on in schools known as higher elementary schools. These institutions should be perfect in every respect.

They would receive pupils of both sexes at the age
of thirteen years, and retain them until the completion
of their fifteenth year. The male and female teachers
should be highly trained and well paid, and should be
carefully chosen. I would have no teachers in these
schools who were not fully qualified to act as competent
educators, and none under the age of twenty-one.
Workshops, class-rooms, dining-rooms, common rooms,
recreation grounds—all should be provided, and dormi-
tories where necessary. I am of opinion that every
boy and girl in the three kingdoms should pass two
years in a higher elementary school. And for the
benefit of children whose parents live in country
districts, I would have such a school established in
every country town, and in case any children lived at
a considerable distance from the school, I would have
provision made for them to sleep on the premises.
And here it may be as well to state that up to the
age of fifteen I would have all education compulsory
and free; and moreover, I would provide a free
meal in the middle of the day for all the children.
This latter provision I hold to be an indispens-
able one in any scheme of enlightened educational
reform.

The instruction in these higher elementary schools
for both boys and girls should be an extension of that
given in the lower schools. Every effort should be

made to perfect the work so far attempted; but greater attention should now be paid to the specialisation of technical instruction. Where the children expect to become farmers, particular attention should be paid to agriculture, and there should be attached to schools in country towns sufficient land to enable the children to make a practical acquaintance with this industry. Where, on the other hand, the children expect to become artisans, particular attention should be paid to those trades that are predominant in the various localities in which the schools are situated. In a town like Birmingham, for instance, there would be many higher elementary schools, and parents would have a choice, so that one school need not attempt to teach the rudiments of all the various trades carried on in the hardware metropolis. The same remark would apply to Sheffield, and more or less to all large towns. But to Manchester, Dublin, Liverpool, Bradford, Belfast, Glasgow, and similar places, it might be expected that specialisation of technical instruction would not be difficult. It might be attended with unusual difficulties in places like Birmingham, but no one would venture to suggest that such difficulties would be insurmountable by Birmingham people.

But that there are no really insuperable difficulties in the way of such schools as are here proposed is attested by the fact that in France and other countries they already exist. And accordingly, whether there are difficulties in the way or not, it is absolutely certain that advances will have to be made in this direction before very long. A rudimentary knowledge of drawing, modelling, engraving, carving, and type-setting, might readily be imparted to both girls and boys alike of from thirteen to fifteen years of age; while elementary instruction in many other occupations having particular reference to the sex of the children might also be given, as for example millinery, lace-making, embroidery, and domestic economy for girls; and fitting, forging, stone-cutting, and joinery for boys, in addition to general literary instruction. And no one can doubt that, once the urgency of educational reform in this direction was duly recognised, all obstacles would rapidly disappear.

It is perhaps right to add, the programme of elementary education here sketched does not contemplate home lessons—excepting, of course, the moral and religious teaching which it is presumed most parents impart to their children. So far as my observation has extended, it has led me to the conclusion that as far as possible the children should have done with books when they leave the school-room. After that let them amuse themselves to the top of their bent. And whenever possible, playgrounds should be large enough to be used as recreation grounds after school hours. If I could have my way, every elementary school should have at the very least two acres of playground attached.

We have now arrived at perhaps the most critical period in the education of children, but I maintain that if we have been happy in our choice of competent teachers, the instruction which has so far been imparted will have been received gladly, and will have effectually inclined the minds of the children to the pursuit of knowledge. And now that we are about to dispense with the element of compulsion, it is desirable that facilities should abound of which the boys and girls might take further advantage, and that every inducement should be held out to them to do so. Pupils of higher elementary schools therefore should be encouraged by the prospect of obtaining scholarships of moderate amount, but sufficient to enable them to pursue their studies in connection with the yet higher educational institutions that fall now to be considered.

Before passing on, however, perhaps it may be well to mention that the reformatory institutions to which I have already alluded should be exactly the same in this respect as the elementary schools, and that to the children in them scholarships should be awarded also, so that all children at the age of fifteen years should have a fair and an equal start in life.

Our real difficulties now begin. The question of

questions for education reformers is how to organise higher education. Any one passing through the large towns of Great Britain must be struck with astonishment at the vast amount of energy displayed in connection with local educational institutions of a superior kind   Take the town of Birmingham. There is here a splendid Grammar School, an unsurpassed Midland Institute and School of Art, and the Mason College, not to speak of minor institutions. In all the great industrial centres, such as Manchester, Liverpool, Leeds, Bradford, and Glasgow, there are similar institutions. In the smaller towns, also, there are kindred establishments. What is required to multiply many times the efficiency of these institutions is simply organisation! It appears to me that the aim should be to consolidate these often competing institutions, and organically connect them with elementary schools, by taking up the work of education where it is left by the latter establishments. At the age of fifteen it is imperative that the children of the working classes should begin to earn their own living, but it is quite certain that there are hundreds and thousands of parents who would encourage their children to continue their education if they could. How can facilities be afforded them for doing so? Let us suppose that in Birmingham the elementary schools are modelled on the plan here suggested. Let us suppose further that the Grammar

School, the Midland Institute, the School of Art, and the Mason College are parts of one organic school whose curriculum is but an extension of that of the higher elementary schools. Let the institutions named be known as the Birmingham University. Each institution with very little change could continue its work very much on present lines, but the aim should be to have within the University separate schools of literature, science, and art In the science school, say the Mason College, there should be workshops for imparting technical instruction with particular reference to the industries in the locality. In fact the apprenticeship schools of Paris might have their counterpart in the Birmingham Mason College. Now let the work done in connection with the University be of a double character. The day classes should be adapted to the instruction of students who are continuing their education untrammelled by work for daily bread. But there should be evening classes adapted to the instruction of students who have to earn their living in the day time The magnificent results which have been already achieved in Birmingham, Manchester, Liverpool, Glasgow, and indeed in all the larger towns of Great Britain by evening classes, (unfortunately evening classes of this kind are scarcely known in Ireland,) warrants us in hoping for results of which as yet no one dares to dream, if only we can do something to increase the number of those able to take advantage of them. I firmly believe that the improved system of elementary education which is here outlined would result in multiplying many times the number of those who would be anxious to attend these evening classes, and reducing to a minimum the devotees of that unpleasant personage who pays special attention to people with idle hands. How can we respond to this noble anxiety? An essential step in this direction would be to put a stop to work at five o'clock in all factories, workshops, and other employments, making exceptions where absolutely necessary, as in the post office, the newspaper office, and so on. But, generally speaking, an end should be put to the employment of young boys and girls in "offices," warehouses, shops, and so forth, after the hour of five in the evening. Artisans have happily taken care of themselves to some extent in this particular, but there are plenty of artisans who work less hours than their own sons and daughters.

In the next place, the fees for these evening classes should be very small. They might be much higher in the day classes. The prizes in the evening classes should be equal in value to those in the day classes. The scholarships obtained in the higher elementary schools should be tenable for three years at the day classes, and should be worth not less than £20 per annum, in addition to free admission to the classes chosen Many a man having a large family would be able to keep his brightest boy or girl at the University for three years in this way, as well as send the others to the evening classes. Can one measure the exertions which the most intelligent of the artisan classes would make to enable their children to take advantage of these facilities? And let me be quite clearly understood. These scholarships should not be limited in number. They should be the right of all children of higher elementary schools who attain a certain proficiency. The examining Board of the University should every year make their pick from among the children who have completed their course at all the higher elementary schools in the town, and to all who satisfy the Board of Examiners, I would have the University say: "There is at your disposal a scholarship tenable for three years at our University. You can have free admission to the day classes and £20 per annum to provide yourself with food and clothing"

But my proposal is not yet complete. There would be many children without parents or immediate relatives. For the benefit of these I would establish a University Hall, where students might reside on easy terms, say upon surrendering one-half of their bursary. Admission to this Hall should not be an act of charity, but a right to those who should happen to be without other homes, and it should always be at the discretion of the University authorities.

There are doubtless many points which I have not considered, but there is one which I have deliberately omitted. I have not counted the cost; but I am perfectly satisfied that if all that has been here proposed were done at the national expense—say by spending a few millions less every year on "war paint," and devoting the money to "operations" against ignorance and vice-breeding in some such way as that pointed out in these lectures—a saving would be effected in other directions so great as to leave an enormous balance in favour of the general tax-payer

---

WHEN making notes of the preceding lectures I had not had the advantage of reading the First Report of the Royal Commissioners on Technical Instruction. In transcribing my notes I was strongly tempted to make many quotations from this most valuable Report, and especially from the documents in the Appendix. It appears that in France the work of free public education is making great progress, and French education reformers seem to have succeeded to a very large extent in impressing upon the public mind the necessity of combining manual and technical instruction with the ordinary literary instruction of elementary schools. This First Report of the Royal Commissioners is of much value, as showing what has been already accomplished, and what is contemplated by the great French nation, and it is important that education reformers should make themselves thoroughly familiar with the information it contains. But I have not seen reason to modify my views, as set forth in the preceding lecture, for it will be clear to all English, Irish, and Scotch readers that the work now going on in France, as well as that which is proposed to be done, however well adapted for France, is not equally so for Great Britain and Ireland It is nevertheless admirably adapted to impress upon the public of these three countries the urgent necessity of seeking similar ends by a policy less open to the suspicion of being hostile to Christianity, and accordingly I strongly urge all who are interested in popular education to make a careful study of this First Report of the Royal Commissioners on Technical Instruction, which can be obtained through any bookseller from Her Majesty's Stationery Office, for the small sum of fourpence.

LECTURE XXIV.

RATIONAL RECREATION AS A PREVENTIVE OF CRIME.

The Free Libraries' Act—Necessity for its Compulsory Application—Loans of Books from Large to Small Libraries—Museums and Art Galleries—Peel Park Library and Museum, Salford—Unsatisfactory Classification in Museums—Exceptions in the Indian Department of South Kensington—Loans from Large to Small Museums—Travelling Lecturers—Art Galleries—Absurd Division of Subjects—Loans of Pictures and Statuary from Large to Small Galleries—Popular Lectures—Advantages of Extending same to Country Districts—Popular Music and Concerts.

THE end I have in view in making suggestions on education, is, simply, a more generally-educated general public; because I believe that, other things being equal, a well-instructed people could do its daily work much better than now, and would enjoy a much higher degree of general comfort than at present. Such a people would, moreover, in the main, walk in virtue's ways, and would discover not only that these ways are intrinsically excellent, but economically best. The

question, "Is life worth living?" would receive a practical
answer in the affirmative.   Life is not worth living now
to the vast majority of people, for the reason that the
life they live is rather that of mere beasts of burden
than of men infinite in faculty.

Now, it is manifest that the suggestions contained in
the preceding two lectures, even if immediately em-
bodied in legislation, could not effect the end in view
in less than a generation.   But there are other methods
by which the same end may be very greatly promoted,
and of these I propose now to speak.

I would make the adoption of the Free Libraries'
Acts compulsory.   Town Councils, Town Commissioners,
Local Boards, County Boards, should be charged with
the duty of putting these Acts immediately into operation.   There is scarcely any item of intelligence which
should   excite   greater   indignation   than   that   which
occasionally appears in newspapers, to the effect that
such and such a town has declined to adopt the Free
Libraries' Acts.   It is probably not generally known
that the Acts in question are capable of being adopted
by "any borough, district or parish, or burgh of whatever population," but, I fear, it may be assumed that
proposals to adopt the Acts in rural "districts" or
"parishes" would meet with considerable opposition.
Yet it cannot be doubted that in rural districts and
parishes there is as great a necessity for free libraries

as in boroughs. There is only one way of overcoming
the opposition of ignorance, and that is by making
compulsory what the "common sense of most" believes
to be for the common good of all. Does any one
seriously suppose that a people who have gone so far in
the matter of public elementary education would refuse
to go the length of insisting upon the establishment of
the natural complement of public elementary schools—
the public library? However that might be, I am
convinced that all friends of popular education should
apply themselves without delay to an amendment of
the Libraries' Acts in the direction of making it compulsory upon local authorities to adopt them. In the
mean time it is earnestly to be hoped that the working
men of the towns will exert themselves to secure the
adoption of these Acts at once.

For the purposes of the Free Libraries' Act, then,
towns and villages and parishes should be grouped
together; having regard, as far as possible, to the geographical distribution of higher elementary schools, and
the superior schools or colleges, similar to those grouped
together in my last lecture, to form the "Birmingham
University." A maximum rate should be fixed, but it
should be supplemented from the National Exchequer
to the extent of one penny for every halfpenny in the
pound contributed by the local rates. This contribution
from the National Exchequer would naturally involve a

certain amount of supervision on the part say of the Minister of Education.   It should be his duty, for example, to insist that certain books should be added to any particular library, if it should appear to him that there was a real desire on the part of any considerable section of the ratepayers of any particular locality to have such books added to the library. I make this suggestion with some hesitation, I confess, but it is made with a double view. In the first place, the National Exchequer in contributing aid to local libraries ought to be in some way represented in its disbursement.   In the second place, it is only too well known that local authorities often contain some one or two men whose " conscientious convictions " will not suffer them to assent to the placing of certain books in the libraries under their control. Conscientious scruples of the kind referred to should always be respected, but they ought not to be permitted to stand in the way of the desire of any considerable number of ratepayers to have particular books placed within their reach. And there seems to me no better way of respecting these conscientious scruples than that of constituting a higher and generally more enlightened power—a sort of court of appeal   The Education Department, with a Minister of Education at its head, would seem to be a fitting authority to settle disputed questions of this kind, and if it should be said that this would mean that

Parliament would now and then be involved in discussions on the merits of a particular book, I can only say that so far as I have been able to observe, it does appear to me that Parliament is frequently less usefully occupied.

But there is one suggestion that may be made here, with a view to the greater efficiency and more economical working of free libraries. When I have looked upon the magnificent collections of books to be found in existing public libraries, I have often wished that some means could be devised of multiplying their utility. Great central libraries could easily lend collections of their books to smaller libraries in small towns and country districts. It might be made a condition of the grant from the National Exchequer that Birmingham, for example, should make such loans to the libraries of surrounding towns and villages. I was at one time hopeful that there might be established throughout Ireland a number of working men's clubs with small libraries attached, connected with a central institution, in Dublin, having a large library from which loans of books could be made to the various clubs or small public libraries in the country. And I see no reason why such a plan should not be carried out with the Free Libraries' Acts in compulsory operation.

On the same principle we could proceed to the establishment of public museums and art galleries.

Every public library in all towns of say 5000 inhabitants should have in connection with it a museum
and an art gallery, and the entire establishment should
as far as possible be situated in the midst of a public
park.   An illustration of what I mean is to be seen in
the town of Salford.   Peel Park is a fine piece of
ground beautifully laid out as a garden, with extensive
pleasure-grounds attached.   There are gymnasia for
boys and girls, and troops of children of both sexes, and
young men and young women may frequently be seen
availing themselves of these means of recreation.   The
library, the museum, and the art gallery are all deposited
in a noble mansion which is situated on the brow of a
gentle declivity, from the terraces of which the eye can
wander at will over the surrounding landscape.

But I shall have something to say of recreation a
little further on.   What I wish to do now is to make a
few suggestions upon the character of museums.   I
have visited many such institutions in my time, and
one general observation will suffice to convey my
opinion in regard to all of them, with one single exception.   It is that as a rule museums instead of being
a harmonious whole are a confusing collection of more
or less interesting and instructive objects.   Going
through most public museums one sees many wonderful
things, but one is very seldom able to carry away a
clear and definite idea of what one has seen.   The only

exception I remember to this general experience is the Indian Museum at South Kensington. I went there one day with a distinct end in view. It was to ascertain if I could more vividly realize the actual condition of the people of India. The air was full of rumours of "risings." I wanted to ascertain if possible what sort of materials existed in India for a revolt, and if there was any hope that an agitation would grow in that country to such an extent as to favour a corresponding agitation in Ireland. I had read a good deal about India, but all the information gathered from books fell into order as I examined the contents of the Indian Museum The pictures and the models illustrative of the life of the people; the specimens of their handicrafts, the examples of their arts; and then the illustrations of the manner of life of the "higher" orders of Indian society—and the characters of the members of these "higher" orders —all combined to give me what I have since found to be a very clear and useful idea of life in India, by means of which I have been able to profit very largely from what I have since heard and read concerning that country. Now, it appears to me that the supreme aim of a museum should be to convey to the mind of the visitor a harmonious conception Accordingly, in connection with all public libraries there should be museums whose contents, instead of being a heterogeneous collection of mere curiosities, should be as far as possible a complete presentation of the leading facts in reference to any particular subject.

From the Indian collection at South Kensington it ought to be easily possible to make a selection suitable for removal from one provincial town to another, on loan. From the British Museum and other sources it ought to be equally possible to make similar selections to be loaned in like manner, and, accordingly, there is no reason why during one year there might not be, certainly in all the larger towns of Great Britain and Ireland, at least two collections such as those described. The loans should be accompanied on their tour by a curator whose services might be available as a lecturer, and on Saturday and Sunday afternoons, at an appointed hour, the curator might well be expected to conduct the visitors round the building, explaining as he proceeded the various objects of interest, and answering questions. Imagine such a loan from the Indian Museum deposited in any provincial town for six months; another from the Egyptian Department of the British Museum. carefully calculated to convey a distinct conception of the past history of India and of Egypt, the present social condition of the two peoples, and the industrial resources of their several countries; can any one doubt that the general public would acquire a much more correct view of the great Indian and Egyptian questions than they now entertain?

Hence I am convinced it would be highly beneficial if museums as a whole were more carefully organised. Every town might, of course, have its own permanent collections, but the maximum educational advantage of museums will never be realised until some such plan as that here suggested is generally adopted.

The same remark substantially applies to art galleries. For the most part these remind one of children's scrap-books The pictures are associated mainly with reference to the fitting of their frames Space is so valuable that it is found necessary to huddle pictures most incongruously together. One general division is thought to be sufficient, viz. into water and oil and statuary. Now, without pretending to be an authority upon art, I venture respectfully to submit that a room full of pictures and statuary is not necessarily an art gallery. What is required is that there should be several rooms as spacious and well-lighted as possible, and moreover provided with seats; and the works of art should be classified with the object of producing a good effect upon the mind of visitors. Suppose one room devoted to pictures of the great masters. There should be so much space to spare that upon occasion there would be room for works of a similar character obtained on loan from other galleries. And so on through all the rooms. It is really incalculable to what an extent the utility of works of art might be multiplied by a proper system of loans arranged between the various museums and art galleries throughout the three countries.

Of course everything in this respect would depend upon management. In all places the Public Library, Museum, and Art Gallery should be under the control of a Board of Management, consisting of members of the town council or other local authority, principals of higher elementary schools, professors of colleges, and others interested in educational work. The expenses of such a Board should be paid partly out of the local rates and partly out of the National Exchequer. The chiefs of such institutions, as well as the heads of departments where the institutions were at all extensive, should be appointed directly by the Board of Management, whose constitution would be a sufficient guarantee that jobbery would be reduced to a minimum. Subordinate officials might well be appointed by their chiefs.

I am inclined to think that the result of an organisation of public educational institutions of this character on such a basis as is here sketched would result in the rapid growth of a class of officials of high culture and yet popular sympathies, whose efforts to make their several institutions promote their avowed object would lead to such an interchange of books, pictures, statuary, and objects of interest between different centres, as would keep up a perpetual popular interest.

Thus would the work of education go on, while those who were being educated would be scarcely aware of it.

There are two other methods by which popular education might be very greatly promoted, and after briefly noticing these I shall have done with this branch of the subject. The popular lecture is one of the most efficient means of education. A great deal has been accomplished in this way by leading scientific men in Manchester, Glasgow, and other large centres of population, but only enough to show how much more might be done. The great difficulty is to make such things "pay." It is out of the question to expect that men competent to popularise science, or men of high literary and artistic culture, could undertake work of this description without adequate remuneration. And I therefore venture to suggest that principals of higher elementary schools and professors of colleges should be open to occasional employment as popular lecturers, not only in the large towns, but in the small towns and country districts. There are great numbers of enlightened men living remote from towns, who would be glad to organise a few public lectures during the long winter months if only they could obtain lecturers. It is not that the people are too poor in every case to pay for such things; it is that the taste of the public has not been educated up to that point of appreciation which is equal to a liberal expenditure upon its gratification. People who have to work hard all day "don't see the good" of lectures on scientific, literary, or artistic subjects. If it should be a lecture on "improved methods of agriculture," say, which some earnest clergyman was anxious to have delivered, the difficulty of finding the necessary funds in the locality most urgently requiring improved methods of agriculture would be insuperable. I only select a lecture on this subject as an illustration of what I mean. But it will easily be seen that if the money difficulty is insuperable in such a case, it would be ten times more so in the case of a lecture on the "Life and Writings of Dean Swift," in a similar locality. The fact is, what is wanted is a systematic scattering of good seed up and down the country. In some unlikely spot perchance the seed would fall upon good ground, and good fruit spring forth. But as a general result a very greatly improved public taste might be looked for. Lectures on domestic economy for young women, on thrift for both young men and young women, on historical and other subjects repeated by the same lecturer in a dozen or twenty different places, could not fail to have a very salutary and almost immediate effect.

It will be observed that I lay stress upon the application of the public lecture to country districts. I do so because after all the population of the country is always pouring into the town, and my idea is to do something to have it a less ignorant stream. Young men and young women coming up from the Arcadian simplicity of country life to its exact opposite in the busy manufacturing towns are naturally led away by the glitter and excitement of their new surroundings; but if their tastes had been to any serious extent formed by any such proposal as that just made, I am convinced that the glamour of town life would soon cease to blind their eyes to the more solid advantages to be derived from a diligent pursuit of knowledge through the more abundant facilities presented to them in their new life, and thus instead of adding permanently to the giddy throngs that haunt the public thoroughfares when the day's work is done, large numbers of them would crowd into the evening classes, libraries, and museums, which would stand invitingly open.

One other means of popular education is to be found in intelligent recreation. It is highly gratifying to find how steadily public opinion is growing in the direction of cheap popular concerts. Why should there not be a school of music as well as a school of art in connection with every considerable town? Music is taught in elementary schools, and should be more diligently taught. Let the work be carried on to the highest degree, as in the case of drawing and modelling and other branches of art. Then just as the teachers and professors already alluded to form a staff of public lecturers, so the teachers and professors of music could apply themselves to the work of improving the popular taste by good music. There is nothing in the way of great and successful efforts in this direction. All that is required is organisation and funds. In all the public parks there should be bands playing at least two evenings in every week as well as two afternoons. In all towns and villages, particularly in the winter, local musicians might be encouraged to get up concerts by being assured of the assistance of teachers from the nearest school of music, who should be paid for their services as the public lecturers would be paid for theirs. I confine myself to recreation of this kind, because physical recreation is more readily provided by the people themselves, according to their several tastes, and it is only required that in every town and village there shall be a public park or recreation-ground such as have been already spoken of in connection with public libraries.

However, an exception must be made in the matter of bathing. Free public baths, it appears to me, are an urgent necessity, and they should be connected with the public parks. But beyond the provision of facilities for bathing and gymnastic exercises, it is hardly necessary to go in this direction.

It is necessary, however, to go much further than

we have already gone in the matter of popular concerts, both under cover and in the open air. It is hardly required that the principle of compulsion should be introduced. Everything necessary would be gained by grants either from the local rates or from the National Exchequer. I do not see, for example, why every town or village should not have its public band or musical society, receiving a grant in aid from the local rates or from the National Exchequer. It would be but an extension of the principle now in operation in the science and art department of South Kensington in reference to science classes. The grants might readily be made contingent upon the due performance of certain specified public services. What is really wanted is simply this— something to stimulate local exertion. In every locality a small minority is always to be found more or less enthusiastically devoted to the promotion of education; some are in favour of science classes, some of art classes, some of music classes. I would have the State say to these earnest men and women: "Come now; for every pound which you can raise locally to further your aims we will give you so much more. There are in your midst highly educated principals of schools, and professors in all departments of literature, science, and art. Go to these for help, and if you cannot find sufficient money to accomplish your purpose we will do our best to meet you."

In this way I am persuaded the movement in favour of popular education and rational recreation would be so effectually promoted that crime would speedily diminish, and a healthier moral tone pervade public life.

LECTURE XXV.

CAUSE OF POVERTY.

Contrasts of Wealth and Poverty—Why are the Poor so very poor?
—The Drink Theory—Little or no Inducement for Thrift—
Wages kept to a semi-starvation point by Competition and
Monopoly—Diminution of Population not Increasing Wages
—Relations of Land and Labour—How Land Monopoly has
robbed Labour in Ireland—Industry ground down to the
Bare Living Point of Remuneration—"Population Tending
to Overtake the Means of Subsistence" fallacy exploded as
regards Ireland—Monopoly's Dictum to Labour—The same
Principle behind the whole Industrial System—Power and
Privilege robbing Labour and manufacturing Poverty—
Abolition of Land Monopoly absolutely essential to the
diminution of Poverty

IF ignorance is an evil, scarcely less so is poverty.
And it is with poverty as it is with ignorance; it is
bad in itself as well as in its effects. In the present
and some succeeding lectures I propose to investigate
the causes of poverty.

Perhaps it is necessary to say a few words in the
first place, however, upon the existence of poverty.

We are told that the poor are not nearly so poor as they used to be, and statistics are quoted to show that the incomes of the working classes have increased in a much higher ratio than have the incomes of other classes within the last fifty years. Admitting all this, the circumstance has still little or no bearing on the real questions at issue between labour and monopoly. For in the first place, what is the good of quoting figures which, after all, are more or less the results of estimates formed upon uncertain and insufficient data, when the great industrial centres present us with the most awful contrasts of wealth and poverty? In the richest counties in England, Ireland, and Scotland, the miserable hovel is the inevitable accompaniment of the magnificent mansion. The question, therefore, is not whether or not the incomes of the working classes have greatly increased of late years, but whether or not there is a weight of poverty which is capable of being removed. And again, what is the good of quoting statistics when the question is not whether or not the incomes of the working classes have greatly improved within recent years, but whether or not the working classes have received heretofore, or are receiving now, their just share of the wealth which is the result of their labour. The real questions are—Is there an unnecessary amount of poverty in these three kingdoms and in the world? Does the worker get a fair share of the wealth

which labour produces?   In my humble judgment, the
first of these questions must be answered in the affirmative ; the second in the negative.   It is accordingly
now my aim to submit certain reasons which account
for this state of things, and certain suggestions which,
if adopted, would, I think, tend to remedy the more
glaring evils of the existing social system.

Why are the poor so very poor?   Some people say,
because they are so thriftless, and "give way to drink."
My study of life does not bear out this charge.   Possibly
the poor are thriftless and intemperate, but so also are
the rich, and it is even accounted a fortunate circumstance when a rich man spends his money freely.   But
what have the poor to be thrifty with, and what reason
have they to be temperate ?   Would poverty be abolished
if all working men and women became thrifty and
temperate to-morrow?   I do not think so.   We are told
that wages tend to the minimum upon which the wage-
earners will continue to subsist—that is, to a bare living.
Those who get more than suffices for a bare living may
be thrifty, and will find it to their advantage to be temperate.   But to the great mass of workers who get only
a bare living thrift and temperance are rendered almost
impossible virtues.   If they all managed to subsist on
something less than a bare living, wages would "tend"
to that reduced minimum, and so we should reach that
absurdity which was illustrated in the case of the man

who proposed gradually to reduce the food of his horse to one straw per day, and did so only to find that the unlucky animal died the day after his first meal of one straw. If wages really do tend to this minimum of which we hear so much, is it not clear that greater thrift and temperance on the part of all workers whose wages are but a bare living would but result in still lower wages to them, and still greater profits to their capitalist employers?

Look at what has happened in my own country. Years ago the farmers of Ireland paid their rents partly out of the proceeds of what we may call auxiliary industries. Gradually these have largely disappeared from the country. What remains of them are concentrated now in the towns But rents have gone up, and the struggle for existence has been so severe that population steadily declined. Millions have gone to other lands, yet those who have remained at home are not a whit better off The "wages" of the Irish farmers have gone down, but the rent-rolls of Irish landlords have gone up, and it is now a settled fact that the thrifty and temperate farmer, who invested the results of his thrift and temperance in improvement upon his farm, has paid the penalty in an increase of rent. And again, wherever a railway has been laid down, wherever market towns have sprung up, wherever harbours have been constructed, there have rents been raised yet higher. In fact, in Ireland, where manufacturing industries are so limited in extent, the real relations between land and labour are more clearly seen. It is plain that they are absolutely essential to one another It is plain that land is valueless without labour. It is equally plain that labour cannot exert itself without land. In a country teeming with manufacturing industries these simple but essential relations are largely obscured. In a purely agricultural country, however, such as Ireland, the truth is clearly seen.

Let us in imagination transport ourselves to one of the many beautiful and fertile valleys which entrance the tourist upon his first visit to Ireland. Let us suppose it is summer Scattered through the valley are the thatched homesteads, surrounded by their fields of waving grass and corn and flax; the potatoes are strong and healthy, and there is every promise of a plentiful harvest. In a very short time there will be food enough in that valley to feed ten or twenty times the population inhabiting it. Yet are those who till that land and make it fruitful in the direst poverty; so poor that they dare not eat their own butter and eggs, nor drink the milk of their own cows. The people of this valley, rich with food, must content themselves with a diet of potatoes, butter milk, and occasionally oaten meal. And if that potato crop should fail, the people would positively starve Why are these poor people so very poor? The reply is simple. There does exist, though these poor folks never see him, a man called a landlord, who has the power to appropriate all the results of the industry of these poor people to his own use and benefit, and does appropriate all save what suffices to afford to them in ordinary circumstances a bare living. If any of the crops fail, the landlord does not moderate his demand; the "bare living" of these poor people is reduced to starvation point And that once upon a time it reached that point is evident, as the ruins of many a cottage serve to testify. Why are these poor people so very poor? Can it really be because population tends to overtake the means of subsistence, and thus forces wages down to "a bare living" point? Certainly not in this case, for here nature and the hand of man have combined to redouble the fertility of the valley, while the greed of one man is responsible for the reduction of its population. Clearly it is no increase of population here that has forced wages down to the minimum of a bare living. One thing, and one alone, is the cause of the poverty of these poor people, and it is this—that an unseen but all-powerful hand comes in just when the labourer is reaping the reward of his labour and snatches it from his grasp. Here are land and labour in   py co-operation, but of the land one man is able to say. "This is mine; to me belongs the power of life and death. It is my prerogative to dicta⸱⸱ to you workers the

terms, if any, upon which I will permit you to work
at all   My terms are the whole of the produce, less
what will just suffice to enable you to maintain a bare
subsistence. The moment I see—for though you cannot
see me I can see you—the moment I see any of you
by thrift and temperance making more than a bare
living I shall increase your rent.   The moment I find
that any of you by thriftlessness and intemperance are
unable to pay your rent, I will get rid of you—I will
not permit you to get a bare living even."   Labour has
no resource but submission; for though labour is represented by a thousand pairs of hands, the owners of those
hands must either work or starve. .They cannot take
the owner of the land by the scruff of the neck, and
say, "You, sir, shall either work or starve," for the
owner of the land has law on his side, and the British
army at his back.

Now the advantage of this illustration is that in this
typical valley the problem is reduced to its simplest
terms.   There were land and labour, and no complex
industrial system to obscure their relations or to conceal
the operation by which the land monopolist appropriated the produce of labour. It was quite easy to see
that the population of the valley entirely depended
upon the monopolist of the land. He would allow just
so much subsistence as would secure him the largest
amount of wealth. If, for example, he found that five

hundred men working for a bare living could hand over to him as much wealth as a thousand men working on the same terms, he would take care to deny even a bare living to the unnecessary five hundred. Hence it is clearly not population pressing on subsistence which compels men to work for a bare living, but a privileged class, for its own advantage, limiting the subsistence available to workers. The wrong is due to "the injustice of society," and *not* "to the niggardliness of nature"

Of course it is easy to say that even though there were no land monopolist in the case, and the valley belonged wholly to its inhabitants, the population would rapidly multiply and very soon overtake the means of subsistence—so that it is still true that population tends to overtake subsistence. But I answer, a tendency on the part of population to overtake subsistence does not necessarily mean that the tendency will be carried on to the bare living point. If Labour were its own master it would elect to live a higher life than is possible to it so long as it is a slave; and accordingly, though population might increase to a bare living point, it is absolutely certain that the bare living with which Labour in a state of freedom would be satisfied, would be luxury compared with the bare living with which in a state of slavery it must perforce be content. Wherever workers are free to fix the terms upon which they are willing to work, we find that these terms include something more than the bare living for which those are content to work who are not free to fix their own terms.

But why discuss this supposed tendency any further? The catastrophe to which it points, in any case, is as remote as the exhaustion of the coal-fields, if not as distant as the earth's absorption into the sun. Look at the vast areas of uncultivated land in Ireland, and the still larger tracts of land in Scotland and England that are given over to cattle and game; and then think of the capabilities of America and the British Colonies. Add to all this the admitted fact that the productive powers of such land as is already under cultivation might easily be doubled, and in many cases trebled, by improved methods of agriculture, and how can we come to any other conclusion than this—that when the population of the world is within measurable distance of reaching the limit of subsistence afforded by the earth and the waters under the earth, it will be time to be alarmed, but that meanwhile we may go on, though indulging the hope that ere we reach the limit of our resources we shall have hit upon a rate of multiplication which will be consistent with a mode of life at least superior to that which is possible or permissible under the existing social system.

And now if we extend our view, we shall find at the

back of our complex industrial system exactly the same thing that we observed in the simple relation of labour and land to which I have just referred, viz., the hand of power and privilege appropriating most of the wealth produced by labour, and returning only a bare living to the labourers, and thus in effect saying, that subsistence shall only be afforded to the extent which secures the richest results to the class which neither toils nor spins. Who, then, under these circumstances can deny that there does exist an unnecessary weight of poverty, or affirm that the worker receives a fair share of the wealth that is produced by his labour?

The first step to be taken with a view to diminish poverty and secure to the worker a fair share of the results of his industry is, therefore to put an end to land monopoly I do not say that this is all that is necessary, but I do affirm that until this is done nothing is done I admit that changes of a very drastic nature are required in what are known as the relations of labour and capital, and of these it will be necessary to say something a little further on. Here I have only to insist that so long as land is private property, the landed can and will appropriate the wealth produced by labour. For consider what has been the effect of improvements in the methods of industry and labour-saving inventions Go back to the fertile valley to which we have already referred Every improvement

there was quickly followed by an increase of rent The
worker who improved his land, or his tools, or his
methods of cultivation benefited nothing. His condition
was not improved at all, the improvement went straight
into the pocket of the landlord—the land monopolist.
And so it would still be if some fine day labour-saving
machinery or improved methods should double the
produce of that valley. The same thing would go on
if our whole industrial system were suddenly changed
from a system of competitive to one of co-operative
production. The land monopolist could just as easily
dictate terms to co-operators as to competitors.

And as a matter of fact he does. Co-operation, so
far as it has yet been tried, has doubtless been of great
advantage in many ways, but the lesson it teaches
to my mind is the same as that which the repeal of
the Corn Laws taught me. It was idle to abolish the
monopoly in corn and leave untouched the monopoly
in the land which grew the corn. Free Trade is no doubt
a good thing, but the working classes have not yet
realised at all adequately its enormous advantages.
In like manner if a system of co-operative production
—and one may take that phrase to include everything
in the shape of improvements, whether in the worker
or in his methods of working—were to-morrow substituted for that which exists to-day, so long as the land
monopoly remained we should be where we are so far

F 2

as labour is concerned. Co-operative mills and co-operative stores are plentiful in the ·north of England; but they have to pay rent, like their neighbours. And rent not only for the land that the mill or the store stands on, but rent for the houses that the people live in, drink in, worship in; rent for the streets they walk on and the railroads they ride on—and that rent is not what they will give; it is what the monopolist will take.

Land monopoly, landlordism, or private property in land is

> "The leprous distilment, whose effect
> Holds such an enmity with blood of man,
> That swift as quicksilver it courses through
> The natural gates and alleys of the body,
> And with a sudden vigour it doth posset
> And curd, like eager droppings into milk,
> The thin and wholesome blood."

And until we purge the body politic of this "leprous distilment," all our schemes for the amelioration of the condition of the poor, all our efforts to secure to every man a fair day's wages for a fair day's work, are alike vain.

LECTURE XXVI.

REMEDIAL PROPOSALS.

The Abolition of Land Monopoly—Prof Newman's Opinion—The Advantages of National Proprietary, or State Ownership of Land—National and Individual Benefit—How it would tend to increase Wages—Lord Derby and the Sands of Bootle—How National Proprietary would put an end to Speculative Land Values—The effect of throwing tied-up Land open to Labour—Increasing Food Produce, and Enlarging the Field of Industry—Collateral Public Benefits—The Incidence of the Land Tax—Contrast between Class and State Ownership—Conditions of Occupancy under State Ownership—The position of the Farmer under same—Practically the Owner of his Holding subject to just Conditions—How the Agricultural Labourers would benefit through State Ownership—Summary of benefits to the Community from State Ownership.

I WOULD abolish land monopoly by simply taxing all land, exclusive of improvements, up to its full value. By the term improvements I mean such erections or qualities as can be clearly shown to be the results of the labour of those now in the occupation or enjoyment of the land or their predecessors. In other words, I

would recognise private property in the results of labour,
and not in land.   But what of the landlords, it will be
asked?   A similar question was once asked of the late
George Stephenson, in reference to a much more useful
animal.   Mr. Stephenson was asked what would happen
if a cow should get in the way of a locomotive, and the
eminent engineer remarked that it would be "a bad
job for the coo"   Similarly I am free to confess that
if my proposal were carried into effect it would be a
bad job for the landlords   I can only say that I should
be very willing to consider candidly, and with every
desire to be just, any suggestions that might be made
with a view to mitigate the misfortune which such a
change as I here recommend would be to them, but I
do not feel called upon to make any suggestions of my
own.   Various suggestions have been made, but for the
most part they appear to me to be more or less in-
genious and effective devices for perpetuating the evils
of the existing system   I greatly fear that the landlords will have to be sacrificed unless they get out of
the way of their own accord   They have a very bad
case, so bad indeed that Prof. Newman says of them
that   if justice could be wisely and rightly separated
from mercy, they might be treated as rudely and curtly
as their ancestors under Henry VIII treated the farmers and peasants, whom they massacred and hanged by
the roadside"   We must not strain "the quality of

mercy," nor must we permit "offence's gilded hand to shove by justice." But inasmuch as I propose to consider one or two suggestions in regard to the best way of dealing with the landlords in my next lecture it is unnecessary to dwell further upon the point now.

We may turn at once to the consideration of the advantages of a national proprietary of land as opposed to a class monopolisation. I claim that constituting the land the property of the State would tend to annihilate poverty by securing to every worker a fair day's wages for a fair day's work. If the entire annual revenue from the landed property of Great Britain, exclusive of tenants' rights, but inclusive of mines and minerals, were turned into the National Exchequer, it would be found to amount to an enormous sum. The Chancellor of the Exchequer would look at it with glistening eyes and watering lips. He would doubtless turn to that charming romance, "What I can do with a shilling," in the hope that by simple multiplication he might discover what he could do with two or three hundreds of millions of golden sovereigns. If the Minister of Education called upon him, the Chancellor would hail his colleague's advent with delight. But even that functionary's demands, though he should have to administer such a system of education as that previously sketched, would leave the pile not appreciably diminished. And if those who are included in the Civil List should call upon the dazed

Chancellor, they would retire, leaving the "income" practically untouched. The only demand which could possibly be made upon the national treasurer, and occasion him any anxiety in reference to a surplus, would be a demand for the immediate extinction of the national debt. Suppose the Chancellor should, however, elect to respond to a request preferred by the President of the Local Government Board for ten or twenty millions to be expended in the better housing of the poor, he would still have a large balance. At present there is raised in Great Britain by local and general taxation about £100,000,000 sterling per annum. All this the Chancellor of the Exchequer would remit, and defray the entire cost of local and general administration by the revenue from the land and minerals. I have seen it estimated that the ordinary artisan pays between 10 and 20 per cent. of his income in indirect taxation. To this extent at least the change which is here proposed would mean an increase of wages.

But perhaps the most effective and direct way in which national ownership of land would tend to increase wages, is that a stop would be put to speculative land values. Wages are paid out of the produce of labour, but it is clear that if an undue share of that produce is appropriated to the payment of rent, there must be less to appropriate to the payment of wages. Put an end to speculative land values, and you diminish the share of produce falling to rent, and increase the share falling to wages. A single illustration will suffice to make my meaning clear. A few years ago the sands of Bootle, near Liverpool, were a dreary waste. But presently the space was required for docks. Then the Earl of Derby stepped in and demanded a speculative value for the Bootle Sands; no less a sum than £200,000, I believe. The result is, that the Liverpool people pay no less than £8,000 per annum for land that had positively no real value before the docks were constructed. Manifestly this speculative value is a tax upon industry, a limitation of the amount of produce which would otherwise be available for wages. I do not say that the whole of this sum would fall into the pockets of working men; but I do say that other things being equal it would do so. There are others than landowners who reap where they have not sown. But at present I am only concerned to show that the tendency of speculative land values is to limit the share of produce falling to wages, and to point out that the checking of speculative land values would have a contrary tendency.

In point of fact, the State being in reality the people, it would administer its inheritance, the land, with a single eye to the welfare of the entire people. The black mail which the Earl of Derby levied upon the industry of Liverpool is only a sample of what goes on every day. No landlord will permit a railway to cross his estate unless he is "compensated," and the amount of "compensation" always exceeds the value of the land as it stands; the sum demanded approximates as nearly as possible to what it is estimated the land will be worth when the railway has been made. In addition to this, the rents of all lands contiguous to the line are at once raised. So again in the case of mineral deposits. No landlord will permit mines to be opened on his estate without first stipulating for royalties. And thus in a hundred ways black mail is levied upon the industry of the people And this is the natural result of private property in land. The landowners regard their own private interests as paramount. If the State were the owner of the land the public interests would be the paramount consideration. It is plain that the temptation to hold for higher prices would not affect the State as it affects the private landowner, and that accordingly one of the most immediate effects of a national proprietary would be to remove those restrictions upon industry which, as matters now stand, result in that most melancholy spectacle—troops of idle men looking on land they may not touch, and thousands of families living on starvation diet and in miserable city dens while millions of acres of fruitful land are occupied as game reserves, and shut out from purposes of human sustenance or shelter. We read again and again of so many thousands of men

being out of employment in this or that great manufacturing town. And in fact we may at any time
see with our own eyes how bitter, on the very lowest
rung of the social ladder, is the struggle for a bare
living. For let us propose to leave a railway-station
carrying nothing more than a small hand-bag, half-a-
dozen miserable creatures will almost throttle each
other for the privilege of carrying it for a few pence.
And this struggle is repeated with diminishing intensity
in every stratum of society. Amongst the artisan and
labouring classes, however, it is most intense. Now,
what is the immediate cause of this cut-throat competition? Can it be any other than this, that "the
landed" instead of facilitating the access of labour to
the land, positively forbid it, except on monopolist
terms? It must be remembered that the rate of
wages is determined under existing conditions by the
minimum upon which those on the lowest rung of the
social ladder can subsist. Put these, then, in a position
to demand higher wages, and you do the same thing for
everybody who lives by labour. Now, who can doubt
for a moment that once the power and the privilege
of preventing this access of labour to land, except upon
terms which enable the hand of power and privilege
to appropriate the lion's share of the produce, were
checked, a social and economic revolution would be
almost instantly effected? It is the rush of the

unemplo... ...d agricultural population to the towns which intensifies the struggle for existence, and thus enables employers to fix the rate of wages on the basis of the least they will give, viz. bare subsistence. If we can check that rush we shall reverse the position, and enable the workers to fix the rate of wages on the basis of the least they will take. Nor ought it to be very difficult to accomplish this. We have only to make the nation the proprietor of the land. Tax land in city, town, and country up to its full value, and no one would find it to his advantage to hold for higher prices, for he would simply be holding for a higher public tax. The millions ... ...cres of land now lying waste in Great Britain would instantly come into cultivation. The State, from its abundant revenue, could advance large sums for the reclamation of the land, and the result would be that instead of there being, as now, an unemployed agricultural population, there would be a demand for labour so great that many generations must elapse before population could overtake subsistence. The mineral resources would be equally thrown open. It would be the interest of the State to impose conditions that would have the effect of encouraging instead of discouraging the development of these resources, and again in this field the demand for labour would far exceed the supply. And thus, instead of the competition being, as now, between workers seeking employers, it would be between employers seeking workers, and wages would rise all along the line.

Consider, for a moment, what this would mean. It would mean, in the first place, an enormous increase the production of wealth as well as its more equitab.. distribution. It would mean, in the second place, all but the abolition of poverty. Workhouses would have to be revolutionised, if not entirely done away with. The crime, which is mainly the offspring of poverty, would tend to a minimum.

Think, too, what the effect of placing all taxation upon land values would mean in another direction. It is said that of every pound collected for the relief of the poor in these three kingdoms, over fifty per cent. is absorbed in expenses of collection and administration. The same remark applies to a greater or less extent to all other of the existing taxes. The cost of their collectic · is enormous. It may, indeed, be confidently affirmed that there is hardly a single tax which is at once easy to collect, fair in its incidence, and abundant in its yield Taxation of land values would comply with all these conditions Nothing is easier than to fix the value of land irrespective of improvements. It is done every day in the United States as well as in Great Britain. And no tax could be more easily or more cheaply collected. Those in the occupation or employment of the land might readily pay their respective assessments as they fell due, or as they pay their other liabilities, to an authority appointed for the purpose. Or the land tax might be paid into the nearest post office to the credit of the Chancellor of the Exchequer, and a stamped receipt obtained, which would be the tenant's title to the occupancy of his holding.

And then what tax could possibly be fairer in its incidence? Take a plot of land far away from any town; its value would be comparatively small. Take again a plot of land in the heart of a great city, its value would be comparatively large Between these two extremes it is plain that the value of any plot of land would be accurately measured, and it is equally plain that every square yard of the land of any country would by this means be taxed in accurate proportion. Agricultural land would, acre for acre of course, be more lightly taxed than municipal land But so nicely can land values be adjusted that it is absolutely certain that except in very rare cases no one paying a land tax would be called to pay one penny more than the land in their occupation was worth. A factory owner might pay as much for a quarter of an acre as a farmer would pay for a hundred acres, and still the incidence of the tax be absolutely just, for as much wealth might be produced upon the smaller as upon the larger area.

Then upon the abundant revenue which such a tax would yield, it is not necessary to dwell further than I have already done   But I may point out that, inasmuch as only that value which was imparted by the community would be appropriated for common purposes, leaving improvements the property of the person who might make them, we have reserved the most powerful incentive to improvements of every kind. The land tax assessed as thus indicated could never be a burden, for the simple reason that a plot of land would always be worth its value, and accordingly agricultural and manufacturing industries might be pursued with perfect confidence on the part of those engaged in them that all the wealth which they could create by their own efforts would be their own, while the community would have the satisfaction of knowing that the value which attached to the land by reason of the integration of population, would fall into its legitimate place—the National Exchequer.

How simple, natural, and just is such an arrangement as compared with that which now obtain   Under existing circumstances a privileged few appro' 'ate not only the value of which an industrious population is the sole creator, but also practically all the wealth produced by that industrious population itself, less only what is sufficient to give a bare living to actual workers. Under the new order of things of a national proprietary, every individual worker would be in a position to command exactly the' 'hare of the wealth produced which

he had by his labour created; while the community
large would be put in possession of that portion of the
wealth produced of which it was the sole creator. The
worker in every case would get his own, no more, no
less. The community would do the same.

So far I have considered the effect of national proprietorship of the land upon the industrious portion of
the community as a whole. The relation of labour to
the land is always and everywhere the same, but it is at
once more simple and direct in agricultural industry,
and can in consequence be seen there most clear

Let it be remembered that it is the annual value
of the bare land, irrespective of improvements, which
it is proposed to appropriate in the form of taxation.
Accordingly, no question of who the improvements
belong to can arise Under the system of national
proprietary, the tiller of the soil would practically be
the owner of his farm, subject only to such conditions
as the State might impose It would be the interest of
the State to frame such conditions as would serve to
promote the greatest good of the people at large The
conditions might reasonably include—1st, That the land
should be cultivated , 2nd, that it should not be sub-
divided beyond certain limits, 3rd that the cultivator
should not hold more land than he could personally
superintend; 4th, that the State should have power to
grant liberty to work the mines and minerals, subject

to reasonable compensation to the tenant for disturbance or injury of any kind to the value of the occupancy.

I only mention these as samples of the conditions that might be imposed; but it is proper that I should say perhaps that the State would have a perfect right to impose conditions upon the tenure of land, whether used for agricultural or other purposes, for the simple reason that land is a fixed quantity. Of course the farmers generally would be chiefly interested in the amount to be levied as a tax. The tax is to be the annual value of the bare land. Manifestly that would vary according to circumstances. If a farm is situated within five miles, say, of a large town, the value of the occupancy of that land would be higher than if the farm were fifteen miles distant. So far then the effect of such a tax would be to put all farmers on an absolutely equal footing. A farmer residing near a town might be called upon to pay more for the occupancy of the same amount of land than a farmer living twenty miles away; but he would have his equivalent in the facility with which he could put his produce into the market Under these circumstances it is quite possible that the real value of land of equal quality might vary from as much as one pound to one shilling per acre But suppose that an agricultural holding is twenty miles from the nearest market town, and that that is but a small place, and that the produce of the farm when it reaches the market town has to be further conveyed a hundred miles by rail. Naturally the annual value of a farm of land so situated would be comparatively small, owing to its backward situation. Now, in the first place, it could be no hardship to the farmer to be called upon to pay his tax, for he would have its exact equivalent in the bare land. In the second place, it would be no advantage to him to compound with the government for the amount, for if he purchased the land at its true value, he would but be sinking money in the land, which it would be better worth his while to employ in improvements. In the third place, subject to this payment and to the other conditions I have named, the farm would be a freehold. It would be the tenant's to sell to the highest bidder if he so pleased, so that he did not infringe the law as to subdivision. Every improvement he made would realise its full market value to himself and to no other. In the fourth place, the benefit to the farmer would be immediate. He would not have to wander forty years in the wilderness only to catch sight of the promised land at last. In the fifth place, the farmer would have to pay no taxes, for the revenue from municipal and agricultural land would suffice for all purposes. Thus national proprietary or State ownership of the land would instantly constitute every farmer the practical owner of his farm, subject only to the yearly payment to the State of the annual value of the land exclusive of his improvements, and relieve him at once of those taxes and rates which he now pays in addition to his rent. This would mean an immediate practical advantage to the farming class, which could not fail to produce a very healthy influence upon agricultural industry. Farming would begin to pay. The demand for labour would be so great that labourers would be able to secure their full earnings.

Indeed it is in its effect upon the condition of the agricultural labourer that the virtues of national proprietary are most obvious. The fact that all land would be taxed up to its full value, whether it was in use or not, would throw open for cultivation the millions of acres now lying waste or given up to the mere preservation of game. By a system of judicious advances the State would certainly encourage the settlement upon this land of all persons able and willing to cultivate it In so far as the land now lying waste is in need of drainage on a large scale, this could be done at the public expense, and its increased value by reason of this drainage would be quickly returned to the revenue It would be the interest of the State to encourage the cultivation of every available acre of land, because an abundant and a cheap supply of food is the first essential to a prosperous commonwealth. The agricultural labourers would be the most likely class in the community capable of engaging in this enterprise. To them would belong the privilege, therefore, of choosing whom they would serve—a large farmer for weekly wages, or themselves as tenants of the small holdings into which the State would at once divide the vast areas of land now lying waste while multitudes perish of hunger. The cut-throat competition which now exists to obtain the bare living, which is all that the land monopolists permit to the lowest scale of workers, and which shows itself more or less mischievously in every stratum of society, would be destroyed at its very source. The agricultural labourer, instead of being, as now, the object of profound compassion to all men who can feel for their fellowmen, would have his share of the land, or its equivalent in higher wages; he would have his foot firmly planted on the first rung of the social ladder, and it would be his own fault if he did not rise to a position of comfort and comparative plenty.

Each individual would get his just share of the total wealth produced, and the expenses of government would be more than defrayed by the contribution of that annual value which attaches to the land by reason of the aggregation of population upon it. Now is the time for the practice of those eminent virtues temperance and thrift, for every improvement, whether in themselves or in their methods of working, would result in advantage to the workers. Every one would get his own, no more no less, and it would be his own, beyond the reach of any monopoly. How could poverty exist here? Only by voluntary idleness, intemperance, unthrift. Those who gave themselves up to bad habits of this kind would go to the wall. The tendency of the entire system would be in the same direction. The evil results which are the necessary product of the existing system would tend to disappear, for under the new system every encouragement to industry, temperance, and thrift would be present.

Now this same tendency would as certainly obtain in all branches of industry, for the relation of labour to land is the same everywhere, though it is less clearly seen in the busy town than in the open country. Make it possible for the lowest form of labour to obtain a fair day's wage for a fair day's work, and you help to do the same thing for the higher forms of labour, and the problem of how to secure an equitable distribution of wealth would soon be solved.

General prosperity would go hand in hand with progress. It would no longer be necessary to spend a hundred millions of money and more in purchasing the necessaries of life from abroad. They could be as readily produced in Great Britain. And a cheap and abundant supply of food would mean a larger and more prosperous population. Every incentive to improvement in the productive arts would exist; accompanying it we should experience a steadily-growing desire for "nobler modes of life," a community of industrious people removed above the fear of want, and regulating their lives like rational beings

LECTURE XXVII.

RIVAL REMEDIAL PROPOSALS

Prefatory Observations—How the Landlords have treated the People—How it is Proposed that the People should treat the Landlords—Direct and Indirect Robbery of the People—The Remedy of Peasant Proprietary—Its Inefficiency—Tending to Extend the Evil of Private Property in Land—Political and Economic Objections—Why the Tories are in Favour of Peasant Proprietary—How this System would still rob the Community—Various other Objections—Would practically Exclude the Labourers from becoming Land-owners—This System but Landlordism in another Form—Dr Russell Wallace's Remedy—Its Defects—The Financial Reform Association Remedy—Asks People to Demand 4s in the £ when entitled to 20s.—Only Just and Efficient Remedy in National Ownership of the Fee-Simple of all Land

In fulfilment of the promise made in my last lecture, I shall now proceed to the examination of several suggestions at present competing for public approbation as to the best method of dealing with the landlords. But in order that we may approach this task with unbiassed minds, nothing extenuating or setting down 'aught in malice, let us first of all consider briefly how the landlords have dealt with the people. I must recall to your mind that remarkable sentence of Professor Newman which I have already quoted: "If justice could be wisely and rightly separated from mercy, they (the landlords) might be treated as rudely and curtly as their ancestors under Henry VIII. treated the farmers and peasants whom they massacred and hanged by the roadside" If the learned professor had made that observation in Ireland it would have attracted more attention than it has yet done, for it is a truly remarkable observation, and presumably was not made at a "tumultuous public meeting" (Richard Cobden's apology for "strong language"), but calmly and dispassionately written down before being spoken and subsequently printed. Manifestly, then, it is worth while to inquire how the landlords have dealt with the people in the past before we consider how the people should deal with the landlords in the present.

There was a time when the land of England was the common property of the people. It was vested in the Crown as trustee for the people. The process by which the land became what it is now, the private property of a class, has been in the main the same in all three kingdoms. But in England the process by which the nation's property has gradually become the landlord's is very clearly traceable. Under the feudal

system, the expenses of government were defrayed by
the Crown lands, and the barons held their estates
subject to the supply of men and money for the services
of the Crown in time of need. Magna Charta simply
emphasised these arrangements. There was at least
one virtue in this system—it made the people valuable
in the eyes of the landlords, for a landlord was powerful
or otherwise according as he had a large or small number
of fighting men at his command. Presently, however,
when the military power of the barons had declined, it
became their interest to have large rent-rolls rather
than large armies of retainers, and they began to eject
the people from their farms, and to convert tillage land
into sheep-walks. The exportation of wool was a
profitable business, and accordingly sheep were more
valuable than men. Then came evictions and agrarian
discontent. The farmers were "got rid of either by
fraud or force," as one historian says; and the landlords
changed "rent by custom into rent by competition,"
"a change," says Professor Newman, "which converted
the landlord into a landowner." Thus the appropriation of the people's property went on until at last, in
the reign of Charles II., an Act was passed which con-
summated the iniquity. The king relieved the landowners of all payments in consideration of a revenue
which was to be derived from customs and excise.
The Act says, "Be it enacted that the moiety of the

excise on beer and cider, perry and strong waters, now
levied, shall be settled on the king's majesty, his heirs
and successors, as full recompense and satisfaction for
all tenures *in capite* and knight service, and of the
court of wards and liveries and all emoluments thereby
accruing, and in full satisfaction of all purveyance."
In 1692, however, a return was made to the old system,
and a tax of 4s. in the £ was imposed on the land; but
the effect of this measure was quickly nullified, for
the landlords, of course in Parliament assembled, fixed
two millions as the limit of their tax. The revenue from
this source was totally inadequate for governmental
purposes, and accordingly taxes, ever increasing in
amount, were levied upon industry.

But the way in which the landlords dealt with the
people is only half described. Year after year they pursued the policy of enclosing common lands, until it has
been estimated that in the thirty-one years from 1783
to 1814 as many as 2253 Enclosure Bills passed through
Parliament, by which the landlords took possession of
many millions of acres for which they paid absolutely
nothing, and which never were included in the land tax.
But the landlords have taken that which was not theirs
even in another respect. They have succeeded within
the period of the present reign in levying a private tax
upon agricultural industry and the community of over
£20,000,000 a year. "The total increase in this

private taxation by landlords is given in Mr. Caird's book on the *Landed Interest*, in which he informs us, at page 133, that the land-rental of England has risen fifty per cent. since 1836; and at page 97 he gives the aggregate land-rental of England alone, as assessed for income tax in 1875, at £50,125,000; or for Great Britain and Ireland at £66,911,000; consequently the equivalent of the advance of fifty per cent. in land-rentals since 1836 is nearly £22,304,000.

"When the Corn Laws were repealed, trade in Great Britain was in such a state of depression that the clamours about interfering with vested interests, and the other Conservative cries of alarm raised then, as now, were not able to maintain such laws, and they had to go at the imperious mandate of public opinion. Before these obnoxious laws were taken off the Statute Book, they yielded the public revenue £4,000,000 annually; and this sum was proved to be such a serious tax upon trade, and so injurious to commerce, that it had to be relinquished by the Government of the day. As soon as the ports of these countries were thrown open to the free admission of food from other lands, the exports of textile productions from England and Scotland began to correspondingly increase. Thus, while exported manufactures continued to bring back, as imports, largely increased supplies of foreign produce in exchange, rents for land continued to increase insidiously, until they have become, according to Caird, £22,000,000 higher than in Corn Law times. Thus the landlords of Great Britain and Ireland, in effect, are now taxing the trade and commerce of these countries nearly six times as much as these obnoxious Corn Laws taxed them in 1844; and this being so, may it not be expected that this will cause the flow in the tide of prosperity to cease, and the ebb to set in? But mark this difference: the £4,000,000 raised through the duty upon imported corn went into the Exchequer of the nation, whereas the £22,000,000 increased annual tax upon agricultural industry goes into the pockets of the landlords."[1]

This is the way the landlords have dealt with the people—they have literally stolen their property, both directly and indirectly.

There are three principal proposals before us for dealing with the landlords. One is, that with regard to agricultural land the tenant farmers shall, with the assistance of the public funds, purchase the fee simple of their farms. The idea is to increase the number of landowners.

Another proposal is that the State shall purchase the land by giving to the landlords annuities extending over three lives equal in value to their present incomes.

A third proposal is that the land tax of four shillings

---

[1] *Depression of Trade*, by William Lattimer, Carlisle, 1880, p 9

in the pound shall be levied upon the present valuation
of all lands

I shall venture to make a few observations upon
each of these proposals.

The first proposal is to establish a peasant proprietary by purchase on the part of the tenant, aided
by public funds. With regard to this, the first and
most obvious remark to be made is that it is difficult
to see how an increase in the number of those holding
private property in land can possibly remedy evils
which are so easily traceable to that institution as it
already exists. To magnify the cause of an evil is
surely an odd way to cure the evil itself. To my mind
it is clear that it is not in increasing the number of
those holding private property in land that the remedy
for the evils of land monopoly lies. Rather does it
lie in the abolition of the institution of private property
in land altogether.

It is thought that the comparative smallness of the
number of landowners enables them to act more as one
man in the protection of their "interests" than would
be the case supposing the number of landowners
enormously increased. But experience shows that self-
interest suffices to make very large bodies act together
with wonderful unanimity. And it is quite certain
that 300,000 or a million peasant proprietors, or petty
landlords, would act together as cordially as the present

landlord party in the three kingdoms. The voting power of the landlord party at the present time in Great Britain and Ireland is insignificant compared with the voting power of the landless party; yet how much greater is the political power of the former than of the latter? To recruit the ranks of the landlord party by the establishment of a peasant proprietary, and particularly with public money, is, then, nothing short of suicidal from the point of view of popular liberty. The blandishments of Mr. Bright, as they have been called, are no blandishments at all. It is perfectly true, as the right hon. gentleman has many and many a time insisted, that to create peasant proprietors is to add to the conservative force of any country. The English Tories, who number a few long-headed landlords in their ranks, know this very well, and the moment they succeed to office, we shall find that the public funds will be very liberally used to promote a peasant proprietary, particularly in Ireland, as the best of all possible means of sustaining "the institutions of the country," especially that most glorious of all Tory institutions, private property in land.

Now, I am far from undervaluing conservative forces in society, but I prefer those that make for the welfare of the whole community, to those which make for the welfare of a   , at the expense of the community and the peace of society.

But the purely economical objections to peasant proprietary are quite as weighty as the purely political. In the first place, it is a just complaint against the existing system that the landlords appropriate that increased value which attaches to land by reason of the aggregation of population. We have only to ask what have the landed proprietors in the neighbourhood of all the great centres of population in the three kingdoms done that they should become possessed of the great increase in the value of their land in consequence of the growth of these large towns, and the answer is clear. They have done absolutely nothing. And I would ask, in what respect would the case be different if any one of these estates were divided amongst a.large number of small proprietors? It appears to me that a tenant farmer, transformed by the aid of the State into a peasant proprietor, would be simply put in possession of a value which he did nothing to create, but which, on the contrary, was the creation of the community; and the community would thus be handing over to a section that which rightfully belonged to all. Then again, consider for a moment what difficulties such a scheme involves as between tenants themselves. One tenant holding a farm in the neighbourhood of a large town would enjoy an enormous advantage over another residing at a distance; for though they might both purchase on even terms, yet in the course of time, as the large town grew larger, the holding of the former would increase in value, while that of the latter would remain stationary; and while the market would be equally good for both, the farmer who had to convey his produce a great distance would be very heavily handicapped in comparison with the farmer who resided in the immediate neighbourhood of the market, and could put his produce into it at a minimum of cost. And, again, it appears to be forgotten by the advocates of a peasant proprietary that such a system but multiplies the difficulties which are now experienced in regard to the development of the industrial resources of a country. The black mail which a great landed proprietor levies upon a railway enterprise is frequently objected to, but does any one doubt that a thousand such landed proprietors would be quite as exacting in their demands? And if the Legislature should propose to limit the privileges of the peasant proprietors in this regard, how will the purchase price be adjusted? And similarly with respect to the working of mineral deposits. We know only too well how the system of royalties which the landlords are able to exact, operates prejudicially to the development of manufacturing industry. It appears to me that a system of peasant proprietorship would be even worse in this respect than the existing system. A dozen different " proprietors " might be in a position to prevent the opening of a mine, or at all events they might make such long demands upon the promoters of such an enterprise as would result in the forcing down to the minimum of a bare living the wages of those who might have no other resource but to work in such mine. And yet the difficulties do not end here. For one peasant proprietor might purchase his farm, in the expectation that the "mines and minerals" would be his as they had been his landlord's, and he might find that after all he had purchased what was not there. And another peasant proprietor might purchase his farm to find incalculable wealth beneath the surface.

In making a new settlement of the land question, therefore, we shall commit a fatal blunder if we leave out of consideration the great fact that the economic difficulties attached to the institution of private property in land will be simply multiplied by the number of peasant proprietors we create, if we proceed to our settlement on the lines laid down by the advocates of peasant proprietary.

But there are yet more fatal objections to this system. Its advocates appear to be under the delusion that a man who purchases the fee simple of his farm gets rid of rent. As a matter of fact he does nothing of the kind. He simply pays it in a lump sum, that is to say, he capitalises it. Where is the practical difference between a man who pays £1000 down for his farm and another who holds his in perpetuity at a rent of £50 per annum, tenant-right protected? There is a difference, for the former has his capital all locked up in his land, while the latter may employ his in earning far more than five per cent. The fallacy underlying this scheme is not made quite clear until a peasant proprietor comes to realise his property. Then two important facts come to light. In the first place, the purchaser finds that, however easily the seller may have acquired his property, it makes little difference to him, the purchaser; for the Government does not step in a second time to facilitate the process of purchase. The purchaser, in fact, finds that he must pay ready money for what the seller obtained by thirty-five instalments, and then if he has to borrow the money he finds, further, that no one is willing to lend it to him at three per cent. for thirty-five years. And this leads to the second fact, viz. that peasant proprietary, as advocated in the present day, practically excludes the labourers from all hope of ever being able to elevate themselves from their present degraded condition to anything better in connection with the land For if one farmer should find a difficulty in purchasing a farm from another, how much more difficult would it be for a labourer to become the owner of a farm? The difficulty is almost insuperable under existing circumstances; it would be entirely so under the system of peasant proprietary. On the other hand, this difficulty is minimised under a system of national ownership of the fee simple, for the labourer would then have to purchase only the tenant-right, and would enjoy his holding subject to the reduced rent or tax assessed on the value of the land minus improvements. In cases where farms are small and where the tenant-right is not of great value labourers would have an opportunity of becoming farmers, and of thus improving their position

Peasant proprietorship is simply landlordism in another form. The two systems of land tenure are in essence identical, and for that reason if for no other a remedy for social ills traceable to landlordism need not be looked for in the direction of peasant proprietary. Fatal as this objection is, however, there is another not less fatal. By what right are the public funds or the public credit to be utilised for the benefit of a section of the community merely? If public money or public credit is to be used at all it ought to be for the public good, and not exclusively for the good of a portion of the public only. In short, seeing how the landlords have dealt with the people, it is about the most monstrous proposal that ever was made to appropriate public funds to purchase for one class of the community that which another class has acquired from the nation by force and fraud.

The second proposal for dealing with the landlords is that made by Mr. Alfred Wallace. That gentleman proposes that a complete valuation of the landed property of the whole kingdom shall be made, and that then a distinction shall be drawn between the inherent value of the land and that which attaches to it by reason of improvements effected by the occupier or owner. The latter, Mr. Wallace proposes, shall remain the property of the landlord, to sell or to retain; the former, however, is to become the property of the State, and the change of ownership is to be effected in this way. Existing landowners and their expectant heirs are to be paid a fixed sum, or secured in the enjoyment of the full revenue from their lands for a fixed term. Says Mr. Wallace, "The principle that seems most consonant with justice is to continue the annuity successively to any heir or heirs of the landowner who may be living at the passing of the Act, and who may be born at any time before the decease of the said owner." The merit of Mr. Wallace's proposal is that it errs on the side of mercy to the landed interest. It is difficult to imagine a more gentle way of letting the landlords down. At the same time it is equally difficult to imagine a scheme more utterly neglectful of the interests of the community at large. The landlords have no claim either in justice or mercy to such considerations as Mr. Wallace proposes to extend to them. It must be remembered that if mercy may not rightly be separated from justice, neither may justice be altogether ignored. And Mr Wallace approaches perilously near to this in his proposal. The inherent value Mr. Wallace defines as that which attaches to the land by reason of its natural qualities as well as by reason of its contiguity to any considerable town. Surely mercy does not require nor does justice sanction the continuance to several successive lives at all events of that portion of the inherent value which attaches to land by reason of the aggregation of population. Mercy might suggest that the landlord class should not be deprived of what they have been wont to regard as "their property," without some allowance being made for them; but in justice they are not entitled to a fraction of "their property" which can be plainly shown to be "inherent value" And yet even mercy does not require that we should go to such extravagant lengths as Mr. Wallace's proposal involves The price is altogether too high. I do not see why we are called upon to do more than guarantee a bare living to the existing landlords and those depending upon them until such time as they may be capable of earning a living for themselves—say until they reach the age of fifteen years. We must put on one side much of the sickly sentimentality to which we are commonly treated in disquisitions upon this subject. It is nonsense to speak of the hardship which it would be to the delicately-nurtured scions of the aristocracy to be compelled to work. There is no hardship in the matter at all in comparison with the hardship involved in the existing social system to the millions who have worked at starvation point from childhood, and if there be any real suffering to the " delicately-nurtured " in the case, it would soon be got over. For the children of the aristocracy, if they were brought up to industrious habits, would soon cease to feel the " hardship " of their lot. Mr. Wallace's plan, therefore, is so far defective and inadequate.

So also is the proposal that a tax of four shillings in the pound shall be levied upon all landed property, the proposition for which the Financial Reform Association is responsible. No doubt this would be a step in the right direction and an excellent beginning; but it would only be a beginning, and it would take as much labour, education, and agitation to secure four shillings in the pound as it would to obtain the entire twenty. Suppose land taxed four shillings in the pound, what would be the result? This · The land which is now kept idle or waste would, to a large extent, become free to the use of labour and for purposes of food production, and would, for a time, afford some relief from the pressure of population upon the resources of industry. It would also add some thirty or forty millions annually to the National Exchequer. But these results would inevitably cause popular efforts for a further imposition of the tax to cease until economic conditions should again arise which would necessitate a further demand being made upon the privilege of land monopoly in the interests of labour and subsistence. In the mean time, however, the increase and better distribution of wealth which would follow from such a reform (as happened after the repeal of the Corn Laws), would enable the landlords to put back upon the nation the equivalent of the four shillings tax, just as they have succeeded, since the duty upon imported corn was abolished, in levying a private tax of £22,000,000 a year * in the form of increased rents upon the industrial community of Great Britain. We should thus have the struggle against landlordism again renewed; not, however, for a *second* fifth of the annual value of the land, but for the recovery of the *first*.

Under these circumstances, therefore, the full, but just, remedy is that for which all true social reformers should agitate, and that is that the annual value of the land of the nation should fall into the National Exchequer to be used in reduction or abolition of taxation, and in furtherance of the general good of the entire community.

* *See* pages 91, 92.

LECTURE XXVIII.

THE ORGANISATION OF LABOUR.

Existing System of Production and its effect upon the Interests of Labour—The Wages of Labour—Similarity in effect between Monopoly in the Agencies of Production and Monopoly in Land—Co operative Production—John Stuart Mill on Property in Land and Industrial Co-operation—How Co-operative Production might be initiated—Industrial Partnerships inadequate—Whitmore Collieries' Experiment a Failure—Maison Leclaire more successful—Only final solution of Labour Question in complete Co-operative Production.

IT is a wise saying, "You do take my life if you do take the means whereby I live;" and that this is so is nowhere more perfectly illustrated than in the monopoly of land. Ready access to the gifts of nature is essential to human well-being. Scarcely less essential is it that every human being should have the entire result of his own labour when applied to the gifts of nature. We have seen that so long as land is held as private property, access to the gifts of nature is practically denied to the mass of mankind, except upon such terms as the owners of the land are pleased to name. We have seen, also, that the monopoly of land is the efficient cause of the tendency of wages to the minimum of a bare living. And now it is not difficult to see that so long as the land of a country is the private property of a class, it must follow, ' as the night the day," that those who labour can never receive as wages the entire produce of their labour. A very considerable part of the produce of labour must go to those who enjoy a monopoly of the land; and another considerable part to those who stand between the landowners and the labourers, viz. the employers of labour.

No one can doubt that under the existing system of production the wages of the workers represent the least that employers are compelled to give; and equally no one can doubt that the least that employers are compelled to give is very far from being that to which workers are justly entitled. No question can arise that in a fair market the market-price of any commodity is the just price. But who will say that the labour market, under existing conditions, is a fair market? Labour is constrained to take what it can get, but who will venture to affirm that what it can get is what it ought to get?

I have already pointed out that the abolition of land monopoly, in destroying the power of holding land for speculative values, would practically result in a sharp competition between employers for labourers instead of the present cut-throat competition between labourers for work. At present the vast accumulations of capital in the hands of employers virtually operates in much the same way as the monopoly of land in the hands of a class. Great capitalists are able to hold for lower wages or higher profits, just as great landowners are able to hold for higher prices. And the question is, how can we effect such social arrangements as will result in a fair day's wages for a fair day's work—in other words, in the payment to the worker of his full equivalent for the work done by him? To me it appears that the answer to this question is to be found in the direction of co-operative production. The late John Stuart Mill, as any thoughtful student of his *Principles of Political Economy* may see, entertained the presentiment, if not the conviction, that the solution of social evils lay in the direction of making the land the common property of a community and in a system of industrial co-operation. In regard to the land, Mill says, "The essential principle of property being to assure to all persons what they have produced by their labour and accumulated by their abstinence, this principle cannot apply to what is not the produce of labour, the raw material of the earth. If the land derived its productive power wholly from nature and not at all from industry, or if there were any means of discriminating what is derived from each source, it not only would not be necessary, but it would be the height of injustice, to let the gift of nature be engrossed by individuals." In the same chapter of his great work Mr. Mill conclusively shows that private property in land, so far as England is concerned, "is very far from completely fulfilling the conditions which render its existence economically justifiable." And he adds: "In Ireland those conditions are not complied with at all." That remark is as perfectly true to-day as it was on the day when the distinguished economist placed it on record, and it is a happy circumstance that its truth is becoming more and more widely recognised. It is generally admitted by all thoughtful men, "when the 'sacredness of property' is talked of," "that any such sacredness does not belong in the same degree to landed property," and the following sentences, which at the time of their first publication were no doubt regarded as embodying merely the "pious opinions" of a social visionary, are now regarded as the statement of fundamental truths. "No man made the land. It is the original inheritance of the whole species. Its appropriation is wholly a question of expediency. When private property in land is not expedient it is unjust"[1] I remember well the effect which a first reading of these sentences produced upon my mind. To me they

---

[1] *Principles of Political Economy*, Book II ch ii

seemed the articles of a new social charter, and lapse
of time and calmer consideration have but deepened
and strengthened my conviction that Mr Mill's mind
was steadily travelling in a direction that would certainly
have led him to declare the monopoly of land to be the
fruitful source of social ills.

Not less clear is it that Mr. Mill looked to co-operative
production for a solution of the problem how to secure
to every worker a fair day's wages for a fair day's work.
He writes: "In the co-operative movement, the permanency of which may now be considered as insured,
we see exemplified the process of bringing about a
change in society, which would combine the freedom
and independence of the individual with the moral,
intellectual, and commercial advantages of aggregate
production; and which, without violence or spoliation,
or even any other sudden disturbance of existing habits
and speculations, would realise, at least in the industrial
department, the best aspirations of the democratic spirit,
by putting an end to the division of society into the
industrious and the idle, and effacing all social distinc-
tions but those fairly earned by personal services and
exertions.

"Associations like those we have described (viz. co-
operative societies as they existed twenty or thirty
years ago—that is, mainly for purposes of distribution—
and industrial partnerships of the Leclaire and Briggs'

type), by the very process of their success, are a course of education in those moral and active qualities by which alone success can be either preserved or attained. As associations multiplied they would tend more and more to absorb all workpeople, except those who have too little understanding or too little virtue to be capable of learning to act on any other system than that of narrow selfishness. As this change proceeded, owners of capital would gradually find it to their advantage, instead of maintaining the struggle of the old system with workpeople of only the worst description, to lend their capital to the associations; to do this at a diminishing rate of interest, and at last, perhaps, even to exchange their capital for terminable annuities. In this or some such mode, the existing accumulations of capital might honestly, and by a kind of spontaneous process, become in the end the joint property of all who participate in their productive employment, a transformation which, thus effected (and assuming, of course, that both sexes participate equally in the rights and in the government of the association), would be the nearest approach to social justice, and the most beneficial ordering of industrial affairs for the universal good, which it is possible at present to foresee." [1]

It is impossible not to admire the cautious spirit pervading Mr. Mill's suggestions in reference to the

[1] *Principles of Political Economy*, B. IV. ch. vii. § 6

means which might in his view be honestly used to bring
about the change from individual ownership to common
ownership of both land and capital. It appears to me
that he saw very clearly the conclusions to which his
reasoning pointed, but that he shrank from declaring
them in plain terms, preferring to content himself with
indicating the direction in which his conclusions would
reveal themselves, and offering in the mean time a
suggestion as to how the end he had in view might
be reached almost surreptitiously.

Having regard to all the forces which operate in
society, the virtual omnipotence of vested interests and
the firm hold which the doctrine of "every one for
himself and the devil take the hindmost" has upon the
popular mind, it is perhaps wise of social reformers to
follow the line of the least resistance, and present their
views as insinuatingly as may be. But the time has
now come for declaring that in a common ownership of
the land and the means of production is most certainly
to be found the "nearest approach to social justice and
the most beneficial ordering of industrial affairs for the
universal good."

We cannot say of capital, however, that no man
made it, and it appears to me, therefore, that the
community would have no such justification for boldly
appropriating existing accumulations of capital as exists
for the appropriation of land. We should rather aim

at preventing these great accumulations of capital in few hands by adopting a system of production the reverse of that which now prevails, and by virtue of which these great accumulations are possible Instead of a hundred or a thousand workers working for one employer, who by reason of the monopoly of land and his command of capital is able to fix the rate of wages, we should aim at constituting a hundred or a thousand workmen their own employers. And the thing is very simple. All you have to do is, first, to destroy the monopoly of land by taxing it all up to its full value— exclusive of improvements. The immediate result of this would be a rise in wages from the minimum of a bare living, for which the worker is now forced to work, to the maximum which an employer would be willing to pay. As a consequence the wages of the workers would more closely approximate to their earnings, and they would be able to devote a portion of their wages to the accumulation of a capital fund which would enable them to enter upon a co-operative enterprise in which they would be their own employers, and their wages exactly equivalent to their earnings.

It must be frankly conceded, however, that the day is somewhat remote when co-operation or collectivism may be expected completely to displace competition or individualism. I believe, nevertheless, that the day will surely come when self-interest will no longer be the great motive power of human enterprise. John Stuart Mill is probably right in affirming that Socialists are in error in so far as they "charge upon competition all the economical evils which at present exist;" but in my humble judgment Mr. Mill is himself in error in estimating competition so highly as he does. "They" (the Socialists), he says, "forget that wherever competition is not monopoly is." Surely the fact is patent to the simplest observation, that in the existing order of society competition emphatically *is*, and monopoly no less emphatically *is*, also. Co-operation, and not competition, is the real enemy of monopoly. And while I would not deny that competition, within certain limitations, has its advantages, I would venture to hope that in the time to come all the virtues which are commonly supposed to lurk in that principle may be found to arise far more abundantly from the simple endeavour of enlightened men and women to play their part in the social economy as rational beings How much longer are we to drag the banner of human progress in the mire of self-interest and cut-throat competition? How much longer are the apostles of humanity to be guilty of atheism? We are taught to believe that God is Love; yet we are at the same time asked to believe that the children of God must needs each seek his own. I for one repudiate this doctrine, and affirm that not in self-interest, but in self-sacrifice, not in competition, but in co-operation lies the most beneficent motive power of human progress, and to this let us for the future appeal. "Knowledge comes, but wisdom lingers," it is true, and we may be well aware of the right path long before we are courageous enough to walk in it; but if history has any lesson to teach it is this—that it is high time to cease stoning the prophets and commence following them.

Already a beginning has been made. Industrial partnerships, as they are called, are a step in the right direction. They proceed on the lines of least resistance, and alarm no one. Yet it must be said that so far as the system of profit-sharing has yet been developed, it only serves to show that the ultimate and only really satisfactory system must be that in which the workers engage on equal terms, and jointly own the means necessary for the successful prosecution of a given industry. In such industrial partnerships as I have been able to study the management has been vested more or less absolutely in the employers, so that, as in the Whitwood Collieries, for example, the relation of employer and employed has still subsisted. Such profit-sharing as there was in this instance was wholly dependent on the good will of the Messrs. Briggs. No doubt these gentlemen were actuated by the simplest motives, but it is very clear that they always recognised that their first duty was to the shareholders Profits were "shared" only after a certain amount was made, and the scheme resolved itself into a device for inducing the colliers to ensure more regular profits to the owners of the collieries. Indeed, it was publicly claimed that the system of profit-sharing adopted in this instance would "increase rather than diminish the dividend to the shareholders."

In many other partially successful instances of the application of this principle the same features of absolute control on the part of the employers and increased advantage to them are present. But it is distinctly noteworthy that the instances in which the application of the principle has been attended with the most striking success have been those in which these features have been gradually modified. Probably in the Maison Leclaire we have the most conspicuously successful illustration of the application of the principle of profit-sharing, and it is in this case that we have the nearest approach to co-operative production with which I am familiar. Even in this instance, however, "the business direction of the house is placed exclusively in the hands of the two managing partners, who hold half the capital, and undertake personal liability for losses, which does not attach to the workmen, except in an indirect manner through their interest in the reserve fund."[1] A thoroughly successful example of the per-

[1] *Profit Sharing*, ch. i. Sedley Taylor, M.A.

fect application of the principle of co-operative production, therefore, remains to be revealed. The complete
organisation of industry on the basis of joint ownership
of capital and absolute control on the part of the
workers is a thing of the future. That this should be
the end to be kept clearly in view I am satisfied. The
first and most necessary means to this end is to abolish
land monopoly. Thus by removing the cause of the
tendency of wages to the minimum of a bare living
workers will be in a position to exact their whole earnings, instead of the moiety, or even less, which they
now receive; and they will then have but to set apart
a portion of their earnings as capital, and combine in
the employment of their own capital and labour in any
given industrial enterprise. Some time must elapse,
no doubt, before the blessings of education will be so
widely diffused as to render the workers, as a whole,
equal to the management of any considerable number
of great concerns; but in the ranks of the working
classes, to my own personal knowledge, are to-day to be
found many men quite equal to the work requiring to be
done. Is it not reasonable to predict, therefore, that ere
long examples of the successful application of the genuine
principle of co-operative production will present themselves in sufficient numbers to lead the industrial classes,
with growing persistence, to look in this direction for their
emancipation from their present state of dependence?

LECTURE XXIX.

STATE SOCIALISM.

State Organisation *versus* State Regulation of Labour—Individualism *versus* Communism—Growth of State Socialism—Beneficial Results—Comparative Risks of Labour and Capital—Insurance on Workmen's Lives should be paid out of Profits of Capital—Necessity for further State Regulation—Co-operative Functions of Municipalities—Natural Evolution of State Functions.

THE organisation of labour, on the principles laid down in my last lecture, if it could be carried out to any considerable extent, would have the effect of directing attention very steadily to what must be the ultimate solution of the social question, viz. the independence of labour, an equitable distribution of the wealth produced by labour, and State ownership of the raw materials to which labour must be applied. It is greatly to be desired that some earnest attempts at such an organisation of labour as that indicated should be made at once; for, after all, the human mind is intensely practical, and the question with regard to any scheme, no matter how theoretically perfect it may be, always is, How does it work? Indeed, it must be frankly admitted that it is not desirable to make great changes without ascertaining as far as possible how the proposed changes will work. The undiscovered country naturally puzzles the will.

The organisation of labour in a few cases on the principle already referred to would have the further advantage of indicating how far the idea of the State organisation of labour is practicable or not. For my own part, I am bound to admit that the difficulties in the way of the realisation of such an idea appear to me to be so enormous that social reformers would do wisely to direct their attention, for the present at all events, rather to the State regulation of labour. It will be through State regulation that we shall obtain State organisation of labour, if we ever do attain to such a thing, for regulation imperceptibly shades into organisation.

A careful observation of the existing social system goes far to show that there is a distinct tendency in the direction of a golden mean between the extremes of individualism and communism. We have a large body of legislation directed to the regulation of the relations between labour and capital; and we have many great enterprises, either under the supervision, or altogether in the hands of local or Imperial authorities. The famous dictum of the Utilitarian School, "the greatest good of the greatest number," is steadily disrupting the philosophy of selfishness, which asks, "May I not do as I will with my own?" It is conceded on every hand that the interest of the individual is subordinate to the interest of the community, and recent history is full of instances showing that when the two interests clash the former goes to the wall. And there is happily also a growing feeling that the compensation of individuals for the subordination of their interest to that of the community must be confined for the future within more reasonable limits than has heretofore been customary. We may take it, therefore, that with the growth of popular enlightenment and popular power, we shall see further developments in the same direction. It is the line of the least resistance; in other words, it is the natural course of events, and social reformers would in my judgment do well to exert themselves to extend the application of the principle of the State regulation of the relation between labour and capital and governmental control and ownership of enterprises similar in character to those which are already subject to such supervision or ownership. We need not be alarmed by the cry that State regulation of industry is in restraint of trade. So far as the principle has yet been applied, it has on the whole been productive of very great good; and it is not unreasonable to assume that it is capable of much wider application with corresponding advantage. Of course it would be exceedingly beneficial if we could hit upon some well-defined limits within which the principle might be permitted to work freely ; but after giving much earnest thought to the subject, I am free to confess that I have no better rule to offer than this—that every case must be decided on its own merits. Where it can be clearly shown that the application of the principle of State regulation would be distinctly for the general good of the community, there the principle should be boldly applied. Where there is any doubt about it, there we should do well to wait for fuller light.

To my mind, for example, though I freely admit my early experiences may incline me to take a partial view of the matter, workers might well demand much more drastic measures of compensation for injuries sustained in the prosecution of their employment than they are now entitled to receive. For, after all, the risks of capital, of which we hear so much, are as nothing in comparison with the risks of labour, of which we hear so little. The risks that are run every day and every hour by workers in coal-mines, and indeed in almost all trades, are risks of life and limb But what are the risks which a colliery owner or a factory owner or a railway shareholder runs? They are never risks of life and limb, but always risks that are reducible to a minimum by prudence and foresight. No amount of these qualities, however, on the part of ninety-nine out of a hundred colliers or factory hands or railway *employés* can shield them from the folly of the hundredth man, or the neglect of an employer to observe the most elementary precautions against disaster. Workers, then, I say, might with perfect propriety insist that the State should go much further than it has already gone in the way of making employers liable for injuries sustained by their workmen, unless it can be clearly proved that the injury has resulted from the negligence of the person injured. It is a distinct hardship that a man or a boy, from no fault of his own, should be maimed for life and cast upon the world without the means of livelihood; and it is a still greater hardship when the head of a family is struck down, leaving behind him a number of young children totally unprovided for. The capitalist who takes from his enterprise a yearly sum often equal to the aggregate wages of his workers, may be fairly, I think, called upon to set aside a much larger porportion of his income than he now does as a sort of insurance fund upon which his workers may draw in such cases as I have mentioned. It is idle to say that a workman should be provident, and should set aside a portion of his own earnings to meet such cases, for, in the first place, under existing arrangements, no workman gets what he earns; and in the second place, what he does get amounts on the average to no more than a bare subsistence. Thrift is an excellent social virtue, but so far as the great body of the working classes is concerned its practice is all but impossible. I am quite aware that pages of statistics can be adduced to show that the working classes are much better off now than was formerly the case; but I take my facts from actual experience amongst the working classes; and the net result of my observation is that not one workman in five is in a position to save a sum of money equal to the necessity occasioned by his permanent disablement or death. And, besides, to throw the responsibility upon the workman in such a case as that to which I am referring, is to beg the whole question. If it were in the pursuit of his own interest alone that he sustained injury or met with death, something might be said as to the obligation resting upon him to make provision for such contingencies. But the workman unhappily is generally promoting the interest of his employer rather than his own, and upon the employer therefore rests, in my judgment, the obligation to set aside, as a first charge upon profits, an annual sum for the purpose mentioned.

In the matter of the hours of labour, the employment of women and children, sanitary inspection, and other kindred matters, there is ample scope for a beneficial extension of the principle of State regulation. For it is obvious that though the organisation of labour would render the workers less and less liable to the tyranny of capital, it would afford no guarantee against either overwork or work under unwise conditions. It is quite conceivable, indeed, that a community of workers owning their own capital, and being in fact their own employers, might be worse tyrants to themselves, their women and children, than even the most grasping capitalists of the present day. Competition between co-operative associations or organised industrial communities would tend to produce evils as great as any resulting from competition between capitalist employers of labour. Therefore the interference of the State would be as imperatively called for as now. Regulation of industry would be necessarily carried to its extremest point, and it would be more clearly seen to what extent it would be desirable to make the complete organisation of industry a function of the State.

My own conviction is, that the common sense of the community will prove to be the co-ordinating power which socialist philosophers aver must be developed as the social organism becomes more complex. I doubt whether it will ever be necessary for the State to become a universal employer in the sense in which I think it should become a universal landlord. For once labour discovers that it may make capital its instrument by the principle of association, and thus secure to itself the entire produce of its exertions; and once the gifts of nature by being vested in the State are free to all under equal conditions, I am convinced that "the common sense of most" will suffice to secure all that will remain to be secured. The common sense of the community will dictate the conditions under which industry should be pursued, and the further interference of the State will be rendered unnecessary. And happily we need have no fear of the growth of common sense, nor of its sufficiency as the co-ordinating power of an increasingly complex social system. There is undoubtedly much to deplore in the condition of society to-day—enough perhaps to drive men of strong passions to a despairing resort to the resources of savagery for a radical remedy; but to men of stronger faith it is clear that there are moral forces at work portending peaceful revolutions more mighty than any the world has known since the dawn of Christianity. To all true reformers the growth of popular enlightenment is a source of supreme satisfaction, for it is the one power which is sufficient to cope with social ills.

The function of the State is much less disputed in regard to the regulation of such matters as have a more distinctly apprehended relation to the welfare of the community. If we glance at the duties discharged by the local authorities, or the governments of the larger and more enlightened towns of the three kingdoms,

we see that there is a rapidly-increasing tendency
in the direction of co-operative association. In many
of the great towns the gas and water-works are the
property of the corporation. Public schools, libraries,
parks, baths, and workhouses, are among municipal
institutions. The corporation not only lights but paves
the streets, and drains the town. Some corporations
even provide their constituents with gas cooking-stoves.
In England and Scotland local authorities employ and
control the police   And so far has this tendency to
multiply the duties of corporations extended, that some
years ago Mr. Chamberlain proposed that the town of
Birmingham should acquire and work all the public-
houses.[1]

[1] At the time of writing, I have before me the prospectus of a
singularly interesting enterprise, of which the midland metropolis
is the scene   A company has been formed for the supply of com-
pressed air, through mains and pipes, over a considerable area of
the town   The expectation is that many small manufacturers
will avail themselves of the motive power thus supplied, and that
it will ultimately be availed of by builders and contractors, by
owners of fire-pumps, by tramcar companies, and that it will be
used for a great variety of purposes : such as ventilating noxious
spaces, blowing organs, and the production of electricity. The
company has entered into an agreement with the corporation, by
which it binds itself to keep a constant supply of power, and to
supply on demand any one within reasonable distance of the mains.
Profits are regulated under the scheme to the extent that none are
to be divided beyond ten per cent., until fifty per cent. of the
profits beyond that amount have been applied to the reduction of
rates and charges. Provision is also made for the acquirement of

The truth is that it is impossible to lay down any hard and fast line as the limit of State regulation or enterprise. The principle underlying all these functions which municipalities now discharge, is that the enterprises which are subject to regulation, or are directly owned by corporations, are either of the nature of monopolies, or are monopolies pure and simple. Public utility alone dictates when and to what extent all such partial or complete monopolies shall be under the control or entirely in the hands of municipalities. And it is not likely that corporations will shrink from extending their functions in this respect. The growing complexity of the social system is matched at all events by the growing capacity of communities. The question is very simple—What reason have we to suppose that the people of this generation are not equal to their duties? No municipality has yet gone so far as to propose to acquire the land upon which the town is built, but I cannot believe that the day is far distant

---

the undertaking by the corporation after the lapse of a certain time, and if the company cease for twelve consecutive months to use any of the pipes put down they become the property of the corporation. If this enterprise should succeed—and it is but a new form of what has already been done with gas—may we not expect that, if ever electricity takes the place which many people believe it is destined to take in our social economy, corporations will not only light factories and streets, but furnish motive power in them? In the face of facts like these who will define the limits of the co-operative functions of corporations?

when some daring spirit will propose that the corporation of some large town should acquire the land upon which it stands, and devote the revenue to the benefit of its citizens

And when our survey of the enterprises, which are admittedly functions of State, is further extended, we find that prisons, hospitals, asylums, armies, dockyards, libraries, museums, telegraphs, are all owned by the State, which also distributes letters and parcels through a vast postal organisation, and saves the people's money in its post-office savings' banks, and insures their lives even by the same agency. Indeed, it is almost as difficult to say what the State already does, as to say what it may not be expected to do in the near future. So far the State has never relinquished its primary right in the land, and it may be expected ere long to go very great lengths in the way of regulating the tenure of land. The Irish Land Act of 1881 is but a prelude to English and Scotch Land Acts, which will put Agricultural Holdings' Acts and Irish Land Acts completely in the shade. Whenever the English and Scottish people come to deal with the land question as a question involving something more than an adjustment of relationships between landlord and tenant, they will hardly be content with such a measure as they thought should satisfy "the mere Irish." Already "the landed" betray a nervous anxiety to secure places of refuge in

America and the Colonies. They have an instinctive feeling that State regulation of the tenure of land will merge very rapidly into State ownership of land Once let it be made quite clear that 'landlords' are reduced to the level of mere pensioners, and the thing will be done. There is a strong feeling against the pension list as it now stands. It has but to be augmented to be swept away.

So far, again, the State has confined itself in these countries, at all events, to the regulation of railways. But it is very plain that public opinion is steadily growing in favour of the acquisition of these great properties by the State, so as to cheapen the cost of travel and goods transit for the community.[1]

The arguments which may be adduced in favour of the State ownership of the postal and telegraph services apply with tenfold force to the acquisition of the

[1] Curiously enough, in a recent Irish Act we see State control merging into State ownership in a very significant manner. The Tramways Act provides for a baronial guarantee of a dividend of five per cent. to those who will advance capital for the construction of tramways But if at any time the Tramway Company should fail, then the Grand Jury of the county are charged with the management of the enterprise at the expense of the guarantors. If a straw will show the way the wind blows, we may take it that we have in the Tramways (Ireland) Act a measure embodying the state ownership principle in a more pronounced form even than any other measure relating to internal communications The acquirement of the railways by the State is, therefore, merely a matter of time

railways by the State. It is perfectly true that the
railways of England and Scotland are not a complete
monopoly in the sense in which the land is; but they
are a practical monopoly of the most flagrant character,
and the community would undoubtedly derive many and
great advantages from their transference to the State.
They should be a means of public income, and might
readily be made to supply the place of a much less
creditable source of revenue, the liquor traffic, which
a good many people think all respectable governments
should be glad to get rid of.

I have in previous lectures laid down the lines upon
which the State should go in matters of education, and
also in reference to the land; and it is not necessary to
do more now than to say that in regard to the functions
of the State, and especially in reference to the limits of
State regulation of industry, or supervision or ownership
of enterprises that either approximate to or are complete
monopolies, no one can pronounce a dogmatic opinion.
No one can say absolutely what is and what is not the
duty of the State. It is for every successive generation
in any given community to say what duties shall be
discharged independently by individuals or collectively
by the State. With growing intelligence on the part of
the people we may fairly expect a wider comprehension
of common interests, and a consequent extension of the
area of State control, and it is, therefore, in earnest

painstaking effort to advance popular education, that we may bring the workers of all countries to see in what direction their highest interests may be most safely and surely sought, in equally earnest and painstaking effort to organise and direct popular power, that the popular will may find most clear and emphatic expression, and in unceasing endeavours to simplify the methods of government, by separating what is local from what is general, that both local and general governments may be equal to the due discharge of the additional functions which the near future has in store for them; it is, I say, upon efforts of this character that social reformers would do most wisely to expend their energies. It is, I repeat, the line of the least resistance, or the natural course of events. It is the path illumined by the Star of Hope. If we pursue it faithfully for a single generation even, those who come after us, realising the advantages of co-operative association seen in the possession by the State of a vast body of common property held and directed for the common welfare, will wonder that we could have hesitated at all in doing that the very mention of which now excites the smile of derision

LECTURE XXX.

STATE OWNERSHIP OF RAILWAYS.

Professor Jevons on the Functions of the State in relation to the
State Ownership of Railways—Objections considered.

IF any objection is offered to what has been so far
advanced, it is most likely to be directed against
the suggestions that land should be constituted the
common property of the people, and that the railways
should be owned by the State. I have already so far
anticipated the objections that may be raised to a
national proprietorship of land, that it is not necessary
to pursue that matter any further now. It is desirable,
however, to attempt some answer to objections raised
against the acquisition of the railways by the State.
The late Professor Jevons is the most vigorous opponent
of the proposal, with whose writings I am familiar, and
an address delivered by that gentleman about ten years
ago, and published at the time, embodies, I believe, all
that there is to be said against the acquisition of the

railways by the State.[1] Mr. Jevons is not altogether opposed to the extension of the functions of Government, for he was one of the most powerful advocates of the Government purchase of the telegraphs and the establishment of a parcels post. So far back as 1867, in a paper read at a meeting of the Manchester Statistical Society, Mr. Jevons gave it as his own "strong opinion" that "no abstract principle and no absolute rule can guide us in determining what kinds of industrial enterprise the State should undertake, and what it should not... Nothing but experience and argument from experience can in most cases determine whether the community will be best served by its collective State action, or by trusting to private self-interest." And many years later, in a most admirable little work—*The State in Relation to Labour*—Mr. Jevons unhesitatingly declared with regard to the grounds and limits of legislation: "I conceive that the State is justified in passing any law, or even in doing any single act which, without ulterior consequences, adds to the sum-total of happiness. Good done is sufficient justification of any act, in the absence of evidence that equal or greater evil will subsequently follow." It would be a fair representation of Mr. Jevons' views to say that he was not in principle

---

[1] This address, with some others, has since been republished in a volume entitled *Methods of Social Reform*.

opposed to State control of the railways, or any other
enterprise so closely approximating to a monopoly;
but that he was very firm in demanding that the case
for their acquisition should be made out with as near
an approach to perfection as possible. There appeared
to him to be "four principal conditions under which
State management of any branch of industry" could
be successful, and therefore justifiable. These were
as follows.

"1. The work must be of an invariable and routine-
like nature, so as to be performed according to fixed
rules.

"2. It must be performed under the public eye, and
for the service of individuals who will immediately
detect and expose any failure or laxity.

"3. There must be very little capital expenditure, so
that each year's revenue and expense account shall
represent with approximate accuracy the real commercial
success of the undertaking.

"4. The operations must be of such a kind that
their union under one all-extensive government monopoly will lead to great advantage and economy."

Mr. Jevons was willing to admit that so far as all
these conditions save the third were concerned, they
might reasonably be expected to be fulfilled in the
State management of the railways. The third condition,
he felt, presented an insuperable obstacle. I confess

I am quite unable to see why it should necessarily
be so.   Mr. Jevons lays much stress upon the fact that
the State paid a premium of about a hundred per cent.
in effecting the compulsory purchase of the telegraphs,
and he asks us to contemplate the prospect before us if
we should venture upon the acquisition of the railways
with their vast capital, amounting to not less than
£600,000,000.   It appears to me little short of absurd
to expect that any Government would acquire railways
on any such terms as are here suggested.   I am not
prepared to say that the railways should be simply
taken over by the State without purchase, but I have
no hesitation whatever in declaring that any such thing
as compensation for compulsory purchase is altogether
out of the question.   The institution of terminable
annuities, estimated with due regard to the fact that
the annuitants would have the security of the Government for their payment, might meet the case, and it
must always be remembered that the railway property
of these three kingdoms is scarcely a whit less dependent for its value upon the industry of the people than
is the land   The railway companies have enjoyed for
many years the privilege of levying a heavy toll upon
industry, and they have taken very good care to compete with each other only in the effort to discover at
what point they had better cease to compete.   The
community will have scrupulous regard to facts of

this character when the time comes for converting railway shareholders into holders of terminable annuities, and transferring the management of the different railway systems to the governments of the three countries. The objection that the cost of effecting the transfer renders the proposal for ever impossible is therefore invalid. The railway companies will have to submit to be dealt with in such a way as the community thinks fit. For it is exactly as Mr. Jevons himself declares · "It may be fearlessly said that no social transformation would be too great to be commended and attempted if only it could be clearly shown to lead to the greater happiness of the community. No scheme of Bellew, or Babeuf, or Robert Owen could be resisted if only their advocates could adduce scientific evidence of their practicability and good tendency, No laws, no customs, no rights of property are so sacred that they may not be made away with if it can be clearly shown that they stand in the way of the greatest happiness. *Salus populi suprema lex.*" [1]

Now, Mr. Jevons frankly admits that there would be many advantages in State control. The objections are mainly two : first, that it would realise very few of the prodigious advantages anticipated from it, and second, that it would probably be a disastrous financial speculation. With regard to the first of these objections, it

---

[1] *The State in Relation to Labour*, pp. 11, 12.

appears to me that its whole force lies in the word prodigious, and I see no reason why the community should look for any such advantages. It might well be content with such advantages as satisfy existing share-holders, and such additional advantages as Mr. Jevons himself admits would accrue from State ownership, such as "the union of all railways in one complete system," allowing of "much economy in superintendence, in the use of the rolling stock, the avoidance of competing trains," "the arrangement of rates of passenger and goods traffic in regard to the interests of the people rather than the interests of shareholders," and so forth; not to speak of the unquestionable advantage of obtaining for the community that increment of value inevitable in prosperous and progressive countries. It is very easy to draw up a catalogue of "prodigious advantages," and then object to the acquisition of railways by the State, because such advantages are impossible of realisation; but to do so does not really affect the argument.

The second objection is not more real than the first. I see no reason to suppose that State control of railways "would probably be a disastrous financial operation" Mr. Jevons' reason for supposing so is that the vast amount of capital involved, "represented by property of the most varied and complicated character," destroys all analogy to the post office; and he says, "if we want to know how the Government would manage such a property we should look not to the post office, which owns no property of any consequence, but to the Admiralty, which holds the dockyards and maintains a large fleet, or to the department of public works." And we are then treated to a melancholy disquisition on the iniquities of these departments. But it is most surprising to me that Mr. Jevons, who is ordinarily most scrupulously careful of his analogies, should have overlooked the fact that the dockyards and the department of public works, though they involve a vast expenditure on capital account, differ from the railways in a very important particular. The work they do is not "performed under the public eye, or for the service of individuals, who will immediately detect and expose any failure or laxity." If this condition applied to the dockyards and the department of public works, it is at least open to question whether they would continue to be guilty of that wasteful expenditure of public money with which they are now generally charged. Mr. Jevons frankly allows, with regard to the railways, that "the larger part of the traffic can be carried on according to a pre-arranged and published time-table, so that the public, whether in travelling or transmitting goods, will have apparently as good a means as in the post office of scrutinising the efficiency of the department and exposing any laxity." It is strange that Mr. Jevons should not have observed that in this respect there was practically

all the difference in the world between the dockyards
and the railways. But it may safely be said that, in so
far as the validity of the second objection depends upon
the perfection of the analogy between the dockyards and
the railways, it is sufficiently rebutted when it is shown
that the analogy fails in the vital point I have specified. But I may go yet further, and point out that
after all capital expenditure is only a question of degree,
and that, when there is a department like the post-
office, subject to close and popular supervision, and
involving a tolerably large expenditure, working satisfactorily in every respect, it may be safely assumed
that, all other things being equal, we may proceed
further in the same direction, even to the length of
constituting the railways a department of the State
It is not a valid objection that simply by reason of their
becoming a Government department the finances of the
railways would get into confusion. That, as Mr. Jevons
affirms, "no English Government department has ever
yet furnished a real balance-sheet" is no argument
against the State acquisition of railways, but rather an
argument for the reform of Government departments.
It might even be argued that it would be well to constitute the railways a department of the State if for
no other purpose than to have at least one department
that could present a balance-sheet, for it would be idle
to suppose that the moment the railways become public

property the officials would all turn rogues, and present the nation with unreal balance-sheets.

Indeed, it may be said generally that all the objections urged by Mr. Jevons are based upon the assumption that there is in a Government department some necessary inefficiency. Now, I am quite ready to admit that Government departments are not what they should be. Nor are they what they might be. Nor, again, are they what they will be in the very near future. As the masses of people grow in competence to appoint governments, governments and government departments will increase in efficiency. Then things that may be regarded as impracticable now will be found to be perfectly practicable. At all events we may hope that then some way will be found of giving practical effect to proposals the theoretical soundness of which Mr Jevons himself does not venture to dispute. "The general conclusion at which I arrive," he says, "concerning the schemes of Government purchase is that they are impracticable." He does not say they are bad in principle. And his conclusion that they are impracticable must be accepted, if Government departments are necessarily corrupt and incompetent and not subject to efficient supervision, and if in purchasing the railways the State must necessarily pay double their market value, or even the "market value" itself. But these are altogether arbitrary and totally inadmissible assumptions, and the reasoning of which they form the basis is accordingly inconsequential.

But there is another objection of quite a different character of which some notice must be taken. It is, that to constitute the railways a department of Government would be to place in the hands of the Minister and officials in charge of the department an amount of political influence so large that it could not fail to be a source of political corruption. There is no doubt that an increase of officialism of the kind that is now so common is not a thing to be desired. But my contention is that officialism tends to improvement with every improvement in the body politic; and particularly with reference to officialism of the special type connected with 'those departments of the public service that most directly touch the people, do I think we may rest assured that corruption would be reduced to a minimum. In any case, however, it is doubtful if there could possibly be placed in the hands of any Minister a power equal to that which is exercised by the railways now. If the railways were a department of Government, the power of the Minister would on the whole be exercised in the interests of the community, since " Her Majesty's Opposition " would carefully watch " Her Majesty's Government," and bring before the great tribunal of public opinion any political jobbery which might be attempted for individual or party purposes.

But as matters now stand, the power of the railways is practically unlimited, and it is wholly directed to serve the interests of the shareholders. We have really no adequate idea of the enormous influence which the railway interest exercises in these countries. But recent experience has brought to light the fact that big interests can practically paralyse parliaments, and overthrow governments when they are pleased to do so. When Mr Gladstone was thrown out of office in 1874, it was admittedly because his "five great legislative achievements" had interfered with as many 'great interests"[1]

Although things may not be quite as bad here as they are in the United States, still everything points to the conclusion that either the State must manage the railways or the railways will manage the State. That is the conclusion at which Mr. Henry George and many other eminent men have already arrived with regard to this question in America, and I confess it seems to me that these countries are scarcely less completely in the power of the railways than are the United States

---

[1] Only lately we have seen how the shipping interest can stand in the way of legislation. All Mr. Chamberlain's suavity is thrown away upon an "interest" which has self for its object, and any one who should say that ultimately the interests of the ship-owners and railway shareholders must be identical with the interests of the community at large, has only, it appears to me, to look at what has happened to the Merchant Shipping Bill to be convinced that they are talking arrant nonsense

of America. Instead, then, of being alarmed that the power which a Railway Minister might exercise would tend to corruption, we should do wisely to ask whether the railway interest, as it at present exists, is not only one of a dangerous political character, but a kindred interest to that of a monopoly antagonistic to the general interests of the nation, and on these grounds a subject for an immediate legislative remedy.

A careful balancing of considerations forces the conclusion that the acquisition of the railways by the State is perfectly practicable, and that it would be conducive in the highest degree to the welfare of the community, and that it ought therefore to be done with the least possible delay. Places of rest and recreation now beyond the means of working men to reach during the summer months, could be made accessible under a State control of the railways, which would look to the benefit of the industrial masses instead of the dividends of non-productive shareholders. Cheaper fares than those now imposed upon the public, and lower rates of goods transit, would necessarily follow from this advance in State socialism.

LECTURE XXXI.

GOVERNMENT BY PRIVILEGE AND WEALTH

Monopoly of Power by Privilege and Wealth—Obstruction to Social Reforms—Constitution of the British Parliament—"Vested Interests" in the House of Lords—"Vested Interests" in the House of Commons—Interests of Labour consequently Obstructed—Opposition to payment of Members—Just Distribution of Political Power dependent upon a more Equitable Distribution of the Products of Labour—Evil results of existing Distribution of Political Power—"After Sedan"—Inhumanity of War—Impoverishment caused by War—Cost of War to Tax-payers—Formation of European Labour Party check upon War—Effects of just Distribution of Political Power—British Rule over Dependent Nations—British Officialism in Ireland and India—Testimony of Sir James Caird—A Model Magistrate—Immediate Practical Remedies.

THE social reforms outlined in the preceding lectures have for their object the steady and permanent improvement of the condition of the people. I believe that the results of their embodiment in legislation would be a rapid rise of the general level of intelligence, and an almost equally rapid increase in the average of comfort, consequent upon the wider and more equitable distribution of wealth. There are few things more to be desired for any country than that its inhabitants shall be well fed, well clothed, and well educated; and if there be any considerable probability that the embodiment in legislation of the reforms specified in earlier lectures would have any such results for the people all earnest social reformers would do wisely to lend their energies to the cultivation of public opinion in the direction indicated.

But it must be clear that this greater extension of enlightenment and wider distribution of wealth would be followed by great and important political consequences. I believe we should have, in the first place, a more real and just distribution of political power; and in the second place, a much more humane and wise exercise of that power. Can any one doubt the desirability of such a state of things?

Political power in these three kingdoms is now practically monopolised by the privileged and wealthy classes. And the consequence is, that almost if not quite all of the more important measures which have been introduced into Parliament in recent years have been confessedly not such as ought to pass, but such as could pass. The art of statesmanship is in a woful plight. It is a humiliating thing to hear a minister recommending the House of Commons or entreating

the House of Lords to pass a particular Bill on the
ground not of the good it will effect, but of the trifling
injury it will inflict upon vested interests. To hear
a minister saying of a so-called "great reform" Bill,
that it is the least he can do, and adjuring privilege
and wealth to permit it to pass on that account; and
to hear the same minister in his next breath saying
of the same measure, but to a different audience, the
common people, that it is the most he can hope to do,
and adjuring the common people to accept it on that
score, is a melancholy testimony to the power of the
few and the impotence of the many. It would be an
interesting thing to know how many Bills involving
social reform, to say nothing of political reform, have
been introduced into Parliament during the last ten
years, but never to reach a third reading, and then it
would be yet more interesting to have an analysis of
the voting or abstinence from voting in respect of such
measures. The extension of the franchise during the
last forty years has not been attended by any such
marked increase in the power of the labouring classes
as we were led to expect; and hence it is that social
reforms having any reality in them are retarded by
those whose success in life leads them to believe that
this is the best of all possible worlds, and that accordingly there is no necessity for any change of system.
A "self-made man" says, "Look at me, go thou and do

likewise," and thinks he has settled the social question. He assumes that everybody else has an equal chance with himself, and then rates those who fail, and holds up those who succeed, himself included, to the admiration of the world. How, indeed, should such men look upon the efforts of social reformers otherwise than as the exploits of lunatics altogether beneath the notice of sensible men of business?

For consider the constitution of the British Parliament. There is, to begin with, the House of Peers, concerning which it is not necessary to say anything further than that it probably contains more bigots, ignoramuses, profligates, and good-for-naughts than any similar assembly in the civilised world. These poor peers have been reared in the amazing delusion that they are the salt of the earth; and conscious as many of them must be of how savourless they are, what can we expect them to think of the miserable creatures who in relation to them are merely the earth? But what is the use of talking about this utterly worthless, meaningless anachronism? May one not as well expect to make a silk purse out of a sow's ear as hope to obtain the co-operation of this assembly in the enactment of any real reform? Indeed, take it altogether, is it possible for the human mind to conceive a more thoroughly and exhaustively stupid institution?

Its stupidity as an institution, however, does not

mean that all its members are stupid. Many of the peers, indeed, are men of exceptional gifts and splendid attainments. Man for man, perhaps, of those who take active part in the business of government the peers have not the worst of it. Unhappily, these men, who are better than the institution, are its bulwark. And they are astute enough to know that there is scarcely any institution, short of the Crown, which is more secure than the House of Lords   It is in the presence of these exceptional men, therefore, that the obstructive power of the House of Peers chiefly consists. Next, there is the fact that nearly 200 peers are directly interested in the Army and Navy; while nearly if not quite all the peers are indirectly interested in these services   Then it seems that sixty peers are associated with as many as 114 railways, as chairmen or directors, while many mo·· ··· deeply interested not only as chairmen and directors, but as shareholders, in many hundreds of great commercial enterprises.

Let us turn now to the House of Commons. Its members have been carefully analysed with regard to their various "interests."[1]   It appears that 168 members are directly interested in the Army and Navy; 282 represent land; 122 represent law; 18, liquor; 25, banks; 84, literature and science; 113, railways, including 21 chairmen, 6 deputy chairmen, 85

[1] *Financial Reform Almanack.*

directors, and one contractor; 155 members represent
commerce, *and two represent labour!* If we but think
for a moment what all this means, we shall have no
ground for surprise that the art of British statesmanship is the art of making a little reform go a long way.
Privilege and wealth, naturally on the side of things as
they are, enjoy a practical monopoly of political power.
The peers have a branch of the legislature entirely to
themselves, and wealth has another branch entirely to
itself; and between the two the smothering or the obstruction of real reforms is a very simple business. So
long as the people assent to the continuance of privilege
to the peers, and so long as the existing unequal distribution of wealth obtains, so long must labour of brain or
hand expect to occupy its present subordinate position.
For what privilege fails to do wealth suffices to accomplish
in the way of keeping labour in " its place." None but
a rich man can enter the House of Commons as a
general rule; and the House of Lords is recruited from
the ranks of the rich, the stupid, and the cranky who
get into the House of Commons. That House as at
present constituted is not likely to make it easier than
it now is for any but the exceptionally wealthy to pass
its portals, and any proposals to make the official expenses
of parliamentary candidates a charge upon the rates, and
to pay an annual salary to all members of Parliament have
so far been met with the most insidious and determined

opposition. For wealth controls the fourth estate—the press—to an enormous extent even yet, and the press is almost unanimous in declaring that the payment of members would lower the tone of the House of Commons. I repeat that extensions of the franchise have so far added little or nothing to the political power of labour. The Reform Bill of 1832 checked the power of mere privilege and increased the power of mere wealth. Subsequent extensions have done no more. The facts above enumerated with regard to the various "interests" of the members of both Houses sufficiently attest the truth of this statement. And so it will continue to be until—as a natural result of the growth of popular enlightenment, and of the wider diffusion of wealth, consequent upon the abolition of land monopoly and the steady and progressive application of the co-operative principle to industry—labour exercises directly that power which it now blindly delegates to its employers.

But the growth of popular enlightenment and the more equitable distribution of wealth would not only result in a more real and just distribution of political power. There would follow of necessity a more humane and wise exercise of that power. Can any one doubt that such a thing is most sorely needed? To me it appears that unjust wars and unjust political rule are a necessary consequence of the practical monopoly of political power by mere privilege and wealth, and that both these evils would be reduced to a minimum, if not wholly abolished, if that monopoly were destroyed.

War! glorious war! Here is a picture of a famous field of battle.

"Let your readers fancy masses of coloured rags glued together with blood and brains, and pinned into strange shapes by fragments of bones. Let them conceive men's bodies without heads, legs without bodies, heaps of human entrails attached to red and blue cloth, and disembowelled corpses in uniform, bodies lying about in all attitudes with skulls shattered, faces blown off, hips smashed, bones, flesh, and gay clothing all pounded together as if brazed in a mortar extending for miles, not very thick in one place, but recurring perpetually for weary hours; and then they cannot, with the most vivid imagination, come up to the sickening reality of that butchery. No nightmare could be so frightful." [1]

This is one side of the picture. But there is yet another. About the middle of the Franco-German War, "there were in the province of Westphalia 11,817 married women, the wives and widows of soldiers, together with 22,713 children obtaining relief from the public funds. In Hanover 9624 women and 26,418 children were dependent upon the public for support.

[1] Dr. Russell in the *Times* on the battle of Sedan.

In the Rhenish provinces there were 14,312 married women, and 29,619 fatherless children who were utterly destitute." Of course, this is only a fragment even of this side of the picture. A reliable estimate gives two millions as the number of men slain by war in the eighteen years between 1853 and 1871. What suffering that means to women and children it is impossible to realise Another side of the picture is the cost of war. But here, again, though we use figures, they represent facts which cannot be at all adequately realised. It is estimated that the Crimean War cost £340,000,000; the American War, £1,841,000,000, or about five times the estimated cost of liberating the slaves by purchase; the Franco-German War cost France £400,000,000. As to Great Britain and Ireland it is authoritatively stated that in the fifteen years previous to 1871 £434,000,000 was spent on the army and navy services, and during the ten years between 1870 and 1880 the amount rose to £500,000,000. These figures, I say, are too large for realisation; it is only when we reduce the statement to terms such as this, that four out of every five shillings of taxation are spent on "the services," that we are at all able to comprehend the cost of war.

And yet when we ask for a justification of any of the wars of modern times we ask in vain. The real reason why Europe has poured out so much blood and treasure on war, is simply because in every country on that continent, political power is monopolised by mere privilege and wealth, and incidents which aristocratic and wealthy people would never dream of converting into causes of war if they had to do the fighting themselves or pay the cost, are magnified into insults to the British flag or the German flag or some other nation's bunting, which can only be referred to the arbitrament of war. As matters now stand, so far as Great Britain and Ireland are concerned, with the fighting interests firmly settled in high places, their ramifications extending through both Houses of Parliament as well as the press, and with wealth and "British interests" synonymous terms, we can look for little change in the exercise of political power. But with the acquisition of real power by an enlightened and an independent industrial democracy, we may safely look for a very startling and beneficent change. The peoples of the different nations of Europe, and also of America, have no interest in war. Their highest interests are all summed up in the Divine words, "On earth peace and good will among men." In their present disorganised and subordinate condition, however, the peoples of Europe are no match for their rulers. And there is only one way by which the inhuman exercise of political power, which characterises the ruling classes in all nations, can be at all adequately checked. Diplomacy may do much, arbitration may do more, the establishment of a great international tribunal might do more still; but until the people have real power, all such things will be lacking in the one element of importance—reality. I venture to think that there is more reason to expect an effective check upon war to come from an international federation of labour interests than from any other quarter. If in Great Britain, where the formation of a Labour party ought to be possible, the enterprise were at once entered upon, the workers of other nations of Europe would follow suit to the best of their limited opportunities; and there can be no doubt that a European Labour party would be an uncomfortable factor in European politics, so far as the interests of the privileged and wealthy classes are concerned, while so far as the moral and material interests of the peoples are concerned, there can be equally no doubt that the influence of such a party would be in the highest sense beneficent. Though it might be inconsiderable in point of numbers, and insignificant for a time in point of wealth, its potency would be wonderful so long as it preserved solidarity. A Labour party in all the countries of Europe would meet with many difficulties it is true; but if it could withstand the seductive influence of privilege and wealth, if its leaders could shake hands with lords and millionnaires without having their principles shaken out of them, all the rest would be easy. Such a party would be of necessity the determined enemy of the fighting interests and their allies; and by acting in concert could virtually, in almost every case, compel the reference of international disputes to arbitration. Such a party would, at all events, be in a position to demand, and would require, a much more definite reason why human beings should slay each other than is usually felt to be necessary by the well-to-do people who never have to fight. If real political power lay with the people, the people would refuse to act like savages for the delectation of their ornamental rulers.

In another matter, closely akin to the preceding, I venture to think, if the people of these three kingdoms enjoyed real power, they would exercise it more wisely than do those who now monopolise it. I refer to the character of British rule over dependent nations The aristocracy of these kingdoms have been trained to regard themselves as the favourites of heaven. It is no wise surprising, therefore, that those who at home have been accustomed to regard the common people as dirt beneath their feet, should manifest a yet more supreme contempt for those nationalities whom the English people have conquered or subdued, and whose government has been committed to their hands. It is very unfortunate for English rule that it should have had such unhappy representatives; but under the circumstances it is not surprising that among the

nations subject to their rule the English people should
be regarded as a nation of bullies; an opinion which
the subject nations may be pardoned for entertaining,
seeing that, according to Mr. Gladstone, the people of
England "had the reputation in Europe—he was afraid
not altogether unjustly—of being rather an arrogant
people."[1]   The English people have many excellent
qualities, but they are certainly not exempt from the
inability to rule other people, which is an infirmity
common to all the nations of the earth.   How, indeed,
should meddling with other people's business be more
successful amongst nations than amongst individuals?
Community of interest may serve as a basis for
voluntary association; but when the interest is all on
one side, voluntary association is impossible, and
meddling is only mischievous.   And when the meddling
is committed to the hands of heaven's favourites—the
British aristocracy—the force of folly can no further go.
The scions of birth make bad enough officials, yet the
scions of wealth out-Herod them, and between the two
English rule becomes a thing of such pitiful character
that the English people would be heartily ashamed of
it if they only knew what its real features were.   But
officialism born of privilege and wealth is supremely
cunning, and aided by its parents, is able to gull the
English people with an ease which is amusing to itself,

[1] Speech at Whitby, Sept 3, 1871

but supremely exasperating to those who have to endure its insolence So omnipotent are the forces such official-ism has at its command, that it is able to treat with the utmost indifference any glimpses of truth as to its real character which may find their way into print. During the recent agitation in Ireland several Englishmen of eminence, notably Mr. John Morley, Prof. Leone Levi, Mr. Boyd Kinnear, Mr. Samuel Storey, and Mr J. L Joynes, visited that country, and looking on, satisfied themselves that the Land League agitation had righteous aims. Some of these gentlemen published their views of the real state of the case, but we have had no reason to suppose that Irish officialism has suffered to any extent Indeed, to cure its effects, we have had actually a more stringent dose of it.[1]

But if the real character of English officialism in Ireland is so readily concealed from the English people, what can be expected with regard to the same thing in India? The common belief with reference to India is that British rule is regarded with the most passionate

---

[1] Existing officials, sitting on a volcano, complacently assure England that law and order once more reign, and England is deluded into believing that the comparative quietude of Ireland is due to the benevolent despotism of Earl Spencer and Mr. Trevelyan. It is a simple matter of fact that these gentlemen and their malodorous underlings are no more responsible for the absence of agitation than the man in the moon. The responsibility rests on quite other shoulders.

adoration by the people of that country. It is altogether impossible to imagine a more complete delusion.
Any student of revolutionary symptoms knows perfectly
well that the overthrow of British rule in India is only
a question of time. It is delayed pending the organisation of a concerted movement. The supreme difficulty of such a movement consists in the variety of
races inhabiting the country, and in the condition of
comparative beggary to which the people have been
reduced. Nevertheless India is seething with discontent. The officials despise the people, and the
people know it, and resent it as they ought to do.
The officials minimise concessions, and delay them until
they are devoid of any virtue. And if the native press
complains or bluntly criticises it is threatened with
suppression; while every care is taken that its com-
plaints and criticisms shall either not reach England at
all, or shall be tortured into crimes. Evidence of the
truth of all this is abundant, but I shall content myself
with adducing the testimony of Sir James Caird, who
was a member of the Famine Commission appointed by
the Marquis of Salisbury, and during his travels through
the country made use of his eyes and ears, and subsequently published a good deal of what he saw and
heard, in the *Nineteenth Century*. In the grand gate-
way at Secundra, Sir James says, "the gaols at present
are overflowing with prisoners for thefts in consequence

of the famine and high price of food." This was one of
the famine districts, but "so silent are these people
in their distress that the settlement officer, who had
been here two months encamped on the land, had not
observed any particular poverty, nor had become aware
either that the people were in a state of famine, or
were dying of it. And to my astonishment the Government representative learnt all this for the first time as
the result of our visit." Sir James would not have been
astonished if he had been an Irishman! But here is
another beautiful fact. "At another place I visited the
courts of law. In one the assistant-magistrate was
dispensing justice. Twelve persons had been tied up in
a row on the previous day and whipped with thirty
stripes for theft. *The magistrate said to me with some
satisfaction that he had at last got a policeman who could
break the skin at the third stroke!*" Sir James naively
adds that this was the only instance of such a feeling
he met with; but it is an obvious remark that he would
not have met with this if the magistrate in question
had had any idea that his amiable remark would have
found its way into print; and, besides, it is not every
village tyrant who will acknowledge to a man like Sir
James Caird his peculiar gratifications. I have not
heard that this particular brute has been cashiered.
Sir James had abundant evidence of the character of
English officials in other respects. He says: "If you

ask the European officers the condition of the people in any village or district, they can seldom tell without making a special inquiry!" And here is a general remark of some significance: "India seems to suffer much from secretaries, men of ability and clever with the pen, some of whom for these convenient qualities rise to high positions without the opportunity of gaining experience out of doors, or any accurate knowledge of the people;" and "as there is neither parliament nor public opinion to criticise or control" the secretaries, "and as their influence in questions of promotion is great, they possess a power, not only quite beyond that of official persons in the same position at home, but greater than that of our parliamentary heads of departments. The interference which they exercise is very properly creating a strong desire for independence and self-government by each Presidency, and cannot be too soon placed under some effectual control." Other difficulties there are looming in the near future. A legal gentleman, a pleader in the Courts of Lucknow and Calcutta, called on Sir James, and gave it as his opinion that the higher education now being given to the people of lower caste will in fifty years make it impossible for England to hold the country, and the legal gentleman regarded that evidently as a calamity. Officialism comes in for the most emphatic condemnation at the hands of Sir James, as, for instance, "The tend-

ency of officialism is to bring every person into subjection to the rule of the leading officials in the capital;"
and again, "Here, as in other parts of India, officialism
is said not to favour the introduction of European
capital;" yet again, "Disaffection is aroused; we are
hated by the Mussulmans and disliked by the Hindoos.
This is not likely at present to take tangible form, as
there is no head under whom the various dissatisfied
persons could unite. But a crusade is being preached
here (Baroda) against the infidel government by the
Mahommedans, and on all sides there is a readiness
to blame it on every occasion. There was lately a
tumult at Surat, during which the civil authorities had
to take shelter in a public building from the violence of
the people, and which might have led to direful results
but for the sharp interposition of the troops. It is
singularly illustrative of our rule, that though the
people for six generations have known no other, we are
still strangers among them. Our representatives come
and go, now faster than ever, and we and they look
on each other with distrust."

Now I have hope that by the testimony of Sir James
Caird with regard to India, and by subsequent testimony
of my own with regard to Ireland, I shall at least
succeed in convincing the people of England that their
rule is and must be evil so long as political power is
monopolised by privilege and wealth. And I have faith

that when that monopoly is destroyed, and political power is more justly distributed, it will be more wisely exercised. It will not be directed to maintaining "the balance of power" by inhuman ways, nor will it be employed to stifle the legitimate aspirations of other peoples.

And now ere passing on, I will answer a question which has frequently presented itself. Can anything of a practical character be immediately done to check the baneful monopoly of political power exercised by mere privilege and wealth? In my judgment a very great deal can be done, and done at once. Labour organisations have only to effect a slight change of tactics. Instead of waiting on political parties, they have only to permit political parties to wait on them. If they would do this, as they might very easily, we should witness remarkable changes. We should have to listen to many admonitions from our "real friends," as they call themselves—the privileged and wealthy classes. But if Labour would adopt as its motto, "He has most friends who has least need of them," and would organise itself as a distinct party in the State, it might work wonders in a very few years. "Bossed" as the press is for the most part, yet it is not so completely bossed as are the constituencies, and there is hardly any enterprise in which labour might more readily and withal more usefully engage co-operatively than in running a powerful

press. By this means the constituencies might be
educated up to the level of combination to return a
Labour party fifty or sixty strong to the House of Commons, instructed to act independently of political parties,
and with a view to the interests of labour. Thus an
excellent beginning would be made. Then the House
of Lords would go—and it will not go until then—for
Wealth to propitiate Labour would make a holocaust of
Privilege.

Mr. Trevelyan, speaking at Glasgow, on the 6th of
September, 1884, upon the subject of the Franchise
Bill, combats the theory that the Bill would destroy
the agricultural interest in the House of Commons.
He argued thus with reference to the labourer: "For
the first time, if this Bill is passed, his voice will be
heard, his wishes will be known through the mouth
of his representative, instead of by a petition, which
the member who presents it hardly takes the trouble
to read." But Mr. Trevelyan is careful to show that
the labourer need have no hope of being represented
by any of his own class, for he goes on to say: "Nobody
pretends that the manufacturing interest is swamped
because the operatives of such places as Glasgow, Paisley,
and Dundee, have votes. Why should the agricultural
interest be anything but strengthened by the votes
of the agricultural labourers of Northumberland and
Berwickshire? . . . Has the power of employers of
labour in towns been destroyed or diminished by the
extension of the Borough Franchise? Let any one
take a list of the principal manufacturing centres in
England and Scotland, and check off their parliamentary

members, and I will venture to say that he will find that *three-fourths of them are employers of labour.* And if this Bill passes, the tenant farmers, who are *the employers of labour* in the rural districts, will have a chance of getting into parliament, and making *their power* felt there" Mr. Trevelyan could hardly have let the cat out of the bag more neatly. Further testimony in support of what has been here advanced is to be found in the remarkable and interesting Report of the Parliamentary Committee of the Trades Union Congress, presented to that body at its sitting at Aberdeen, also on the 6th of September. The Report notices that the Employers' Liability Act is defective—a circumstance which will occasion no surprise to thoughtful readers of Mr. Trevelyan's remarks—and adds, "We have increasing evidence of the necessity of preventing employers contracting out of the Act of 1880, and hope that at no distant period we may be able to do so." Further on the Report alludes to the Merchant Shipping Bill in the following pregnant terms: "While some of the clauses could undoubtedly have been improved from the workman's point of view, the Bill on the whole was one of the most effective and courageous attempts to deal with a great scandal ever introduced by a Cabinet Minister. But *the combination of shipping interests, like an avalanche, crushed this humane attempt to protect the victims of rapacity.* The sacrifice of human life on the altar of personal interest and greed is still going on, and will, we fear, continue until the people make a mighty effort to support the protection of our sailors, and declare in a voice that cannot be disregarded, that men and fathers of families are more precious than profits." Further, the Report describes Mr Chamberlain's proposed Railway Regulation Bill, as one which would have been most valuable to railway *employés,* but *the determined opposition of the railway interest,* it appears, has compelled its withdrawal. The Report also alludes in terms of condemnation to the *"interested opposition of the banking interest* in the House of Commons to the Savings' Bank Act Amendment Bill." Perhaps, however, the most interesting portion of the entire Report is that which refers to the Paris Conference of last year, on International Trades Unionism, as to which the conclusion of the Parliamentary Committee is "that a compact labour party, working steadily for itself, may not be out of place in this country."

PART III.

POLITICAL CRIME

HOW IRELAND IS RULED AND RUINED

POLITICAL JUSTICE·

HOW THE ANGLO-IRISH PROBLEM MIGHT BE SOLVED.

LECTURE XXXII

POLITICAL CRIME.

A Reminiscence—My "Crime"—Definition of Irish Government —The "Castle" System—England put in the position of Ireland under same—Exploits of the Irish Lord-Lieutenant of England—The Castle training of the Irish-English nief Secretary—The London "Castle Ring"—Power and Functions of its Members—How England would be governed by Anti-English Irishmen—Political Police and Political Judges —What Englishmen would do if their country were thus rule 1 and ramed

WE have now reached the time, Mr Chairman, when you are clearly entitled to your liberation. We have arrived at the end of the task which we set ourselves to accomplish, and I promised, as a reward for your attention, that when this task was finished, I would loose you and let you go. We have talked of crime and criminals, ignorance and its evils, poverty and its causes. We have also discussed how such drawbacks to a better state of society, and impediments to higher and happier conditions of social life for the masses, could be removed from the path of human progress. This was the motive and object of these lectures, and now that they are drawn to a close, the hour of your freedom has arrived.

Liberty! Who that has not himself been once imprisoned can appreciate what this means? Who that has not had to look forward with aching heart and longing soul for days, months, years, to the time when he would once again find himself unfettered, free to talk to his fellow-man—at liberty to exercise the rights of his nature's manhood, undeterred by prison rules or the threat of warders' reports, can realise what that heaven-born word implies?

I was liberated once—unexpectedly set free, after seven and a half years of close imprisonment, and I am almost inclined to say, that the punishment involved in a penal servitude of that duration would be worth enduring again to enjoy the wild, ecstatic, soul-filling happiness of the first day of freedom. It is a sensation of delight akin to that which Adam must have experienced upon waking to life and consciousness in the Garden of Eden; only Adam's memory could recall neither pain nor sorrow as a contrast to the living pleasure of Paradise, while everything which meets the gaze of the liberated prisoner, every thought of the present and the future assumes a brighter hue and wears a more blissful meaning from the terrible recol-

lection of the felon degradation, the narrow cell, the
stinted sunlight, the loathsome drill task, the brutal
warder, and the weary, heart-longing expectancy for
the hour of deliverance.

This reminiscence of a kindred joy to that which you
are shortly to experience, reminds me that, while I have
described for you the various classes of criminals that
are to be found within this prison of Portland, I have
omitted to enlighten you upon one type with which you
have been the most familiar—myself. Yes, I am "a
criminal" The law has branded me as such ; and the
instruments with whom rest the carrying out of the law's
decree have made me feel that they, at least, believe
that penal servitude was a richly merited punishment,
whatever my own opinion to the contrary may have
been.

"And pray what crime have *you* been guilty of ? "

I must detain you for a few hours more, in order
to answer your question   Your curiosity must be my
warrant for postponing the hour of your release.

I am a native of Ireland, a country rich in almost
everything which makes a nation great—a fertile soil,
an industrious and a virtuous people , but lacking this
one thing, which you and I also lack—Liberty. My
country is ruled by another—by England. And that
rule is maintained by a garrison of anti-Irish landlords and a horde of unsympathetic officials.   Let me

endeavour to convey to you some idea of the nature
of this rule, in order that I may indicate the nature
and the justification of my "crime," which is none other
than that I have attempted to assert my country's right
to rule herself.

If an "intelligent foreigner" were asked the question, "What was the government of Ireland?" he
would most probably answer, "The same as that of
England," or else confess his ignorance on the subject.
An Englishman, who would have neither resided in
Ireland nor cared to acquire correct information on
how the country is ruled, would, of course, reply, "It
has the same constitution as that of England, with a
Viceroy to represent the Q en." While an Irishman's
answer to the same question would simply be, "Dublin
Castle."

The singularity of this last definition of Irish
government consists in its absolute truth, and the fact
that ninety-nine out of every one hundred Englishmen
are as ignorant of what "The Castle" really means, in
the rule of Ireland, as if it were situated at the
mouth of the Yang-tse-Kiang, and was identified
with the government of the Celestial Empire, instead
of standing by the banks of the Liffey, the representative of England's powe and authority in the rule of
the "Sister Island"

Without caring to inquire into the cause of this

unfortunate ignorance on the part of the English people, I will endeavour to do my best to remove such of it as may give way to the convincing force of facts. I hope to succeed in presenting this "Castle" system in its true light to the public of Great Britain. Should I do so, its real character of practical absolutism and anti-Irish feeling will stand revealed before all right-thinking men, as at once the primary, if not the greatest factor in the discontent of the Irish people, and a centralised despotism without a parallel in any European State outside of Russia.

In order that Englishmen may better understand the true working of this headquarters of English rule in Ireland and learn something of the chief cause of our disaffection to that rule, I will try and describe what a similar government would be in England, supposing the relative positions of the two countries were reversed, and the manner of conducting their respective civil and military affairs exchanged.

The Home Office would be "The Castle." All its subordinate officials would either be Irishmen, or Englishmen holding anti-English principles and sentiments. Not only would there be no popular Englishman occupying any post of trust in the administration of his country's government, but the approach of any such to the very building which would represent such government, would be looked upon by the military police in charge of the same as a menace to the authority of "London Castle."

The Queen and the Viceroy would, of course, change residences, and Buckingham Palace would become the "Viceregal Lodge" of St. James's Park. The Irish nobleman who would be the nominal head of the English Government, would also have to be a Roman Catholic, as a law would have been passed in an Irish parliament, sitting in Dublin, declaring that the religion of the majority of the people of England should not be that of the man appointed to rule them. The Irish Lord-Lieutenant of England would be in the hands of an Irish or pro-Irish "London Castle" Ring. He would be taught that the dignity of "Her Majesty's Lord Lieutenant-General and Governor-General of England" would be best consulted by attending, almost exclusively, to the holding of petty levees, or Brummagem Courts, in "London Castle," a building that would stand protected by a military barracks on the one side, and by various police departments and detective officers on the other, as proof that the depot of Irish government in London was (poetically) situated in the hearts of its people, and resting for foundation upon the public sentime of the land.

The people who would receive cards of invitation to these 'Castle" Courts would all be selected by the Ring aforesaid, as neither the Irish Lord-Lieutenant

nor his Irish Chief Secretary would know anything of
the politics of London Society. These invitations would
be confined to the Irish, Scotch, and English officers
whose regiments might be quartered in and near London
at the time, for t protection of "The Castle," and
such few Anglo-Irish Members of Parliament as might
have obtained their seats in the Dublin Parliament
through the influence of the Ring, and who would be
distinguished for their defence of the same in the Irish
House of Commons against the searching attacks of
popular English members. The remainder of the
favoured would be made up of judges, crown prosecutors, government officials, "castle hacks," office-
seeking lawyers, landlords, a few anti-English members
of the London Corporati and such fortunate grocers,
drapers, pawnbrokers, and hotel-keepers as might have
caught the eye of the Ring in the pursuit of their
respective callings, and who would be known as
thorou, 'oyal to Ireland's rule of England, and
opposed all national sentiment and aspirations on
the part of the English masses. When the nobility
and gentry of England (all, or nearly all, of Irish
descent) should condescend to attend one of these
"Castle" levees, the fashionably-dressed consort of an
East End tradesman, who would be fortunate enough to
receive a card of invitation, would have to occupy the
eighty-second place in "the roll of ladies' precedence,"

as established by an English Sir Bernard Burke; and from thence contemplate, with feminine pride and generosity of sex, her eighty-first degree mo. favoured sister in Viceregal notice.

All popular English public men would be rigorously excluded from the "London Castle" Court. Mr. Gladstone (who would probably be an English Gracchus), Messrs. Bright, Chamberlain, Dilke, Labouchere, Morley, Trevelyan, Forster, Sir W Lawson, and others, would all be "ex-suspects," and be held as dangerous enemies to the peace and welfare of England. Mr. Joseph Co ~ uld be an ex-political convict. All these would be debarred from Viceregal society or "London Castle" honours. If the Lord Mayor of London should chance to be a popular favourite, the Castle Ring would succeed in making the Lord-Lieutenant select some public occasion upon which to offer the chief magistrate of the metropolis of England a public insult by refusing to dine with himself and the city fathers

The remaining duties of the Irish Viceroy of England would mainly consist in delivering an annual speech upon an exclusively viceregal topic—the growing prosperity of England under Irish rule, especially since his party came into office and himself into England as its ruler. It would be his duty to show, by a formidable array of figures,—specially prepared by the chief statistician of the Ring, — that notwithstanding bad harvests, depression of trade, increase of pauperism, and continued political agitation by misguided men (like Messrs. Gladstone, Bright, Chamberlain, Forster, and Cowen), the prosperity of England was advancing in a most marked manner. By the amount of deposits (from landlords, graziers, and civil servants) in the banks, it would follow that the average savings of the English people were on the increase. True, thousands of English farm labourers and artisans might be leaving the country, but then the number of cows and horses were multiplying, while pigs were being more economically fattened than twenty years ago; and emigration was after all a humane Irish policy for the congested population of England. Finally, all that England would want, in viceregal estimation, would be rest from political agitation, and a rigorous application of law to all disturbers of order and assailants of the sacred rights of landlord property.

If, after the performance of such onerous duties as these, the Irish representative of royalty in England aspired to make himself appear popular to the public opinion of London, he would visit a Ragged School or two in the East End, and express himself delighted with the management of such institutions. On the anniversary of England's patron saint he might chose to wear a rose in his button-hole, while an Irish military band would be playing "Rule Britannia," and from the top of the boundary wall of " London Castle" show himself and his genero , to e few hundred people and corner boys whom the music would attract by scattering a few pounds' worth of small silver among the audience. If, during the remainder of the year, he had an eye to augmenting his salary of £20,000, he might follow the example of a recent Lord-Lieutenant of Ireland by grazing the cows of the viceregal establishment in St. James's Park, and sell the surplus butter-milk to one of the London workhouses.

The training of the Irish Chief Secretary to the Irish Lord-Lieutenant of England would be the most difficult task which the "London Castle" Ring would have to perform in order to keep the government of England practically out of his, and centre it in their own hands. He would be the virtual governor of the country; but being an Irishman, and member for an Irish constituency, he would be almost entirely ignorant of English affairs, and totally unacquainted with the topography of England. Consequently, he would have to depend upon the permanent "Castle" staff for all information necessary to carry on the business of government, and to answer questions in the Irish House of Commons touching public occurrences in England, character of officials, &c., &c. As Chief Secretary to the Lord-Lieutenant, he would have to be absent in Dublin during six months in each year to attend to the parliamentary duties of his office Actually during this period, and virtually at all times, the government of England would remain in the hands of the "London Castle" Ring, which would be made up as follows from the salaried heads of the various departments of the Castle system:

The permanent Under-Secretary of the Castle.

The assistant Under-Secretary.

The Law Adviser to the Castle.

The Crown and Treasury Solicitor to the Castle.

The Crown Solicitor for the County and City of London.

The Head Inspector of the Royal English Constabulary.

The Commander-in-Chief of the Irish Forces in England.

The Vice-President and three Members of the Local Government Board.

The Chairman of the Board of Works and two Commissioners.

The Resident Commissioner of "National" Education.

The active members of a body known as the Privy Council of England, twenty of whom would be the judges of the land.

The enormous power that would be wielded by this Ring, and the anti-English character of its *personnel*, will readily be understood from the following brief summary of its administrative functions and analysis of its composition.

"The Under-Secretary of London Castle" would not be affected by any change of party government. His temporary nominal superiors might be Whig or Tory, but this would make no practical difference to the permanent official who would have the key of the whole administrative machine of England constantly in his hand. Under a weak Lord-Lieutenant he would be the real governor of the country. The rule of a strong viceroy would but change the mode, not the reality, of his influence; for without his constant advice, and the assistance of the knowledge of persons and things which the permanent Under-Secretary would alone possess, no Irish nobleman or commoner could play the part of Lord-Lieutenant or Chief Secretary of England.

The man in whose hands this enormous power would thus be placed would be the very negation of an Englishman. Alien in blood, in religion, in national feeling, he would scarcely have one sentiment in common with the people whose liberties would be at his disposal. He would be all but absolutely independent of English public opinion, owing his appointment to the exigencies of that policy which would find it necessary to exclude from every post of administrative government all men who might be suspected of sharing the national feelings of the English people. The same rule which influenced the selection of himself would guide him in the disposal of the patronage which the office of Under-Secretary would place in his hands. All his subordinates would have to be pro-Irish in sentiment, anti-English in prejudice, and mostly ultra-montane Catholic in religion. The singing of "Rule Britannia," or "Britons never shall be slaves" would cause the instant dismissal of any English subordinate official of the Castle who should thus manifest his disloyalty to Irish rule. (Such songs would be considered treasonable, and a member of the Royal English Constabulary would be only doing his duty to "London Castle" by arresting any person whom he should hear whistling such tunes "with the intent of intimidating her Majesty's English subjects.")[1]

"The Assistant Under-Secretary"[2] would be an Englishman of ultra loyalty towards Irish rule. As clerk of the Privy Council, he would hold a very important position in the inner circle of the "Castle"

---

[1] During the Land League excitement in Ireland, a little boy, aged 10, was prosecuted for "intimidating her Majesty's subjects" by whistling "Harvey Duff" in the streets of a provincial town

[2] Another assistant Under-Secretary has been added to the Castle government of Ireland since 1882   A new department, that of police and crime, was created after the passage of the Coercion Act of the same year, and the new post has been filled by an Anglo-Indian.

Ring. His advice would be sought in the issuing of proclamations. Matters of private or public interest which the "Castle" system would require to be brought before the Council would have to pass through his hands. In times of cattle disease the power of restricting the sale of stock in certain markets, of exporting or importing beasts, etc., would lie, to a great extent, with this official In religion he would be a Catholic.

"The Law Adviser to the Castle" would fill one of the positions most peculiar to that system of rule, and a post the like of which is not to be found in connection with any other civilised government. He might be termed the consulting lawyer of the Under-Secretary and director-in-chief of all preliminary proceedings leading up to State prosecutions His duties would be manifold He would have to advise the magistrates throughout England how to carry out the wishes of the "Castle" towards prisoners who might have infringed upon "Castle" law and order, whether bail should or should not be accepted, and whether or not a person who committed a crime, say in Rutlandshire, was more likely to be convicted by a jury of that county than by one in Northumberland. His functions would quite easily dispose of that trouble to centralised government which is found in the legal fiction that the prerogative of magistrates is to judge impartially between the subject and the State.

To prevent the pernicious influence which such a fiction might exercise upon the minds of the disloyal English masses, the post of Law Adviser to "London Castle" would be filled by a true and tried "Castle" hack, who should have his own country's aspiration to be free from Irish rule, and who would look upon the religion of the Protestant people of England as constituting a badge of inferiority, and rendering most of those professing it neither fit nor proper persons to constitute a jury in any case in which the Crown should be prosecutor.[1]

[1] "We have recently come upon a document which is in many respects the most instructive piece of official reading it has ever been our good fortune to enjoy. Its title is 'Rules for Crown Solicitors and Sessional Crown Solicitors,' and its compilation is ascribed to a distinguished judge while Attorney-General for Ireland   The rules have been the *vade mecum* these years back for Mr George Bolton and his *confrères* in Crown prosecutions, and some of the puzzling practices in the packing of juries, which are associated with various names among those officials, lose all their mystery in the light of these marvellous directions.   It will be learned with unfeigned astonishment that an entire class of business men in Ireland are described in the rules as unfit to exercise the functions of jurors in certain cases.   Mere Catholics and Nationalists have long been under the ban in political cases, but the Licensed Vintners' Association has been miserably at fault in not discovering before now that its members are deemed by the Crown to be ignorant of the obligations of a juror's oath, or, what amounts to the same thing, are not to be relied upon to give an honest and impartial verdict.   This fact is revealed in Rule 9 of the Crown Prosecutor's Manual   The rule is long in detail, but under it the amplest hints are communicated to the

"The Crown and Treasury Solicitor to London Castle" would be an important member of the "Castle" Ring, and would be of the same anti-English feeling as the preceding members.

"The Crown Solicitor for the City and County of London" would be a highly useful and efficient "Castle" lawyer. His would be the duty of arranging the

---

Crown Solicitor as to how his prisoner may be involved in the meshes of an inextricable net, and then it proceeds as follows :—
'In all cases of *peculiar local excitement* in any particular town or district'—instance the trial of Myles Joyce, or of Cornwall and Kirwan—'it will be prudent, if the panel permit, to set aside all persons returned from such locality, and in all cases every vintner, publican, and retailer of spirits or malt liquors shall, *as a matter of course*, be ordered to stand by' . . . . By another provision of the same Rule 9, . . . the Crown prosecutor may set aside *all persons* whose motives they suspect, 'although some may not amount to a legal ground of challenge, and may not admit of legal proof.' This is an honest bit of brutal candour, but it is, in so many words, the principle which has governed the system of trial by jury in Ireland as far back as the memory goes. . . Where the system is watered down to accommodate the religious and political prejudices of Crown Prosecutors, it is little wonder if, with 'the pulse of the Constitution dead at the extremities,' the Constitution should be sometimes regarded with unmingled contempt. Our experience snows us that in one description of criminal cases a *soupçon* of nationality is an unpardonable disqualification in a juror; in another wide class of cases Catholics, because they are Catholics, must stand aside, and the 'Rules for Crown Solicitors' now inform us that 'in all cases of local excitement' the licensed vintner is 'as a matter of course' a person utterly unfit to act as a juror' (*The Freeman's Journal* Dublin, August 26, 1884)

challenges for the Crown side in all political and
criminal prosecutions. He would be the author of a
manuscript history of the antecedents of every popular
English public man who would be suspected by the
Ring of holding views inimical to Irish rule in
England. The work would be for the private reading
of members of the "Castle" Ring. He would profess
to hold in his hands the threads of all conspiracies
against the "Castle" system. The disposition of a
large share of the secret service money would therefore
be in connection with his office. Like his other
colleagues of the Ring, he would be Catholic and anti-
English in faith and feeling.

"The Inspector-General of Constabulary" would also
be an Irishman and a Catholic. As head of 12,000
military police, which would be scattered over every
parish of England, he would be next in importance to
the Under-Secretary in the councils of the Ring. His
would really be the Irish army of occupation in England.
To him would be allotted the duty of training the sons
of English farmers to become the spies and pimps of
their own country, the janizary force which could be
most relied upon for the repression of any attempt on
the part of their own countrymen to throw off the yoke
of Ireland. Daily reports from every police barrack in
England would be forwarded to the Inspector-General
at "London Castle." If Joseph Cowen should address

a public meeting in Newcastle-on-Tyne, a special report of his speech, with an account of the objects and conduct of the gathering, would be supplied by the police of Newcastle to the head of the force in the "Castle" of London. The same would be done towards Messrs. Chamberlain, Forster, Trevelyan, and other popular English public men, for the information of the Inspector-General and the Ring. Strangers arriving at country places would have their movements watched by the local constabulary, and particulars of their business would be ferretted out and transmitted, along with a description of their persons, to the "Castle." No public body, municipality, or local board could interfere with the police of the Inspector-General. Just as the Under-Secretary could influence the action of magistrates and justices of the peace through the Law Adviser of the "Castle," so could he control the entire police force of England through the Inspector-General of English Constabulary. The prevailing notion, obtaining in most countries, about the police being the servants of the people would be thoroughly exploded under the system of an Irish Inspector-General of Royal English Constabulary. The English people would be taught that the "Castle" police were their masters. They could arrest Englishmen on suspicion; enter the houses of Englishmen on suspicion, at any time, day or night;

keep a constant espionage upon suspected Englishmen; bludgeon Englishmen on the smallest provocation, and prosecute their victims for insolence and intimidation afterwards; they would allow no Englishman to carry arms except those who would be known to be of the Anglo-Irish garrison; while they would intimidate Englishmen by carrying rifles and side-arms themselves in the ordinary discharge of "police" duty.

"The Commander of the Forces" would be an Irish general, who would have distinguished himself in the military service of Ireland. He would be a Roman Catholic, and hold anti-English ideas on all matters affecting the government of the country. The 30,000 Irish soldiers which would be constantly under his command in England would render him one of the most formidable factors in the maintenance of Irish rule, and a man of weight in the deliberations of the "London Castle" Ring.

"The Vice-President and (three) members of the Local Government Board" would bring under the immediate influence of the Ring the whole Poor Law system of England. By this centralised control over the action of Boards of Guardians, enormous power would be wielded against popular ideas. All the accounts of these public bodies, as well as those of all the municipalities throughout England, would have to be submitted to the Local Government Board to be audited.[1] Small items of expenditure on account of municipal honours shown to popular public men—such as Gladstone, Chamberlain, Bright, and Forster—would be disallowed, while any expense incurred in a similar way in connection with the Irish Lord-Lieutenant of England, or members of the Royal Family of Ireland, would be passed unquestioned.

The Poor Law system which "London Castle" rule of England would inflict upon that country, would be framed with the specific intention of giving whatever power could not be centralised in the "Castle" Board into the hands of the landlords of England, who would be Ireland's territorial garrison. This would be effected by a system of multiple voting, and the provision that an *ex-officio* guardian (from the landed interest) should be selected out of each Union district for each guardian elected by the rate-payers of the same district. This would insure, at least, as many "Castle" guardians as popular ones, on each Board throughout England;[2] and such *ex-officios* would be the direct representatives of

---

[1] In England, at present, local bodies audit their own accounts. In Ireland the practice is as illustrated above.

[2] In England, at the present time, two-thirds of the Poor Law Guardians are elected, leaving but one-third *ex-officio* In Ireland the *ex-officios* have half the representation. The English system was once applied to Ireland, but it was repealed again in a few years

the Irish garrison of conquest, and the indirect agents of the "Castle" Local Government Board in thwarting the plans, ideas, and actions of the popular party on all these local bodies.

Another important function of the "Castle" Local Government Board would be the inquiry into and reporting upon all the chronic visitations of distress which would fall upon England as a consequence of English landlordism, absence of alternative industries to that of agriculture, and the general impoverishment which would result from centuries of Irish misgovernment, absenteeism, &c. &c. Such reports, as a matter of course, would be coloured by the "Castle" officials on the Board, who would be in thorough sympathy with the institutions and laws from the operation of which such periodical distress would spring. One member of this Board would be a Protestant; the other two would be Roman Catholics, as would also the Secretaries of the Board, and ten out of the twelve Inspectors who would be deputed, when occasion would arise, to hold inquiries in connection with the management of workhouses, suspicious deaths of paupers, &c. &c., in any Union in England.

"The Chairman and (two) Commissioners of Public Works," with secretary, architect, engineer, accountant, solicitor and superintendent of national monuments, would all be Roman Catholics. Not a single member of the Protestant faith, or man tainted with popular sympathies, would be found in connection with this the most important Board of the "London Castle" system of ruling England, saving, perhaps, a hall-porter or messenger. To give an idea of the influence which this Board would wield, and of the patronage that would be at its disposal, it is only necessary to indicate what its special functions would be under a "London Castle."[1] It would have control over all public works, piers, and harbours, it would control all famine relief works; arterial drainage, inland navigation works; and be in addition the Loan Board under the Irish Treasury for the whole of England.

"The Resident Commissioner of National Education" would be the only head of a Castle department who would be of the same religion as the majority of his English fellow-countrymen. He would be a Protestant, but of that type which would be known in England as a "Cawstle Protestant"—*i. e.* an unmitigated English flunkey, who would toady and pander to every Irish Lord-Lieutenant and Irish Chief Secretary, that would be sent from Dublin to perpetuate Irish rule over Englishmen. He would take care to supply the most antiquated set of school class-books to the "National" Schools of England that could be compiled by the most

In England, at present, the Board of Works has only control ⌐r public buildings.

ardent anti-English educationist. They would be fifty years behind the progressive age. Lessons in manufacturing industry would be sought for in vain in these books; and lest a better and more advanced class of school-book might possibly find its way into the schools of England, the Resident Commissioner would provide that no books should be used by schools under the "National" Board but those which would be issued by the authority of the Commissioners.

To better carry out the policy of "London Castle" of effacing the nationality of England, no English history would be permitted to be taught in the "National" schools. Irish, Hebrew, French, Roman and other history might form part of the teaching which English boys and girls would receive; but history of England there would be none allowed inside one of the schools of the country. It would be disloyal to teach it. The memory of King Alfred should die so that the exploits of King Brian Boru of Ireland might become familiar to the future fathers and mothers of the English nation. John Hampden and other confessors of English liberty would never be mentioned in the schools of the country which they died to free from kingly despotism, but the exploits of such Irishmen as would have conquered India, wrested Canada from the French, and trampled upon English freedom, would be made as familiar to the youth of England as household words. To add insult to injury, such a system of education would be known as the " National system " of England !

"The Privy Council of England " would be a make-believe English body to whom the Irish Lord-Lieutenant would relegate certain Executive matters. But no popular Englishman would have a seat at its board, nor could any number of the people of England be privileged or empowered to elect any of its members. They would all be appointed through various Irish Lord-Lieutenants, by the influence of the Ring. The two first names would be those of members of the Royal Family of Ireland, who would never attend a meeting of the " Council " The next would be those of the two highest dignitaries of the English Roman Catholic Church. For the same reason that no Protestant could be a Lord-Lieutenant, no Protestant Bishop could be a member of the " Privy Council of England." Various ex - Lord - Lieutenants, ex - Chief Secretaries, ex - Commanders - in - Chief, all Irish, would follow. Then would come several Anglo-Irish noblemen and landlords; and the list of names would be completed with the Judges who would represent the strength of the Judicial Bench of England under " London Castle." [1]

[1] In England, at present, the Judges on the Privy Council form the Judicial Committee of that body for purely legal business, and never interfere in matters of State In Ireland they act as described

The Privy Council of "London Castle," through its Clerk (who would be, as already described, an Assistant Under-Secretary to the Castle), would be one of the most efficient instruments of the " Castle " system of rule that could be wielded against the liberties of a people. The Judges of England—all true, tried, and promoted " Castle " hacks—would practically constitute the Privy Council. They would always be in a majority at its meetings. All proclamations, under which arrests for seditious conspiracy would be made, would be issued by the Privy Council; and amongst the signatures which these documents would bear would be those of the Judges who would afterwards constitute the Court before which the persons arrested under such proclamations would be tried. The people of England would witness this strange spectacle : they would read the edicts of the Privy Council of " London Castle," by which certain districts of their country would be declared to be "disturbed," and they would next witness in the persons of the Judges sent down to try Englishmen on the charge of a disregard of (Irish) law and order, the owners of the names of those who issued the Proclamation.[1]

---

[1] The following is a copy of a Dublin Castle Proclamation. The asterisks denote the members of the Privy Council signing the Proclamation who were Judges of the land :—

This "Castle" Ring would have many political advisers among the Irish landocracy of England; but

"BY THE LORD LIEUTENANT AND PRIVY COUNCIL
OF IRELAND.

"PROCLAMATION.

"ABERCORN :

"Whereas by an Act made and passed in a Session of Parliament, holden in the eleventh year of Her Majesty's reign, Chapter II , it was amongst other things enacted and provided that, whenever in the judgment of the Lord Lieutenant or other chief Governor or Governors of Ireland, by and with the advice of the Privy Council of Ireland, it should be necessary for the prevention of crime and outrage that the said Act should apply to any County... in Ireland... Now we the Lord Lieutenant-General, and General Governor of Ireland, do by this our Proclamation in pursuance and execution of the said Act for the better preservation of the Peace in Ireland, by and with the advice of Her Majesty's Privy Council in Ireland, declare, that from and after the 12th day of March, in the year of our Lord 1867, the said Act, that is to say the Peace Preservation (Ireland) Act 1856 .... shall apply to and be in force, in and for all those parts of the Queen's County not included in the above recited Proclamations.

"And of this our Proclamation, all Justices of the Peace of the said Queen's County, and all constables, peace officers, and all others whom it may concern are desired to take notice.

"Given at the Council Chamber, Dublin Castle, this 11th day of March, in the year 1867.

"RICHARD C DUBLIN.	JOHN HATCHELL.
NAAS	JOSEPH NAPIER.
*FRED SHAW	*A. BREWSTER
SAMUEL MEATH.	*JOHN E WALSH.
*R KEATINGE	FRANCIS PLUNKET DUNNE.
J. W. FITZPATRICK.	*MICHAEL MORRIS
FITZSTEPHEN FRENCH	

"GOD SAVE THE QUEEN."

the chief exponents of its policy and champions of its
acts would be two ultra-Irish and rabid Catholic news-

"The Irish Judge is a composite official fashioned from very
incongruous elements. In addition to being a Judge, he is also
the Government, the Privy Council, the Castle, he represents
English dominion through the medium of the Viceregal establishment—the most hateful form in which it can be represented
to the popular mind—and he is careful to keep his hand in constant practice by exercising the multiform duties which go to
comprise the bizarre nature of his office. When judicially engaged
in a political case, for instance, or when charging a Grand Jury
on circuit, or whenever an opportunity presents itself, the Judge
improves the occasion by delivering a solemn lecture on nearly
every subject of current public interest. The flimsiest pretext will
sometimes suffice for ventilating the peculiar views of his order
or of his party. If an agricultural case appears on the record, he
will avail himself of the accident to make commentaries on the
Land Act It will be an occasion for extolling the Prime
Minister, for commending the Lord-Lieutenant, and for saying
a good word for the Chief Secretary"—*The Irish Bar Sinister*,
p 45 Simpkin, Marshall and Co., London, 1872.

"In Ireland, that paradise of lawyers, there are (including the
Recorder of Dublin, who is practically a County Court Judge)
thirty-four Chairmen, or County Court Judges, as they are called
on this side of the Channel, in England the number of County
Court Judges is fifty-seven Now when we recollect that the
population of England is more than four times and its wealth
more than eleven times greater than Ireland's, and when we
further ascertain that the jurisdiction of the County Courts is
much more extensive than in the latter country, we may well ask,
How can the thirty-four Irish Chairmen possibly make out occupation for themselves? That they find it difficult to do so is evident
from the Parliamentary Returns which were made out in 1870
and 1871, at the instance of the Right Hon. G. Ward Hunt, from
which we learn, that in the year 1869, the average number of days

papers published in London. The editor of one of these papers would be the special correspondent of the chief

---

on which each County Court Judge in England sat, was one hundred and forty, while for the same year the average sittings of each Irish Chairman numbered forty-seven days. In other words, if each English County Court Judge performed the same amount of work as each Irish Chairman, and no more, it would take one hundred and seventy Judges to get through the business of the English County Courts, or to reverse the case, if we could prevail upon the Irish Chairmen to work as hard as their English brethren, eleven Chairmen instead of thirty-four would suffice for Ireland. It is doubtless some consolation to the taxpayer to know that if the work of the Irish Chairmen is very small, still, on the other hand, their pay is very large. An English County Court Judge receives a salary which is at the rate of £11 for each day he sits in Court, and from the date of his appointment he must resign all practice at the Bar ; the Irish Chairmen, up to the year 1871, received just £20 12s for each day's sitting, with liberty, moreover, to practice at their profession as much as they pleased. The Irish Land Act (1870) having thrown upon each of the Chairmen additional work, averaging eleven days in each year, these hard-worked and badly-paid public servants raised such a cry, that they succeeded in wringing out of the State additional pay, averaging £221 per annum each."—Article "Irish Judges" *Fortnightly Review*, March 1875.

The origin of the institution of County Chairmen is thus given by the able author of the above :—

"In the year 1798, Lord Clare, who, under the direction of Mr. Pitt and Lord Castlereagh, was moving heaven and earth to carry the Act of Union, found his efforts greatly clogged by the strenuous opposition offered to the measure by the Irish Bar. In December of that year, a meeting of the profession was held, at which, by a majority of 162 to 32, they passed a resolution protesting against the proposed Union, which, they asserted, would entail countless evils upon their country. Lord Clare organ of public opinion in Ireland. The apparent sole object of these journals would be, to offer daily insult to the national feeling of the English people; hold them up to the contempt of Ireland and the world as at one and the same time the best governed and most ungrateful people on the face of the habitable globe, and contend that the only persons in England worth reckoning as civilised beings were the Irish landlords, Irish officials, and pro-Irish section of the English community, who would be all ultramontane Catholics. The general tenor of the writings in these semi-official organs of " London Castle " would be, that there could be no real security for landlord life ·and property in England, nor peace or prosperity in the land, until Irish statesmen would have the courage to govern the country by means of a continuous suspension of the Habeas Corpus Act, abolition of trial by jury, and

---

saw the gravity of the situation; the Bar was a dangerous opponent, and should be silenced. Forthwith he established the system of County Chairmanships, which from that time to the present has constantly supplied thirty-three Irish barristers with salaries ranging from £700 to £1000 per annum, and which has consequently proved very useful, if not to Ireland, at least to her governors. As there were not Judgeships enough vacant to reward each of the thirty-two barristers who voted for the Union, the creation of the Chairmanships was most opportune. Sixteen of them were distributed among such of the thirty-two lawyers as had not received Judgeships. "

suppression of all seditious newspapers—which would mean, all anti-Irish or English national journalism

The "London Castle" Ring thus particularised would comprise about thirty-five persons, and adding the Lord-Lieutenant and Chief Secretary as *ex-officio* members, the united salaries which these individuals would draw from the public taxes of England would amount to over £120,000 per annum. They would have in addition the entire disposition of the revenue of the country in their hands, the management of all government business; control of all government offices; disposal of some 3000 government posts, the legal drilling of all resident magistrates in "Castle" tactics; the appointment of all county justices through their created county lord-lieutenants; the appointment of lord-lieutenants and deputy-lieutenants of counties; selection of high sheriffs for counties, and also of cities and boroughs from the lists returned by their municipal bodies to the Lord-Lieutenant, with whom the final selection would remain; appointment of grand juries (through Judges and Castle county high sheriffs) and indirect control over the expenditure of the county rates levied by these unrepresentative and irresponsible bodies.

One of the most serious duties that would devolve upon this "Castle" Ring would be the English State training of the Irishman who should, for the time being, hold the office of Chief Secretary to the Irish

Lord-Lieutenant of England. This Minister upon
visiting London (probably for the first time) after his
appointment by the Irish Cabinet, would be taken
in hand by select members of the Ring, and be immediately inoculated with the alarmist doctrines and rule-
by-state-of-siege principles which would have obtained
in the council chambers of "London Castle" since the
time when an Irish Pitt and an English Castlereagh
succeeded in robbing the English nation of legislative
independence.[1]

Should the new Chief Secretary be imbued with
liberal opinions towards the English people, and give
any symptoms of coming to the performance of his
duties with a mind prepossessed against the promptings

---

[1] Lord Hartington (then Chief Secretary to the Lord Lieutenant
of Ireland) in the debate on the Peace Preservation Act, Dec. 9, 1872,
said : "I can hardly undertake to describe the feeling of painful
dismay with which I undertake the task that is before me, *for in
addition to the inexperience and want of acquaintance with Irish
affairs which I labour under*, I have to approach that very difficult and painful task which has perplexed English statesmen for
many years," &c. Further on in the same speech, Lord Hartington
shows how ignorance of Irish affairs, on the part of an English
Chief Secretary, can be compensated for by arguments in favour
of more coercive laws—the stock remedy of the Castle Ring :
"The police have arrested," continued the noble lord, "numerous
persons under the provisions of the Act of last year (1871), for
being out at night under suspicious circumstances, but in very
few instances have the magistrates been able to inflict a penalty,
*for the men arrested have always been provided with a reasonable
and lawful excuse for being where they were found !*"

of the salaried English underlings who had guided
the policy of his predecessor, a serious danger would
at once confront the absolutism of the Ring. The
wrongs which a stupidly unsympathetic legislation had
for generations inflicted upon the English masses might
have made some impression upon the mind of the
Chief Secretary, to which fact his appointment might
be due; and if, in addition to these dangerous pro-
clivities, he should have the reputation of being a man
of independent character, firmness of will, and recognised honesty of purpose, the obstacles that would be
thus placed in the way of the continued supremacy of
the Ring, would be most formidable.

The genius of the "Castle," however, would be equal
to such a critical emergency.

The occasional experience of such more or less
perversely-disposed Chief Secretaries would suggest the
ways and means by which the newest appointment
to the post would be won over to the hereditary policy
which generations of absolutism had fixed as that
without which constitutional government would become
inevitable, and "Castle" rule overthrown, in England.

There is scarcely any feeling so keenly disappointing
to a public man as that which results from the suspicion,
or seeming discovery, that a people whose cause he has
more or less advocated are the ungrateful, perverse, and
unworthy nation their enemies have always declared

them to be. He may have maintained, in senate and on platform, that such alleged traits of character were foreign to the observed natural dispositions of such people. Or, if their demeanour did occasionally form an unfavourable contrast to that of another race residing among them, it could be both logically and charitably accounted for and extenuated by recollecting the numerous deteriorating moral and national agencies which centuries of admitted unjust rule had engendered. But let the belief that he was in error, after all, once approach his mind, and he becomes a prey to doubts as to the wisdom of extending popular liberties to them —doubts which accidental circumstances may appear to confirm, and which will ultimately throw him into the arms of a policy without which, he is assured, it will be impossible to keep the people in subjection to the rule of his own country. He feels like a man who was willing to succour a poor cripple who had experienced grievous wrong, but discovers that the police have arrested the object of his sympathy, and convicted him as an impostor. Political sympathy like human law would not, in such an instance, be proof against appearances.

Those influences which in a more or less degree guide the class of public men who are above the consideration of salary in the performance of the duties of responsible statesmanship, are thoroughly understood by the class of mercenary officials who are heard of by the public for the first time when they become berthed in some important Government situation. Salary and the possession of influence for the advancement of self and friends, are everything to them; while motives of self-denial or sacrifices for the common weal are the very principles of public action which threaten with opposition the exercise of such influence and the permanency of such stipends, and are dreaded when recognised in chiefs of departments as a dangerously infectious disease would be by the father of young children.

The advent of a Chief Secretary to power, who by his previous utterances or acts should exhibit any evidence of a reforming spirit, would call forth all the inventive faculties of the "London Castle" Ring. The absence of the popular English leaders from "Castle" levees would be explained as symptomatic of their disloyalty to the Crown, and desire for an English republic. Their speeches to English public meetings would be interpreted as incentives to a breach of law and order, and contempt for the authority of Ireland in England, while it would be broadly hinted to the new Secretary to the Lord-Lieutenant, that these leaders were in secret alliance with deadly enemies of the Irish empire in America and elsewhere, and that their real purpose was red revolution

In giving this complexion to the acts and motives of
the Gladstones, Brights, Chamberlains, and Forsters of
a subjugated England, and in the support of the tradi-
tional "Castle" policy, the King would have the active
aid not only of all the officials throughout the country,
but of the entire landed aristocracy also, including its
agents, lawyers, and dependants; and from very obvious
and intelligible reasons.

All the land of England would be in the possession
of a few thousand Irish and Anglo-Irish peers and
commoners, who would hold the same in virtue of
certain deeds performed by their ancestors in the conquest of England by Ireland. This right, by force of
violence and fraud, together with the entire neglect of
duties with a front of brass and exaction of rights by
a hand of iron, would make the landocracy hated and
dreaded by the mass of the English people. Their
rights to the soil of the country would not be worth a
month's purchase but for the protecting bayonets of
the Royal English Constabulary and an Irish army
of occupation, 30,000 strong. But this would not be
enough. Physical force must be supplemented by the
moral force of civil administration, consequently all the
administrative powers of the country must be either
in the hands of the landlords, or in those of their
adherents or nominees. Therefore, the incoming Chief
Secretary would find Irish rule and the interests of

the loyal English class thus "secured" upon taking office :

The direct Government of England would be centralised in "London Castle," and be in the hands of the Ring of permanent officials, as described. The conservatism of mercenary motives in these officials would correspond with the nature of the "vested interests" of the landlords, and make the continued rule of the one a necessary condition to the upholding of the territorial abuses of the other. The law of reciprocal dependence would render the supremacy of the Ring the perfection of government to the landlords, while the continuance in full swing of the rights, privileges, and monopolies of the latter in levying of county rates, functions of rural magistracy. and dispensation of petty patronage, would be guaranteed them by the Ring, in return for such disinterested confidence.

The Chairmen of Quarter Sessions and County Court Judges, before whom cases of eviction and breaches of landlord privileges would be brought for adjudication, would be the nominees either of the Ring or of the landlords. The high sheriff of a county in whom would be vested the power of calling the Grand Jury, would be a landlord, while the sub-sheriff would be either another landlord or an agent. The Lord-Lieutenant of each county would be a landlord or a peer, while the various deputy-lieutenants would all be recruited from the same territorial class. Of the four or five thousand rural magistrates, who would be scattered throughout England as Justices of the Peace, eighty per cent. would belong to the class most hostile to the social and political rights of the English people— the landlord class. The resident or stipendiary magistracy would be recruited from retired military and naval officers, ex-inspectors of constabulary (promoted policemen), and legal hangers-on of the Ring.

While the vast majority of the people of England would be of the Protestant religion, not above twenty per cent. of the foregoing administrators of law and justice would be of that faith. Eighty per cent. of England's paid and honorary magistracy would be ultramontane Catholic [1]

The Grand Jury system under which county government would be conducted—as in Ireland at present— would work as follows, under a "London Castle" Government —

---

[1] By a Return moved for by Mr Sexton, in Nov. 1882, and which was presented to Parliament during the last Session (1884), it is shown that the Protestant Justices of the Peace in Ireland number 4509, while those of the Catholic faith are but 884. The Protestant population in 1881, including "Church of Ireland," "Irish Church," "Protestant Episcopalians," "Presbyterians," "Methodists," "Baptists," &c., was 1,198,948; the Catholic population 3,960,891.

The Judges of Assize, who, as already explained, would be promoted "Castle" hacks, and members of the Privy Council to the Irish Lord-Lieutenant, would have the power of submitting the names of persons qualified to act as high sheriffs to the Lord-Lieutenant, who would be empowered to make the final selection. A high sheriff thus selected—who would invariably be a landlord and of strong anti-English feeling—would have the power of "calling" the Grand Jury for the county. This body would necessarily and invariably be composed of county landlords, all pro-Irish in their sympathies, mostly Roman Catholic in religion, and of strong anti-English prejudices. The people in the county would have no more voice in their selection than in the nomination of the President of the French Republic. This landlord and un-English body would have the management of roads, county asylums, &c The levying and expenditure of county rates would be among its functions, as would also the disposal of such offices and patronage as such fiscal administration would require If a murder should be committed or property be maliciously injured within any portion of a county thus governed, the Grand Jury would be empowered, upon application by friends of the murdered person, or the owner of the injured property, to levy a special tax upon the people of the district in which the deed would have been perpetrated, for compensation to the claimants—though the perpetrator might belong to another county, country, or continent.

The members of the various Boards of Guardians for the administration of England's Poor Law would be of a mixed representative character. The people's guardians and the landlord guardians would be in about equal force, owing to the system of multiple and proxy voting, which would enable the landlord interest to put in by a few landlord multiple votes as many members of the Board as the ratepayers of a whole union. Thus the ex-officio system, by which a landlord or property-holding guardian is entitled to sit for every elected guardian, would virtually hand over the huge machinery of the Poor Law into the hands of the great anti-English land-owning aristocracy. But this would not exhaust the vast centralising power of the " London Castle " Ring. The Local Government Board, already described, would be the virtual controller of the Poor Law administration in England. Everything done by every Board of Guardians would have to be approved of by the Local Government Board. Not a ten pound note of the people's rates could be expended without every item being submitted to the Local Government Board. A new water-closet in a workhouse at Berwick-on-Tweed could not be erected until plans, specifications, and estimate of costs should first be submitted to the Local Government Board.

Thus from the functions of the Lord-Lieutenant down to the meanest detail in the economy of rural government, everything would be under the absolute rule and control of the "London Castle" Ring on the advent of a new Chief Secretary.

The "police force of England" he would find a purely military body, and entirely under the control of the Ring. Under the "Castle" system he would find six policemen in England to one in Ireland, proportionately to population. They would all be trained in a central depot before entering upon police duties throughout the country. They would be drilled, dressed, and armed like any other military body, and would never be seen without either a rifle or a sidearm   Not a single railway station from Land's End to Berwick but would have two or more of these military police watching the arrival and departure of trains. They would be present, under arms, at every public gathering of the people, whether an open-air meeting, fair, athletic sports, or races   They would be empowered, under special Coercion Acts (fifty of which would have been passed by a Dublin Parliament at the instigation of "London Castle" in the space of eighty-two years), to enter any Englishman's house at any hour of the night in search of arms or treasonable documents. Englishmen found out of their homes after certain hours would be liable, at times, to be locked up until the police should be satisfied as to the reasons why they were abroad English Protestant ministers, noted for their patriotism and national principles, would have to tolerate policemen taking notes of their sermons on Sundays at Church. Finally, no municipal body or local authority in England would be allowed to exercise the least control over the police force of England. Not even the Metropolitan police force of London would be permitted as an exception to this rule. London, Manchester, Liverpool, Birmingham, and every other large centre of population would have their police officered by the Ring, directed by the Ring, promoted by the Ring, like every county in the country; and to "London Castle," and not to any local authority in the land, would such police look for pay, promotion, and favour.

The Chief Secretary would thus find England divided, in an unmistakable manner, into two clearly-marked parties—the national and anti-national, or the English and the pro-Irish. Numerically, the former would comprise four-fifths of the population, and would be paying an equivalent share of the rates and taxes of the country. The remaining one-fifth would constitute the anti-English party, and would have almost the entire wealth and all the government of England in its hands. This arrangement would necessarily separate the inhabitants of England into antagonistic classes—

one, the popular, and the other, the ascendancy class. The former, by their representatives in Parliament and the force of popular feeling outside, would naturally strive to obtain the control of the administration of their own affairs, while the latter party would, just as naturally, strain every nerve to keep down popular power in order to retain possession of the ruling machinery of government, social wealth and privilege, and the supremacy of the "Castle" system. To effect this the more securely, the ascendancy class would constitute itself and its dependents an Irish garrison of England, made up of soldiers, police, judges, magistrates, and other "defenders of law and order." It would be represented on all occasions of popular (English) feeling or agitations, that the continued supremacy of the Irish empire in England, and the maintenance of Irish rule over the English masses, would depend upon the support which the Imperial Government would give to its loyal and devoted English garrison. Any concession to popular English demands would be but a recognition of disloyalty and turbulence, and such a suicidal policy, if persisted in, would be strenuously opposed in the Dublin Parliament by the representatives of the "London Castle" Ring as measures that would be fatal to the integrity of the Empire and a supreme danger to civilised society. Every movement in England, aiming at an extension of popular liberty or a curtailment of class despotism, would be denounced by the "Castle" organs as "seditious proceedings," "attempts to supplant the constitution and destroy the Catholic religion," &c.; while "additional forces," with which "to strengthen the hands of the Executive" (the "Castle" Ring), would be loudly and persistently called for all along the line of the garrison. The leaders of such popular movements (Gladstone, Chamberlain, Dilke, Bright, Forster, &c.) would be branded as self-seeking agitators, enemies of law and order, emissaries of English-American revolutionists, communists, and socialists; while such newspapers as should propagate their subversive doctrines (the *Daily News, Pall Mall Gazette, Spectator, Echo*, &c.) would be denounced or prosecuted for inciting the gullible English masses to disorder, confiscation, and revolution.

The foregoing would be an outline of the government of England under the "Castle" Ring, on the advent of an Irish member of an Irish administration to the post of Chief Secretary to the Irish Lord-Lieutenant of England. The higher branches of the Administration would be under the heads of the various departments— the members of the permanent Ring. The subordinate and provincial part of the same would be in the possession of the landolrds, or "Castle" nominees.

Not a solitary individual would he discover in any responsible post of government who would be, in the

remotest sense of the word, a representative of the
industry, popular feeling, or national longings of the
people of England. The millions of tax and rate-paying
citizens would be intensely English in everything apper-
taining to the honour and welfare of their country; but
not a voice would they be permitted to have in the
actual management of their own national affairs; not a
single popular English nationalist would be found
entrusted with administrative responsibility. A law
actually prohibiting the chief post of England's government from being held by any person holding the same
religious belief as three-fourths of the English nation
would brand with an insult the conscientious belief of
the English people, and remind them, though religious
freedom might have been virtually won by their fathers,
that their faith was still a badge of political servitude
in the estimation of the rulers of their country—the
Irish "Castle" government of England

LECTURE XXXIII.

POLITICAL CRIME (*continued*).

Castle Rule of the Judicial Bench—Its " Impartiality "—Contrast between the Irish Constabulary Force and the Police System of England—The Irish and English Franchise—English defence of the Dublin Castle System of Government answered.

THAT the preceding lecture presents no fancy or over-drawn sketch of Dublin Castle and its system of ruling Ireland, few will venture to doubt who are familiar with the way in which the Irish people are governed. The law of the Castle has never commanded more than forced obedience, because there has existed, and there does still exist, in the popular mind of the country, the conviction that such law is not and cannot be impartial under the system which enforces it. While the vast majority of our people are treated as enemies, denied the ordinary privileges of free citizens, and ostracised from every responsible function in the government of their country, a small class, alien in almost every respect to the feelings and wants of the Irish nation, is permitted to speak and write and do almost whatever its ascendancy interests may require, no matter what law or precept of government may be virtually trampled upon by such procedure. What wonder, then, that there have been, and are still, treasons and plots among wronged and insulted Irishmen to overthrow this detested and miserable despotism? If such a system of government should fall to the lot of Englishmen, is there a man with English blood in his veins, and feeling for the honour of his country, who would not plot, plan, and conspire to hurl such an infamous rule into the Thames? There never can and there never will be peace in Ireland, or a respect for the administration of law, while its sensitive people see their beloved fatherland and their own rights and liberties in the clutches of a Ring of unscrupulous mercenaries, who flaunt the stigma of official, race, and religious ascendancy before their face in almost every transaction of administrative government.

In the law proceedings and administration of justice in England, the judge is expected to be, and invariably is, either a neutral power between the accused and the Crown which prosecutes, or an umpire who inclines more or less to the side of the accused until his guilt is clearly established. But who can truly say that this is the character of the Irish Judicial Bench? There is not a score of people in Ireland, outside of the landlord and ascendancy faction, that would not count upon having the judge as an assisting public prosecutor on the Crown side, if arraigned for any offence against the property of the landlords or law of the Castle.

The two latest instances of this open partisanship of the Castle judicial bench happened in connection with the recent State trial, "The Queen v. Parnell and others." A few weeks previous to the commencement of the trial, two of the traversers brought an action for attachment against one of the organs of the Castle, for certain libellous statements that were deemed prejudicial to the chances of a fair trial. The case against the proprietor of this paper was argued by Mr. Macdonagh, Q C, on behalf of Messrs. Parnell and Egan, and was heard by Lord Chief Justice May and Mr. Justice O'Brien. The conduct of the Chief Justice, however, was characterised by such violent and open partisanship against the traversers, whose trial was immediately pending, that the whole press of Great Britain and Ireland—the two organs of Dublin Castle excepted—cried shame upon the intemperate harangue of which Judge May delivered himself from the bench; and he was, in consequence, compelled by force of public opinion to retire from any further part in the trial of Parnell and co-traversers.

No such conduct would be heard of from a judge in England now-a-days, yet Judge May is still one of the heads of English law in Ireland, drawing his salary of £5000 a-year from the taxes of its people.

- The other instance of a Castle Judge acting as assistant to the Attorney-General was on the occasion of the State trial just referred to. Mr. Justice Fitzgerald was the president of the court, owing to the compulsory withdrawal of Chief Justice May; and the whole of the traversers without exception accepted him as an advocate for the Crown, having a sympathetic brief from the landlords, with a seat on the bench. Nor did the sequel belie their expectations. In his interruptions of the traversers' counsel, and whole demeanour and conduct during the trial, a looker-on could not possibly recognise a single instance or occurrence which would lead to the most charitable opinion being formed of his impartiality. His summing up to the jury was an elaborate and envenomed indictment of the Land League (up to Christmas of 1880), and supplementary speech for the Crown to that of Attorney-General Law. After the jury returned into court, and one of their number informed his lordship that ten were for an acquittal and but two for conviction, Judge Fitzgerald became white with rage, turned upon the unfortunate juryman, rated him for mentioning the numbers, and then loudly called upon the High Sheriff to bring in sufficient police to clear the court in case any emergency should arise, and—ordered the jury back to their room.

Such, however, is the frequency of these exhibitions of partisanship on the Irish bench that the Irish people cease to wonder at them. They accept such administration of Castle law as one of the many evils inseparable from the rule of that institution; and their undisguised contempt for and antipathy towards such parodies upon justice is but the necessary result of the whole system of Irish government as centred in the establishment on Cork Hill, Dublin.

Glaring as is the contrast between the judicial bench of the two countries, that between the two police systems is still more so. In England "Bobby" is a "popular institution." It very rarely happens that he "runs in" the wrong man, nor can disturbers of the peace or enemies of other people's property hold his vigilance, intelligence, or pluck in defiance or contempt. Yet he is never seen with a rifle slung across his shoulders, or met with a buckshot-pouch and bayonet at his side. He would probably feel as awkward if thus equipped in the task of keeping the peace among his fellow-countrymen as they, on their part, would look astonished and indignant at such an un-English spectacle as a soldier-policeman. "Bobby's" truncheon is at once the symbol of his authority as a public officer and the only weapon with which the law permits him to defend himself in the discharge of his duty. Even when called upon to assist in quelling a riot, he is never seen with any other weapon but his baton. Firing upon crowds and killing little boys and girls by such wanton and infamous licence as frequently characterises the action of the Royal Irish Constabulary would create a feeling of such indignation, if perpetrated in England, as would hurl any ministry from office that should appear to sanction such butchery by a police force.

The results of totally opposite systems of unarmed police under local and municipal control in England, and armed soldiers termed constabulary under Castle administration in Ireland, is clearly seen in the respective attitudes of the English and Irish people towards the particular force of each country. An Englishman loves individual liberty and respects the law which recognises his right to that privilege of free-citizenship; therefore he holds in equal respect the law and its agents, which are never associated in his mind with any other duty than what is to his advantage as a member of society —the duty of defending the property of the community from its enemies and preserving the peace from disturbers. The Irishman has an equal if not a more passionate attachment to freedom of movement, speech, and action, with a corresponding enmity towards whatever maintains a continued espionage upon any or all of these prerogatives of personal liberty. He can, therefore, have no feeling of respect towards the Royal Irish

Constabulary, because he knows that it is an Imperial political force, having none of the qualities of a police body, and that its extra-political duty and *raison d'être* is to form a bodyguard for the system of Irish landlordism.

In England and Scotland the expense of both County Constabulary and Borough Police is defrayed mostly out of local rates, for the well-known reason that Englishmen would object to have such an important factor in the administration of their country under the complete control of even their own (centralised) government. Hence the police of Great Britain are under the control of and dependent upon the local or municipal powers.

In Ireland, as already pointed out, the case is entirely reversed. Since 1846 the charge of supporting the Irish Constabulary has been undertaken by the Imperial government, for what purpose and policy is easy to discern, and the annual cost of this Imperial force is considerably over £1,000,000. While Scotland has but a police force less than 5000, and England and Wales less than 15,000 (not counting the Metropolitan force), Ireland with 5,000,000 of people, has over 11,000 constabulary, exclusive of the city of Dublin police!

From the manner in which this army of political police is distributed throughout Ireland, its equipment, *esprit de corps*, and high pay, it is ridiculous to regard it in any other light than that of 11,000 added to the 30,000 other Imperial troops which make up the physical force government of Ireland,

"But," I think I hear you say, "you have the same franchise in Ireland as in England, and to that extent, at least, your country is not unjustly treated."

Let us see what facts and figures have to say in reply to this erroneous statement (Thom's 'Official Almanac,' 1880).

The Irish franchise is distributed over 170,698 county electors, 57,290 city and borough, and 3548 for Trinity College, Dublin; giving a total number of parliamentary voters to Ireland of 231,536.

England (including Wales) has 903,658 county electors, 1,584,877 for her cities and boroughs, and 13,141 for her Universities, or a total of 2,501,676 parliamentary voters; being 2,270,140 more than Ireland.

England, with little over *four* times the population of Ireland, has *ten* times the number of electors. One in every nine Englishmen is privileged to vote in England; one in every twenty-four Irishmen in Ireland.

The Province of Ulster, comprising nine counties, and having a population of 1,312,879, has 15,966 voters *less* than Birmingham and Nottingham, in England, with but a little more than one-third as many people.

The two provinces of Munster and Leinster, comprising eighteen counties, with a population (not counting that of cities or boroughs) of 2,674,000, have 6218 *less* voters than the two English counties of Cheshire and Derbyshire, having less than one million of people. Dublin, Limerick, Cork, Athlone, Waterford, Mallow, Drogheda, Dundalk, Kilkenny, Ennis, Clonmel, Bandon, Tralee, Carlow, Dungarvan, Wexford, New Ross, Portarlington, and Youghal, cities and boroughs of Leinster and Munster, having a united population of 585,000, have 21,820 voters *less* between them, than the two English boroughs of Salford and Hull, with but a united population of 250,000.

The entire province of Connaught, with over 850,000 people, has 1718 voters *less* than Stoke-upon-Trent, English borough, with a population of 131,000.

Finally Glasgow has 2630 more voters than all the cities and boroughs of Ireland combined; Yorkshire has 180,000 more than all the Irish counties, while Lancashire has near 120,000 more voters than the whole of Ireland put together.

In English Boroughs, *all* rated Householders (whose rates have been paid) are entitled to votes, and, by a late decision of English judges, every room separately held has been considered a "house" under the 1867 Reform Act.

In Irish Boroughs, only rated householders whose

houses are *valued by Government* at *over £4* per annum (equal to a yearly rental of £8 in Ireland, or £10 or £12 in England), and occupiers of lodgings worth 4s. per week (unfurnished), or over, are entitled to votes.

As a consequence, Irish boroughs have less than half as many Parliamentary voters, in proportion to population, as English boroughs.

In English and Irish counties, the Occupiers' Franchise is nominally the same (£12 Government valuation), but from a difference in the methods of valuing, and other causes, English counties have more than one-and-a-half times as many voters in proportion to population as Irish counties

Let us next see what differences there are between the two countries in respect to the municipal franchise

In England every person, *male* or *female*, who has occupied for twelve months any house rated to the poor, is entitled to the Municipal Franchise.

In Ireland, in all towns except Dublin, every *man* only, who has occupied a house rated at *the Government value of* £10 (equal to a rental of £17 in Ireland, or, say, £22 in England), is entitled to the Municipal Franchise In Dublin, though the suffrage is ostensibly household, yet the necessity of three years' residence, and the rating of landlords, instead of occupiers, together with the non-rating of quarterly tenants, annihilate the household franchise

As a consequence, English towns have from *four* to *seven times* as many voters, for Municipal purposes, as Irish towns

I think I have successfully negatived in the foregoing lectures the frequent assertions of Englishmen, that Ireland is governed as England is governed—according to the British Constitution. Government by physical force is contrary to both the letter and spirit of that palladium of British liberty. Its aversion to despotism is such that it places it within the power of the elected representatives of the English people to curtail, or even to abolish, the army and navy (by the provisions of the Mutiny Act) during any session of Parliament, as a safeguard against a possible attempt on the part of the monarch to misuse the nation's forces against popular rights. But the popular liberty so jealously guarded on one side of the Irish Sea is placed entirely at the mercy of an anti-national and unpopular clique or Ring on the other. A system of rule analogous to that for which the Stuart dynasty was kicked out of England is thus maintained by English statesmen over the Irish people in the name of Constitutional government ! The rights and liberties of the Irish people are in the hands of a corps of anti-Irish officials. In the appointment of these officials the people of Ireland have no voice whatever, either directly or through their Parliamentary representatives. Questions can be asked in the House of Commons, and appointments can be criticised, of course; but six times the whole Irish representation in Parliament can be counted upon to stand by any English Minister who is determined to defend a Castle official against a representative of the country which that official helps to rule for an Anglo-Irish Ring and an English party.

I will now endeavour to meet and answer such arguments in defence of Castle rule as are ordinarily advanced by Englishmen who admit it to be an exceptional but necessary system of government for Ireland.

"The continual presence of a large proportion of the British army, and the maintenance of a special military police are needed in Ireland to uphold Imperial supremacy, and to meet any attempt on the part of the Irish people to separate the two countries."

This but concedes to my contention—that England's rule of Ireland is government by physical force, and not by constitutional methods. Such an argument, moreover, makes two admissions that are equally damaging to the institution which they are meant to defend :—(1st.) After seven centuries of rule by physical force, the Irish people are admittedly still disaffected towards England. (2nd.) A system of government which thus persists in keeping alive a feeling of hostility to its rule among the people governed, needs no other condemnation. It stands self-condemned.

"But was not the Act of Union the work of an Irish Parliament, sitting in Dublin?"

Yes; a Parliament of Anglo-Irish landlords, bribed by Lord Castlereagh, as all history acknowledges, to destroy the Irish legislature. A measure passed in this manner, under pressure of an insurrection which was most wickedly and with malice aforethought fomented by Dublin Castle, to aid the treacherous policy of Pitt in terrorising an exclusively Protestant Irish House of Commons into a surrender of its existence, cannot well be said to have been placed upon the statute-book with the sanction of the Irish people. Hundreds of thousands of the people of Ireland, Protestants and Catholics, petitioned against the Act at the time. O'Connell's great Repeal movement was organised to repudiate and overthrow it. The '48 movement was born of the national detestation of the system which the Act of Union substituted for Home Government. Fenianism arose to achieve national independence, as a consequence of the Castle system. Home Rule drew its inspiration from the popular aversion to the Act of Union; and sixty-four Irish representatives in the present Parliament are returned, by even a limited franchise, to demand the undoing of the measure which has given us Dublin Castle rule for a Dublin House of Commons. The national will of Ireland has never for a moment acquiesced in the Act of Union.

Irish popular opposition to it has never ceased during the last eighty-two years, as fifty-two Coercion Acts passed during that period by the Imperial Parliament at the instigation of Dublin Castle most significantly attest; and the longer English statesmen continue to uphold this most unholy union, the more fierce will grow the determination of the Irish race throughout the world to have it repealed, and the larger the number of Coercion Acts that will yet have to be added to those which already illustrate the imbecility of the rule of which they are the inevitable outcome.

"The Castle system centralises the power of our garrison in Ireland, and enables it to cope all the more effectively with the elements of disaffection"

Let me briefly examine the record of this centralised garrison, and see what it has accomplished for the power which it "protects" and represents.

Has it subdued the people of Ireland to a willing acceptance of English rule? No.

Has its administration of the law succeeded in winning popular confidence and respect? Just the reverse: Its Judges are mistrusted, its juries generally believed to be packed, its police hated, its authority defied, and the name and power of English Government, represented by this garrison, held in undisguised detestation by four-fifths of our population

Are the chiefs of this garrison either feared by the

Irish people, so as to inspire respect, or respected as the result of having performed their duty to the country? The contrary is the fact. Their power is defied at the present moment by one thousand representative Irish Nationalists, who are incarcerated in Irish prisons because they are "reasonably suspected" of being inimical to the entire garrison. The country, knowing that this act is perpetrated by England's Irish Executive in its character as the instrument of landlordism, cannot help despising a Government which coerces the majority of a country in order to sustain the unjust power of a class. Neither the English Lord-Lieutenant nor the Chief Secretary dare travel through Ireland without a military or police protection. No Government official could obtain a hearing from the people in any part of three provinces if notice of the meeting were published beforehand. While the imprisoned popular leaders are loved and their names cheered by the people, their Castle jailers are hated, and the mention of their names groaned at every public gathering. Finally, not one of these officials would stand the ghost of a chance of being elected by the Irish people to any position of public trust in their power to give

Let us now, on the other hand, summarise the record of this garrison as far as the country and people subjected to its rule are concerned.

What have been its fruits to Ireland? A loss of

three millions of population during the past forty years;
emigration still depopulating the country; periodical
famines, through the operation of an admittedly infamous
system of Land Laws, land continually going out of
cultivation; over two millions of people living in one-
roomed, mud-walled cabins; manufacturing industry all
but dead in three provinces, and languishing in the
fourth; an agrarian revolution raging throughout the
country at the present moment against the cause of
this depopulation, poverty, squalor, industrial stagnation
and social anarchy; agrarian murders and outrages of
frequent occurrence, moral ruin of thousands of virtuous Irish girls, who are compelled to leave the protecting influences of their homes through what amounts to
compulsory expatriation; and the following Coercion
Acts during the last fifty years:

1830. Importation of Arms Act.
1831. Act to Prevent Tumultuous Assemblies, known as "the
      Whiteboy Act"
1831 Stanley's Arms Act.
1832 Importation of Arms and Gunpowder Act
1833 Change of Venue Act
1834 Suppression of Disturbances Amendment and Continu-
      ance Act
1834 Another Importation of Arms and Gunpowder Act,
1835 Public Peace Act
1836 Another Arms Act
1838 Ditto   Ditto
1839 Unlawful Oaths Act.
1840 Another Arms Act
1841 Outrages Act.

1841. Another Arms Act.

1843 Act consolidating all previous Coercion Acts.

1844 Unlawful Oaths Act.

1845 Additional Constables near Public Works Act

1845 Unlawful Oaths Act.

1846. Constabulary Force Enlargement Act.

1847 Crime and Outrage Act.

1848 Treason Amendment ("Treason Felony") Act.

1848 Removal of Arms Act.

1848 Suspension of Habeas Corpus Act.

1848 Another Oaths Act.

1849 Suspension of Habeas Corpus Act.

1850 Crime and Outrage Act.

1851 Unlawful Oaths Act.

1853 Crime and Outrage Act.

1854 Ditto   Ditto

1855. Ditto   Ditto

1856 Peace Preservation Act.

1858 Ditto   Ditto

1860. Ditto   Ditto

1862 Ditto   Ditto

1862 Unlawful Oaths Act.

1865 Peace Preservation Act

1865 (August) Suspension of Habeas Corpus Act

1866 Suspension of Habeas Corpus Act.

1867 Ditto   Ditto

1868 Ditto   Ditto

1870 Peace Preservation Act.

1871 Protection of Life and Property Act

1871 Peace Preservation Continuance Act.

1873 Peace Preservation Act

1875 Peace Preservation Act (for five years)

1875 Unlawful Oaths Act.

1881 An Act for the better Protection of Life and Property [1]

---

[1] Since the above list was compiled, the Prevention of Crimes Act (1882) and the Arms Act (1882) have been added to post-Union coercive legislation.

It may be objected, by such Englishmen as are not familiar with the facts of recent Irish history, that the foregoing Coercion Acts were measures which the perverse lawlessness of Irish character rendered necessary on the part of a just and enlightened Government, which that of England is generally declared to be by those who believe their country can do no wrong.

For the information of such people, I will quote from the following sources what English writers, statesmen, and journalists have said of Irish government and Irish landlordism, within the same period covered by the above Coercion Acts—the lifetime of the present generation.

"With the Government in Ireland, 'the gallows is the only preacher of righteousness.'"—*Froude, English in Ireland.*

"Is a system which can only be supported by brute force, and is kept up by constant blood-shedding, to be perpetuated for ever? Are we still to garrison a defenceless country in behalf of those whose property was, generally speaking, originally conferred on the special condition of residence, but whose desertion occasions all the evils under which she has groaned for centuries?—*property so treated, that it would not be worth a day's purchase, were the proprietors its sole protectors.* But they are aware that their absence is balanced by the presence of a body of military and police, which enables them to conduct themselves with as little apprehension as remorse. The possessions of the entire empire would be lost were such conduct general; and are these so meritorious a class, that their utmost demands are to be extorted from a distant and suffering country, and themselves protected in the open neglect, or rather audacious outrage, of all those duties, on the due and reciprocal discharge of which the whole frame of the social system is founded? · If they persist in this course, let them do so, but let it be at their own proper peril."—Mr. Sadler (Tory), M P., *Ireland and its Evil*, 1839, p. 161-2

" *We* have made Ireland—I speak it deliberately—*we* have made it the most degraded and miserable country in the world All the world is crying shame upon us, but we are equally callous to our ignominy and to the results of our misgovernment."—*Lord John Russell.*

"The people of England have most culpably connived at a national iniquity. Property ruled with savage and tyrannical sway. It exercised its rights with a hand of iron, and renounced its duties with a front of brass. The 'fat of the land, the flower of its wheat,' its 'milk and its honey,' flowed from its shores in tribute. It was all drain and no return. But if strength and industry fared but ill in a land where Capital was in perpetual flux and decay, how much more poverty and weakness? In an integral part of the British Empire, on the soil trodden by a British sovereign, the landowner was allowed to sweep away the produce of the earth without leaving even a gleaning for them that were ready to perish. And they did perish year by year continually from sheer destitution.

England stupidly winked at this tyranny. Ready
enough to vindicate political rights, it did not avenge
the poor It is now paying for that connivance."—
London Times, Feb. 25, 1847.

"In this self-defensive war, they (the Irish) cannot
cope with the armed power of England in the open
field; and they are driven upon the criminal resource
of the oppressed in all ages and all lands—secret combination. They feel no remorse; first, because it is
war—just as the soldier feels no remorse for killing the
enemy in a battle, and, secondly, because their conquerors, and the successors of those conquerors, have
taught them too well, by repeated examples, the terrible
lesson of making light of human life. Poor, ignorant
creatures, they cannot see that, while the most illustrious
noblemen in England won applause and honours by
shooting down Irish women and children like seals or
otters, the survivors of the murdered people should be
execrated as cruel, barbarous, and infamous for shooting
the me. that pull down the roof-trees over the heads
of their helpless families, and trample upon their household gods These convictions of theirs are very revolting
to our feelings, but they are facts, and as facts the
legislature must deal with them. If there be a people
singularly free from crime, who regard the assassination
of the members of a certain class with indifference or
approbation, the phenomenon is one which political
philosophy ought to be able to explain, and one which
cannot be got rid of by suspending the Constitution and
bringing railing accusations against the nation"—
Godkin: Land War in Ireland.

"Among the many acts of baseness branding the English character in their blundering pretence of governing Ireland, not the least was the practice of *confiscating the land*, which, by Brehon laws, belonged to the people, and giving it not to honest resident cultivators (which might have been a politic sort of theft) but to cliques of greedy and grasping oligarchs which did nothing for the country they had appropriated, *but such its blood in the name of* RENT and squander its resources under the name of pleasure, and fashion, and courtliness in London."—*Landlords and Laws*, by Prof John Stuart Blackie, in *Contemporary Review* for January, 1880.

"Neither liberty of the press nor liberty of the person exists in Ireland. Arrests are at all times liable. It is a fact that at any time in Ireland the police may enter into your house, examine your papers to see if there is any resemblance between the writing and that of some anonymous letter that has been sent to a third person. In Ireland, if a man writes an article in a newspaper and it offends the Government, he has a warning, and if he repeats the offence his paper may be suppressed. They say Ireland is peaceful. Yes; but she is so not because she is contented, but because she is HELD UNDER BY COERCIVE LAWS. These laws may be necessary. I am not here objecting to them. I am a Tory, and, as such, I might favour severer laws myself. But I say it is not honest in the Liberals, whilst denouncing us, to imitate our ways."—*Speech of Benjamin Disraeli*, Feb 10, 1874.

"It is not in human nature—and all history teaches

this—that men should be content under a system of legislation and of institutions such as exist in Ireland. You may pass this (Coercion) Bill; you may put men in jail; you may suppress conspiracy; but the moment it is suppressed there will still remain the germs of the malady, and from those germs will grow up, as heretofore, another crop of disaffection—another harvest of misfortunes   And those members of this House—younger it may be than I am—who may be here eighteen years hence may find another Ministry proposing to them another administration of the same ever-failing and poisonous medicine." [1]—*John Bright, Coercion Bill Debate*, 1866.

"The Irish circumstances and the Irish ideas as to social and agricultural economy are the general ideas and the circumstances of the human race. It is the English ideas and circumstances that are peculiar. Ireland is in the main stream of human existence and human feeling and opinion. It is England that is in one of the lateral channels."—*John Stuart Mill. Hansard*, 17th May, 1866.

"I must say from all accounts and from my own observation, that the state of our fellow-countrymen in the parts I have named is worse than that of any people in the world, let alone Europe   I believe that these people are made as we are, that they are patient beyond belief, loyal, but at the same time broken-

---

[1] The Right Honourable gentleman has verified this prophecy in his own person. A Liberal Ministry of which he was a member received his support, by speech and vote, in passing some of the most despotic Coercion Acts which ever received the sanction of the Parliament of England, those of 1881 and 1882

spirited and desperate, living on the verge of starvation in places in which we would not keep our cattle The Bulgarians, Anatolians, Chinese, and Indians are better off than many of them are. . . . I am not well off, but I would offer Lord Bantry or his agent [Mr. J. W. Payne, J.P.] £1000 if either of them would live one week in one of these poor devil's places, and feed as these people do."—*General Gordon:* Letter from Glengarriff, County Cork, to *The Times*, December 3rd, 1880.

"The most serious and clear-minded of the exponents of Liberal ideas, talks sometimes as if a good Land Bill would settle everything. It will not; and it is deceiving ourselves to hope that it will. This can be brought about only by doing perfect justice to Ireland, not in one particular matter only, but in all the matters where she has suffered great wrong."—*Matthew Arnold.*[1]

As a fitting commentary on the system of rule under which these Coercion Acts have been passed for Ireland, I may add, that there were no less than twenty-eight

---

[1] "The centralisation of the Government was one of the great plagues of the country. Well, immediately after the first Reform Act it was proposed to grant municipal reform to Ireland, but it was opposed by a majority of the House of Lords. It was opposed in 1835, 1836, 1837, 1838, 1839. It passed, I think, in all these years—certainly in nearly all these years it passed the House of Commons and was rejected in the House of Lords (hear, hear). And in the year 1840, at last, it was passed, but passed in a mutilated form, and passed, for instance, with a higher franchise different from the franchise in England, so that the brand should still be left upon that country "—*Mr Gladstone*, Corn Exchange Meeting. Edinburgh, August 31st, 1884.

Bills introduced into Parliament by Irish members between 1870 and 1880, with the object of lessening the social evils of Irish landlordism (and thereby promoting the interests of law and order), not a single one of which was placed upon the Statute book.

Let me now ask, in all seriousness, a few questions *apropos* of the foregoing facts . Suppose that instead of applying to Ireland under England's rule, they could be related of Venetia under Austria, Bulgaria under Turkey, or Poland subjected to Russian rule , and supposing, again, that one thousand Italians, Bulgarians or Poles, were arrested and imprisoned, *without trial*, for open and constitutional efforts to overthrow the cause of such wrongs to their country ; would English statesmen designate them " village ruffians," and English papers applaud the Government which should imprison them ? Would not English sympathy, on the contrary, be voiced, and generous English assistance not be readily volunteered to the men who would be thus battling against an odious tyranny ? If Ireland were only situated by the Danube, and had Turkey or Russia in the position which England now occupies towards " The Sister Island," with a record of centuries of struggle for national as against Turkish or Russian rule, would English prejudice stand arrayed against her aspirations for self-government ?

The eighty years which have elapsed since the Act

of Union, and which have sufficed to bring Ireland to the condition just described, have seen what was a British Colony, almost as stupidly governed as Ireland, develop, when freed from the trammels of alien rule, into one of the most powerful and progressive nations in the world. Had it been possible for English statesmanship to have crushed out the spirit of American independence, before Liberty had won that continent for itself and mankind, the United States might be to-day a trans-Atlantic counterpart of a discontented Ireland. Within the same period we have seen France delivered more or less from the deadly sway of social and Bourbon servitude, and find herself, at the present hour, a Republic, however imperfect, as well as a fairly prosperous and progressive nation. Prussia, from being a small kingdom of Germany, has become the first of European military powers, and the greatest of European Empires   Italy,[1] when Ireland had her own Parliament, was divided into petty kingdoms and dukedoms, while being, at the same time, a prey for her powerful neighbours, France and Austria, to plunder and conquer at

[1] "Half a century ago, what was Italy? An idling-place of dilettanteism or of itinerant motiveless wealth, a territory parcelled out for papal sustenance, dynastic convenience, and the profit of an alien Government. What were the Italians? No people, no voice in European counsels, no massive power in European affairs; a race thought of in English and French society as chiefly adapted to the operatic stage, or to serve as models for painters, disposed to smile gratefully at the reception of half pence, and by the more

will. To-day she is a United Nation, and almost the equal of her former masters in the councils of Europe. Russia, though still an odious despotism, has progressed from the confines of barbarism and political insignificance to a position which places her second in importance to no other of her contemporary empires. England, within the same span of time, has reached the very pinnacle of political and commercial greatness.

Belgium is a still more telling instance of the transforming power which corporate nationhood has exercised in recent years over the social fortunes of an industrious people, whilst Greece, from being the degraded vassal of the Mussulman at a time when Ireland was self-ruled, is now, with a recognised national existence, a living evidence of the elevating power of self-government over the demoralising tendencies of political subjection In no single instance in modern history do we find a people who have won the right of ruling themselves, or to whom political autonomy has been conceded, retrograding either in civilisation, material prosperity, the arts or sciences.

---

historical remembered to be rather polite than truthful; in all probability a combination of Machiavelli, Rubini, and Massaniello. Thanks, chiefly, to the Divine gift of memory which inspires the moment with the past, present, and future, and gives the sense of corporate existence that raises man above the otherwise more respectable and innocent brute—all that, or most of it, is changed "
—George Eliot, in *The Modern Hep! Hep! Hep! Theophrastus Such,* p 261

" But, if we abolished the Castle, repealed the Act of Union, and granted you self-government, you would use an Irish Parliament as a means for effecting total separation and the establishment of an Irish Republic."

The best reply to this stock objection to our just demand for self-government, is to see, by a comparison of actual facts, whether Ireland could *possibly* separate herself from Great Britain, without the consent of England or the fall of her greatness.

Facts Relative To

Great Britain	and	Ireland.
Population, 1881—30,190,920		5,088,079
Wealth—£?		£—Nothing in comparison
Army		None
Militia } —626,123		None
Volunteers		None
Navy—81,318 men		None
„ —594 war vessels		None
Great Britain united in maintaining connection with Ireland.		One-fifth of Irish population averse to total separation

" Well, suppose we admit the impossibility of separation under such conditions; would not the Roman Catholic majority persecute the Protestant minority under a native parliament? Would not ' Home Rule ' mean Rome Rule ? "

Nothing of the kind. The religious interests and other rights of Irish Protestants would be as safe from molestation in an Irish parliament as they are to-day in that of Westminster. Why not? They are Irishmen, and it is as Irishmen, and not as Catholics, that Irish Nationalists are striving for the self-government of their country. Without the influence arising from the sacrifices and the teachings of Irish Protestants like Tone, Fitzgerald, Emmet, the Sheares, Flood, Grattan, Curran, Mitchel, Martin, and others, the Irish National cause would not possess the vitality which it has to-day. The canonised political saints of Ireland's struggle for nationhood during the last one hundred years are chiefly Protestant; and any Irish parliament which would dare to deny to a countryman of Robert Emmet's faith the same religious, social, and political rights which might be won for all the Irish people, would be repudiated by the mass of the Catholics of Ireland There is not in any civilised country in the world a body so free from political bias on account of religious differences, as the Catholic Hierarchy and priesthood of Ireland; nor a people so indifferent to "religion in politics" as Irish Catholics. This is so obvious to every student of Irish political life that evidence to substantiate its correctness is unnecessary. Where then is there any reasonable ground for the supposition, that an Irish parliament, elected on manhood or universal suffrage, would be inimical to the Protestants of Ulster?

His Holiness the Pope, as head of the Catholic Church throughout the world, can have no special desire to see self-government granted to Ireland, except in so far as he is influenced by moral considerations to desire the triumph of justice. A native parliament could not make Ireland more Catholic than she is to-day. It would not convert Ulster to Catholicism to have her send one-fourth of Ireland's representatives to legislate in Dublin in company with the members from the other provinces; all of whom would no more be Catholic than would those from the north be all Protestant. It would rather tend to give our Protestant fellow-countrymen greater prominence in the public life of the most Catholic people of Europe, than they now exercise, to have them conspicuously represented in Dublin

Viewed from the stand-point of the head of the Catholic Church, then, the concession to Ireland of a measure which would transfer forty or fifty Roman Catholic members from the most conspicuous legislative Protestant assembly in the world, to a Parliament House in Dublin, could be no victory for the cause of the Catholic Church. The interests of the Universal Church must be paramount to those of Irish nationality with the Vatican. Would those interests be as equally represented and as faithfully guarded in a British House of Commons, having no Roman Catholics among its members, as when forty or fifty Irish members are resent to defend their faith from misrepresentation and the Sovereign Pontiff from the attacks of enemies? This is how the question of Irish self-government *must* be viewed by the Propaganda, and if, as no one will deny, the interests of the Church *are* of greater moment to the Vatican than those of Irish nationality, the granting of a local parliament to Ireland could not be viewed with any extreme satisfaction by Pope Leo XIII It would leave the Parliament of the British Empire—an empire embracing many million Roman Catholics—almost without a single Roman Catholic representative; while many men of Mr. Bradlaugh's opinions may confidently be reckoned upon as members of that assembly after the next extension of the franchise

"Well, supposing we made the Irish leader Chief Secretary and a member of the English Cabinet, and allowed him to re-official Dublin Castle out of his own following; would that not satisfy the Irish people and abate the popular demand for an Irish parliament?"

Most certainly not It is not only a question of officials, but one of principles of government that is at the bottom of the Anglo-Irish strife. Our grievance is national, as well as constitutional and social, and none but a national and constitutional remedy will suffice for its removal It is well that this should be clearly understood by Englishmen. We demand the restoration of the right to make our own laws, to rule our own country. This right we have never voluntarily surrendered; and without its restitution by the power which deprived us of it, there can be no real peace in Ireland while one liberty-loving Irish nationalist is alive.

Apart from the injuries inflicted upon Ireland through Castle rule, what are our claims to the right and advantages of nationhood? John Stuart Mill lays down [1] the doctrine that "a portion of mankind may be said to constitute a nationality, if they are united among themselves by common sympathies which do not exist between them and any others—which make them co-operate with each other more willingly than with other people, desire to be under the same government, and desire that it should be government by themselves, or a portion of themselves exclusively. This feeling of nationality may have been generated by a variety of causes. Sometimes it is the effect of identity of race and descent, community of language and community of religion greatly contribute to it. Geographical limits are one of its causes. But the strongest of all is identity of political antecedents; the possession of a national history, and consequent community of recollections; collective pride and humiliation, pleasure and regret, connected with the same incidents in the past." The Irish people, both in their antecedents and present political attitude, fulfil all these conditions

---

[1] *Representative Government,* chapter xvi.

of distinct nationality   The struggles from 1172 on to
1642, 1782, 1798, 1800, 1803, 1829, 1844, 1848, 1867,
1879-80-81, attest the unbroken character of our
resistance in one form or another, to a power which
denied us the right of ruling ourselves.   From 1172
until the present hour, we have contended as a distinct
nationality, against what Charles James Fox declared
to be " the false and abominable presumption that the
English could legislate better for the Irish than they
could do for themselves—a presumption founded on the
most arrogant tyranny."   The root of the Anglo-Irish
difficulty, therefore, is not altogether who shall administer but who shall make the laws of Ireland.   We
do not want the Castle system reformed.   We demand
its abolition.[1]

[1] " No Government can exist in any country that is not
based upon one of two things, conquest or the good-will of the
governed   The Czar's rule is based upon the first of these, our
own upon the second   Which of these is it that supports the
Irish Government ?   Ask of the soldiers that garrison the cities
and towns of Ireland   Ask of the enormous constabulary and
police force.   Ask of any Irishman, no matter of what party, and
the answer will be—conquest.   True, our Government merits the
good will of one-fifth of the nation, and even receives it so long as
the Executive is careful not to offend that section by a rash interference with their hereditary privileges.   But we annexed the
real body of the Irish nation, and though we have been liberating
them by inches ever since, they stedfastly refuse to acquiesce
cordially in our presence as rulers   There is only one alternative
We must either rule them by force or let them go free.   And

[NOTE —Of the many fallacies which make up the sum-total of the ordinary Englishman's ignorance of his country's rule of Ireland, there is none so firmly believed in as that which asserts that the government of "the Sister Island" is a most costly business to the British taxpayer. John Bull's housekeeping expenses would, in the opinion of nine out of every ten Britons, be considerably reduced if Ireland were only "cast off," and compelled by the disassociation to keep house for herself. To maintain the connection, therefore, is, according to the aforesaid prevalent English belief, an act of political charity on the part of England for which she receives in return the proverbial ingratitude of the Irish people. To explode this fallacy is an easy task Facts and figures are the only arguments required to accomplish it By a parliamentary return which was laid on the table of the House of Commons last March, it appears that the cost of governing Ireland during the year 1882-3, was £7,110,000. Not only was this sum contributed by Ireland herself to the Imperial Exchequer—strange as it may appear to the incredulous Briton—but £1,183,000 of a balance, according to the same return, remained to our credit after we had paid every item of the expenditure which was incurred in the luxury of Dublin Castle government.

One fallacy overthrown only begets another, when the rule of Ireland is the subject of discussion in

---

while we continue to rule them we must make them contented by punishing discontent. As some minister so beautifully puts it, we must endeavour to reconcile them to our Government, while putting down crime with a firm hand. It is a noble task, and one in which we have glorious encouragements to persevere, from the example of the Czar in Russia, the Austrians in Italy, and other enlightened governments elsewhere "—*The Truth about Ireland*, by an English Liberal. London: Kegan Paul & Co., 1884, p 15

England. It may possibly be admitted that this parliamentary return (moved for by Col. Nolan, M P) was right, and that the Irish people have paid the expenses incurred by English officials in ruling them, but then look at Scotland ! See how much more *she* contributes, and mark how much less is *her* bill for Government housekeeping than Ireland. True. But before a just comparison can be instituted between the two countries in these respects, we must take into account their respective tax-paying capacity. We must consider the wealth of Ireland and Scotland

In 1882, the property upon which legacy and succession duty was paid in Ireland, amounted to £7,142,912. In Scotland, it was £16,473,542. The annual value of the property assessed to income tax was as follows in the two countries :—

	SCOTLAND.		IRELAND
Houses	£11,838,269	...	£3,210,50
Railways	3,055,464	...	1,128,22_
Land	7,711,895		9,980,650
Mines	803,122		17,205
Ironworks	484,874		100
	£23,893,624		£14,336,683

It will be seen, from this comparison, that the taxable wealth of Ireland is but 7-12ths of that of Scotland, and if Scotland's just share of Imperial revenue amounts to £9,137,000 (the figures given in Col. Nolan's return) Irelands relative contribution should be only £5,330,000, instead of £8,194,000, or £2,864,000 less than is now exacted from the Irish people

It is also true that the rule of Scotland cost but £2,665,000, while that of Ireland amounted to £7,000,000 in the above year. But this only shows that a country which is virtually ruled by its own people can be governed for one-third the expense which the government of another country, not much larger, entails, when it is carried on by alien and obnoxious officials.

In this connexion the following figures ought to convey an instructive lesson on the cost of Castle rule to Ireland   Compare, from the official returns, the two countries in regard to—

	(SCOTLAND)	(IRELAND)
Law and Justice	£605,011	£1,028,285
Constabulary	——	1,530,144
Military Forces	558,439	1,854,466
Naval Forces	105,629	223,036
Pensions	300,016	555,148
Viceregal Household	——	30,501
	£1,569,095	£5,221,580

A study of these figures will not induce Scotchmen to agitate for a North British system of Castle rule Perhaps Englishmen may also conclude from the arguments which these statistics enforce, that the Irish people have good and substantial reason for their detestation of a kind of government which robs the taxpayer while it insults the nation]

LECTURE XXXIV

POLITICAL JUSTICE. HOW THE ANGLO-IRISH PROBLEM COULD BE SOLVED.

"What will satisfy the Irish People?"—Stock Opinions and Arguments of Englishmen—Ireland learning "to make the Ruling Power uneasy"—Difficulties in the way of a Formulation of Ireland's Demand for Political Justice—Degrees of Intensity of Irish National Sentiment—Physical v Moral Force Ideas—Serious Considerations for Irish Leaders—Outline of a Scheme of County and National Government for Ireland—Duties of Elective County Board—Functions of a National Assembly—Conclusion—Liberation of the "Chairman"—A Lesson in Liberty

THE question is frequently asked, "What will satisfy the Irish people?" And the answer is as frequently volunteered, "Nothing Nothing will satisfy them but total separation—and that they won't get" It is an illogical way of answering a question, but pardonable in an Englishman, and the impatience which it manifests is also strikingly characteristic. Your ordinary Englishman entertains the pretty conceit that English rule is of such a beneficent character that any people who do not tamely submit to it are to be pitied and—dragooned. While in particular, the Irish people, for their obstinacy in refusing to see any virtue in English rule in Ireland, "must be clearly made to understand," and "must be told once for all," that England will maintain her hold upon Ireland at all costs. All this talk is indulged in really for the sake of concealing the chagrin which England experiences in consequence of the fact, revealed in recent years, that the people of Ireland have discovered how to make it more difficult for England to rule Ireland, than to govern all the rest of her vast empire put together. English Statesmen, even now, are devising a middle course between things as they are, and total separation. They are casting about for a scheme which will combine the characteristics of modern statesmanship—a scheme, for example, which will involve as small a concession as possible to the demand of the people concerned, and have a fair chance of passing the House of Lords Eminent statesmen have more than once challenged Irish public men to say what they want, but the required answer has not been forthcoming. There have been answers, but they have been too reasonable. English statesmen have not been able to offer upon them the comment, "We told you so, the thing demanded is utterly out of the range of practical politics, and, in point of fact, is absolutely out of the question" The answer really required is such a one as English statesmen can meet with a *non possumus* And for this reason, English statesmen, I repeat, know that a substantial concession will have to be made to the genius of Irish nationality within the next few years The demand for it is too strong to be resisted; for the Irish race have to be dealt with now If at home on Irish soil the people can "make the ruling powers uneasy" to such an extent as I have indicated, in Westminster their representatives can clog the wheels of legislation and endanger the very existence of government by parliamentary methods; while abroad, in Great Britain, America, Australia, Canada, the exiled Irish have discovered how to operate on the flank, so to speak, by elevating the Irish question into the position of a national or colonial issue Further, England's guilt towards Ireland is known and commented on all over the world Further still, the real people of England—the working men of England—have of late been asking for the reasons why Ireland should be perpetually discontented, and the answers they have received, to the credit of their common sense, be it said, do not appear to have satisfied them Respectable England is very angry, and, to conceal their annoyance at the inevitable, and to pave the way for a concession, English statesmen ask the question of Irish public men—" What do you want ? "

and require an answer to which they may return an
emphatic "impossible." But this is only diplomacy
They only desire us to say how much we want, in
order to say in reply how little they will give. They
ask us to "formulate our demand," that they, in
formulating their concession, may assure their oppo-
nents of its comparative innocence. Responsible Irish
public men have declined to fall into the trap. And
they have acted very wisely. For why should Irish
public men show their hand rather than English Prime
Ministers ?

Apart altogether from considerations of this character, however, there are others of a distinctly Irish
nature which the leaders of the National movement
in Ireland have to take into account. The varying
shades of National sentiment may not be ignored. Let
us therefore analyse the degrees of intensity of Irish
Nationalist aspirations.

We have first, the Extremists, those who believe that
total separation from England is the only thing that
would satisfy Irish genius or develope it properly.
These include the most self-sacrificing Irishmen. They
represent, in their aspirations for Irish liberty, those
who have made the most illustrious names in Ireland's
history. They include many cultured men, especially
among the expatriated portion of the race, but their
main strength is in the working classes Patriotism

is purer among the industrial order because less modified by mercenary motives and less liable to corrupting influences. But the Extremists or Separatists are divided among themselves upon the question of method. There are Separatists who advocate physical force, believing moral force, that is constitutional means, ineffectual and demoralising This section includes men who have never tried moral force and who believe solely either in "honourable warfare" or "dynamite" It also includes those who have tried moral force, and given it up in despair Then there are the Separatists, who, with the experiences of '48 and '67 before their minds, rely upon constitutional action alone

Next in importance to the Extremists, come the Home Rulers, or Federalists, who may be divided into those who disbelieve in the possibility of Separation and those who do not see its necessity This section of the National party includes some of the ablest and most earnest men in Ireland. Their methods, I need hardly say, are strictly constitutional.

No Irish leader can afford to ignore either of these two principal phases of Irish National sentiment. Were such a man to commit himself to a definite scheme, at the mere invitation of an English Minister, he would run the risk of alienating that section of his supporters whose views were not represented in his proposals It is an obvious remark that such a contingency would not be unwelcome to English statesmen. From what I have just said, it will be readily perceived how difficult is the task to which Irish popular leaders are asked to address themselves.

Nevertheless, I shall venture to outline a scheme of local and National self-government which, I believe, would command the support of the majority of the Irish people at home and abroad, and which would probably receive a fair trial at the hands of the Extremists, though its operation would undoubtedly be watched with a jealous eye.

In the first place, there should be established in Ireland a system of county government, by means of Elective Boards, to take the place of the existing un-representative and practically irresponsible Grand Jury system. The functions of such Boards should be more comprehensive than those exercised by the Grand Juries. For example, in addition to the duty of administering purely county business, these Boards should be per-mitted to initiate measures of general application; such as schemes of arterial drainage, tramways, railways, canals, docks, harbours, and similar enterprises, which would be of more than local importance and character. Such schemes, after being fully discussed by these elective bodies, would be submitted to the National Assembly to be subsequently described. Then the County Boards should control the police within the county, and appoint the magistrates, and be entirely responsible for the preservation of law and order.

Further, should the land problem be justly and satisfactorily solved on the lines of national proprietary, the duty of assessing and collecting the land-tax would naturally devolve upon the County Boards, which, deducting what was necessary for the expenses of county government, would remit the balance to the National Exchequer. In fact the object of such a system should be to constitute each county, as far as practicable, a self-governing community

Manifestly any system of local self-government for Ireland involves a corresponding one of National self-government as its natural and inevitable complement To extend the principle of local self-government at all in Ireland, without radically changing the system of Castle rule, would only have the effect of increasing the friction already existing between the people and their rulers Hence, it is absolutely necessary that legislation for National self-government should go hand in hand with any scheme for the creation of Elective County Boards. I am well aware that the hope is indulged, in some quarters, that the inclusion of Ireland in a general measure of county government, with the sop of an Irish Parliamentary Grand Committee thrown in, will suffice to choke off the demand for Irish legislative independence, but English statesmen need not delude themselves with the idea that any such West-minster expedient will satisfy the genius of Irish Nationality

There could be established in Dublin a National Assembly, composed of elected members from the constituencies of Ireland, who should proceed to the administration of all Irish affairs, in the manner which obtains in Colonial parliaments, excepting the substitution of one for two Chambers, here proposed. That is to say, the Representative of the Crown in Ireland would call upon some member of the National Assembly to form a government, the different members of which should be constituted the heads of the various Boards, which at present are practically irresponsible bureaucracies, but which, under the system here proposed, would become departments of a popular government, and open to the supervision of the people through the National Assembly. Such a government, subject to the control of the governed through their elected representatives, would be the practical solution of the Anglo-Irish difficulty. It would be but the common definition of constitutional rule carried into practice. It would, as already remarked, be the application to misgoverned and unfortunate Ireland of a constitution kindred to that which British statesmanship has long since granted, wisely and well, to a consequently peaceful and contented Canada

Certainly if a similar act of political justice and sound policy does not solve the Irish difficulty, nothing less will. What possible danger could England run from such an application of constitutional rule to a country much nearer to the centre of Imperial power than Canada? But what a beneficent change for Ireland —nay, what a relief to England herself—would be involved in such an act of simple political justice!

Now, Mr Chairman, our task is done, and your right to liberty can no longer be resisted by me　I shall feel our separation keenly, for our companionship has been to me a source of singular happiness　You have robbed solitary confinement of its inhuman features, while the little care and attention which your simple wants required at my hands, have kept in play those better attributes of poor humanity that manifest themselves in the solicitude which one being exhibits for the welfare of another, but for the exercise of which there is neither scope nor opportunity in penal servitude.　But with to-morrow's advent I will surely open your cage, and you shall be as free as the air upon which your wings are longing to unfold themselves

CONCLUSION.

IT was a lovely morning in the autumn of 1881, and the infirmary garden in Portland Prison was aglow with the bloom of the late summer flowers which the Governor had kindly permitted me to sow in the early portion of the year. The English Channel, which often lulls the weary Portland prisoner to sleep by the storm-chorus of its waves as they dash against the rocks underneath the walls, lay in unruffled calm From the headland upon which the great convict establishment stands could be seen the picturesque shadows which the Dorsetshire cliffs flung out upon the bosom of the sea. Away beyond the coast-line appeared harvest-fields and homesteads, melting into the distance, and so sadly suggestive of what imprisonment was not—liberty, home, and friends—conjuring up that contrast between the manacled and the free which constitutes the keenest mental pain in the punishment of penal servitude.

It was a day which would fill one's whole being with a yearning to be liberated—a day of sunshine and warmth and beauty, and the moment had arrived when my resolution to give freedom to my little feathered "chum" could no longer be selfishly postponed. I opened his door with a trembling hand, when quick as a flash of lightning he rushed from the cage with a wild scream of delight, and in a moment was beyond the walls of the prison! The instinct of freedom was too powerful to be resisted, though I had indulged the fond hope that he would have remained with me. But he taught me the lesson, which can never be unlearned by either country, prisoner or bird, that Nature will not be denied, and that Liberty is more to be desired than fetters of gold.

THE END

London: P. Clay, Sons, and Taylor, Bread St. Hill.

11, HENRIETTA STREET, COVENT GARDEN, W.C.

(*Late 193, Piccadilly, W.*)

NOVEMBER, 1884.

CATALOGUE OF BOOKS

PUBLISHED BY

CHAPMAN & HALL,

INCLUDING

DRAWING EXAMPLES, DIAGRAMS, MODELS, INSTRUMENTS, ETC.

ISSUED UNDER THE AUTHORITY OF

THE SCIENCE AND ART DEPARTMENT, SOUTH KENSINGTON,

FOR THE USE OF SCHOOLS AND ART AND SCIENCE CLASSES.

MILITARY BIOGRAPHIES.

Messrs. CHAPMAN & HALL are preparing for publication a Series of Volumes dedicated to the Lives of Great Military Commanders.

The volumes are designed to form a set of critical Biographies, illustrative of the operations and the art of war, by writers of distinction in the profession of arms, whose competence to weigh the military qualities and deeds of the Chiefs can be accepted. Maps will, when necessary, accompany the volumes, for the convenience of students.

The aim of these volumes is to be both popular and scientific, combining the narrative of the most romantic and instructive of human lives with a clear examination of the genius of the soldier.

"FREDERICK THE GREAT," by Col C B BRACKENBURY, containing Maps. Large crown 8vo, 4s

"MARSHAL LOUDON," by Col. MALLESON, C S.I ; the two Lives presenting the opposing aspects of the Seven Years' War. Containing Portrait and Maps. Now ready. Large crown 8vo, 4s.

"TURENNE," by Col. HOZIER, will follow shortly.

BOOKS

CHAPMAN & HALL, LIMITED.

THE ARMIES OF THE NATIVE STATES OF INDIA.
Reprinted from the *Times* by permission. Crown 8vo, 4s.

BADEN POWELL (GEORGE)—
STATE AID AND STATE INTERFERENCE. Illus-
trated by Results in Commerce and Industry Crown 8vo, 9s.

BARTLEY (G. C. T.)—
A HANDY BOOK FOR GUARDIANS OF THE POOR.
Crown 8vo, cloth, 3s.

BAYARD: HISTORY OF THE GOOD CHEVALIER,
SANS PEUR FT SANS REPROCHE Compiled by the LOYAL SERVITEUR;
translated into English from the French of Loredan Larchey. With over 200
Illustrations Royal 8vo, 21s.

BELL (DR JAMES), *Principal of the Somerset House Laboratory*—
THE CHEMISTRY OF FOODS. With Microscopic
Illustrations
PART I TEA, COFFEE, SUGAR, ETC. Large crown 8vo, 2s. 6d
PART II. MILK, BUTTER, CEREALS, PREPARED STARCHES, ETC.
Large Crown 8vo, 3s

BENNET (WILLIAM) *The Late*—
KING OF THE PEAK: a Romance. With Portrait.
Crown 8vo, 6s.

BENSON (W)—
MANUAL OF THE SCIENCE OF COLOUR. Coloured
Frontispiece and Illustrations. 12mo, cloth, 2s 6d

PRINCIPLES OF THE SCIENCE OF COLOUR. Small
4to, cloth, 15s.

BINGHAM (CAPT THE HON D)—
A SELECTION FROM THE LETTERS AND
DESPATCHES OF THE FIRST NAPOLEON. With Explanatory Notes
3 vols. demy 8vo, £2 2s.

BIRDWOOD (SIR GEORGE C M), C S I—
THE INDUSTRIAL ARTS OF INDIA With Map and
174 Illustrations New Edition Demy 8vo, 14s.

BLACKIE (JOHN STUART) F R S E —
THE SCOTTISH HIGHLANDERS. Crown 8vo.
[*In November.*

ALTAVONA: FACT AND FICTION FROM MY LIFE
IN THE HIGHLANDS. Third Edition Crown 8vo, 6s.

BLATHERWICK (DR)—
PERSONAL RECOLLECTIONS OF PETER STONNOR,
Esq. With Illustrations by JAMES GUTHRIE and A. S. BOYD Large crown 8vo, 6s.

LORD BLOOMFIELD'S MISSION TO THE COURT OF
BERNADOTTE. By GEORGIANA, BARONESS BLOOMFIELD, Author of "Reminiscences of Court and Diplomatic Life." Two Vols. demy 8vo, w Portraits, 28s.

BOYLE (FREDERICK)—
ON THE BORDERLAND—BETWIXT THE REALMS
OF FACT AND FANCY. Crown 8vo, 10s. 6d.

BOULGER (DEMETRIUS C)—
GENERAL GORDON'S LETTERS FROM THE
CRIMEA, THE DANUBE, AND ARMENIA. Crown 8vo, 2nd Edition, 5s.

BRADLEY (THOMAS), of the Royal Military Academy, Woolwich—
ELEMENTS OF GEOMETRICAL DRAWING. In Two
Parts, with Sixty Plates. Oblong folio, half bound, each Part 16s.

BRAY (MRS)—
AUTOBIOGRAPHY OF (born 1789, died 1883).
Author of the "Life of Thomas Stothard, R.A.," "The White Hoods," &c.
Edited by JOHN A. KEMPE. With Portraits Crown 8vo, 10s. 6d

MRS. BRAY'S NOVELS AND ROMANCES.
New and Revised Editions, with Frontispieces. 3s. 6d. each.

THE WHITE HOODS; a Romance of Flanders	THE TALBA; or, The Moor of Portugal
DE FOIX, a Romance of Bearn.	THE PROTESTANT; a Tale of the Times of Queen Mary

NOVELS FOUNDED ON TRADITIONS OF DEVON AND CORNWALL.

FITZ OF FITZFORD, a Tale of Destiny	COURTENAY OF WALREDDON
HENRY DE POMEROY	
TRELAWNY OF TRELAWNE	HARTLAND FOREST AND ROSE-
WARLEIGH, or, The Fatal Oak	TEAGUE

MISCELLANEOUS TALES
A FATHER'S CURSE AND A DAUGHTER'S SACRIFICE.
TRIALS OF THE HEART

BROADLEY (A M)—
HOW WE DEFENDED ARABI AND HIS FRIENDS
A Story of Egypt and the Egyptians Illustrated by FREDERICK VILLIERS.
Second Edition Demy 8vo 12s.

BROMLEY-DAVENPORT (the late W, M P)—
SPORT. With numerous Illustrations by General CREALOCK.
[*In December*

BUCKLAND (FRANK)—
LOG-BOOK OF A FISHERMAN AND ZOOLOGIST.
Fourth Thousand With numerous Illustrations Crown 8vo, 5s.

BURCHETT (R)—
DEFINITIONS OF GEOMETRY. New Edition. 24mo,
cloth, 5d.

LINEAR PERSPECTIVE, for the Use of Schools of Art.
Twenty-first Thousand With Illustrations Post 8vo, cloth, 7s

PRACTICAL GEOMETRY· The Course of Construction
of Plane Geometrical Figures With 137 Diagrams Eighteenth Edition. Post
8vo, cloth, 5s.

BURLEIGH (BENNET G)—
DESERT WARFARE: Being the Chronicle of the Eastern
Soudan Campaign Demy 8vo, with Maps, 12s

CAMPION (J S)—
ON THE FRONTIER. Reminiscences of Wild Sports,
Personal Adventures, and Strange Scenes. With Illustrations. Second Edition.
Demy 8vo, 16s

ON FOOT IN SPAIN. With Illustrations. Second Edition,
Demy 8vo, 16s.

CHAMPEAUX (ALFRED)—
TAPESTRY. With Woodcuts. Cloth, 2s. 6d.

CHRISTIANITY AND COMMON SENSE. A Plea for the
Worsh῾᷾ of our Heavenly Father, and also for the Opening of Museums and
Galleᵣᵢ on Sundays. By a BARRISTER. Demy 8vo, 7s. 6d

CHURCH (A H), MA, Oxon —
ENGLISH EARTHENWARE. A Handbook to the
Wares made in England during the 17th and 18th Centuries, as illustrated by
Specimens in the Natural Collections With Illustrations *[In December.*

PLAIN WORDS ABOUT WATER. Illustrated. Large
crown 8vo, sewed, 6d

FOOD: A Short Account of the Sources, Constituents,
and Uses of Food. Large crown 8vo, cloth, 3s.

PRECIOUS STONES: considered in their Scientific and
Artistic Relations. With Illustrations. Large crown 8vo, 2s. 6d.

CLINTON (R. H.)—
A COMPENDIUM OF ENGLISH HISTORY, from the
Earliest Times to A.D. 1872 With Copious Quotations on the Leading Events and
the Constitutional History, together with Appendices. Post 8vo, 7s. 6d.

COBDEN, RICHARD, LIFE OF. By JOHN MORLEY. With Por-
trait. 2 vols. Demy 8vo, 32s.
New Edition. Portrait. Large crown 8vo, 7s. 6d.
Popular Edition, with Portrait, sewed, 1s ; cloth, 2s.

CHAPMAN & HALL'S SERIES OF POPULAR NOVEL
New and Cheaper Editions of Popular Novels. Crown 8vo.

ZERO A Story of Monte Carlo By MRS. CAMPBELL PRAED
THE WORLD WE LIVE IN By OSWALD CRAWFORD. 5s
MOLOCH A Story of Sacrifice By MRS. CAMPBELL PRAED, Author of "Nadine,"
Crown 8vo, 6s.
INTRODUCED TO SOCIETY. By HAMILTON AÏDÉ.
THE RIGHT SORT A Romance of the Shires. By MRS EDWARD KENNARD.
Illustrated, 6s.
FAUCIT OF BALLIOL By HERMAN MERIVALE. 6s.
AN AUSTRALIAN HEROINE. By MRS. CAMPBELL PRAED. 6s.
HARD LINES. By HAWLEY SMART. 6s
STORY OF AN AFRICAN FARM. By RALPH IRON 5s.
NADINE A Study of a Woman By MRS. CAMPBELL PRAED. 5s.
TO LEEWARD By F MARION CRAWFORD. New Edition. 5s.

COOKERY—
OFFICIAL HANDBOOK FOR THE NATIONAL
TRAINING SCHOOL FOR COOKERY Containing Lessons on Cookery,
forming the Course of Instruction in the School. Compiled by "R. O. C."
Twelfth Thousand. Large crown 8vo, 8s.

HOW TO COOK FISH. A Series of Lessons in Cookery,
from the Official Handbook to the National Training School for Cookery, South
Kensington. Compiled by 'R O. C." Crown 8vo, sewed. 3d.

SICK-ROOM COOKERY. From the Official Handbook
for the National School for Cookery, South Kensington Compiled by "R. O C'
Crown 8vo, sewed, 6d.

CRAIK (GEORGE LILLIE)—
ENGLISH OF SHAKESPEARE. Illustrated in a Philo
logical Commentary on his "Julius Cæsar" Sixth Edition. Post 8vo, cloth, 5s

OUTLINES OF THE HISTORY OF THE ENGLISH
LANGUAGE Ninth Edition Post 8vo, cloth, 2s 6d

CRAWFORD (F MARION)—
TO LEEWARD New Edition. Crown 8vo, 5s.

CRAWFORD (OSWALD)—
THE WORLD WE LIVE IN. New Edition. Crown
8vo, 5s

CRIPPS (WILFRED)—
COLLEGE AND CORPORATION PLATE. With
numerous Illustrations. Large crown 8vo, cloth, 2s 6d.

DAUBOURG (E)—
INTERIOR ARCHITECTURE. Doors, Vestibules, Stair-
cases, Anterooms, Drawing, Dining, and Bed Rooms, Libraries, Bank and Newspaper Offices, Shop Fronts and Interiors Half-imperial, cloth, £2 12s 6d

DAVIDSON (ELLIS A)—
PRETTY ARTS FOR THE EMPLOYMENT OF
LEISURE HOURS A Book for Ladies. With Illustrations. Demy 8vo, 6s.

DAY (WILLIAM)—
THE RACEHORSE IN TRAINING, with Hints on
Racing and Racing Reform, to which is added a Chapter on Shoeing. New
Edition   [*In the Press.*

D'HAUSSONVILLE (VICOMTE)—
SALON OF MADAME NECKER. Translated by H. M.
TROLLOPE 2 vols. Crown 8vo, 18s

DE KONINCK (L L) and DIETZ (E)—
PRACTICAL MANUAL OF CHEMICAL ASSAYING,
as applied to the Manufacture of Iron. Edited, with notes, by ROBERT MALLET.
Post 8vo, cloth, 6s.

DICKENS (CHARLES)—*See pages 20-24*
THE LETTERS OF CHARLES DICKENS. Edited
by his Sister in Law and his Eldest Daughter Two vols. uniform with " The
Charles Dickens Edition" of his Works Crown 8vo, 8s

THE CHARLES DICKENS BIRTHDAY BOOK.
Compiled and Edited by his Eldest Daughter With Five Illustrations by his
Youngest Daughter In a handsome fcap 4to volume, 12s.

DRAYSON (LIEUT-COL. A. W.)—
THE CAUSE OF THE SUPPOSED PROPER MOTION
OF THE FIXED STARS. Demy 8vo, cloth, 10s.

THE CAUSE, DATE, AND DURATION OF THE
LAST GLACIAL EPOCH OF GEOLOGY. Demy 8vo, cloth, 10s.

PRACTICAL MILITARY SURVEYING AND
SKETCHING Fifth Edition. Post 8vo, cloth, 4s 6d

DYCE'S COLLECTION. A Catalogue of Printed Books and Manuscripts
bequeathed by the REV. ALEXANDER DYCE to the South Kensington Museum
2 vols Royal 8vo, half-morocco, 14s
A Collection of Paintings, Miniatures, Drawings, Engravings,
Rings, and Miscellaneous Objects, bequeathed by the REV ALEXANDER DYCE
to the South Kensington Museum. Royal 8vo, half-morocco, 6s. 6d

DYCE (WILLIAM), R A —
DRAWING-BOOK OF THE GOVERNMENT SCHOOL
OF DESIGN, OR, ELEMENTARY OUTLINES OF ORNAMENT Fifty
selected Plates Folio, sewed, 5s., mounted, 18s.
Text to Ditto. Sewed, 6d.

EGYPTIAN ART—
A HISTORY OF ART IN ANCIENT EGYPT. By
G PERROT and C. CHIPIEZ Translated by WALTER ARMSTRONG With over
600 Illustrations 2 vols. Royal 8vo, £2 2s.

ELLIS (CAPTAIN A B)—
WEST AFRICAN ISLANDS   8vo.   [In the Press
THE LAND OF FETISH. Demy 8vo. 12s.

ENGEL (CARL)—
A DESCRIPTIVE AND ILLUSTRATED CATALOGUE
OF THE MUSICAL INSTRUMENTS in the SOUTH KENSINGTON
MUSEUM, preceded by an Essay on the History of Musical
Instruments. Second
Edition. Royal 8vo, half-morocco, 12s.
MUSICAL INSTRUMENTS.   With numerous Woodcuts.
Large crown 8vo, cloth, 2s. 6d.

ESCOTT (T H. S)—
ENGLAND. 1 vol Demy 8vo.   [In the Press
PILLARS OF THE EMPIRE : Short Biographical
Sketches Demy 8vo, 10s 6d.

EWALD (ALEXANDER CHARLES), F.S A.—
REPRESENTATIVE STATESMEN : Political Studies.
2 vols. Large crown 8vo, £1 4s.
SIR ROBERT WALPOLE.   A Political Biography,
1676-1745. Demy 8vo, 18s.

FANE (VIOLET)—
QUEEN OF THE FAIRIES (A Village Story), and other
Poems. Crown 8vo, 6s.
ANTHONY BABINGTON · a Drama.   Crown 8vo, 6s.

FEARNLEY (W)—
LESSONS IN HORSE JUDGING, AND THE SUM-
MERING OF HUNTERS With Illustrations. Crown 8vo, 4s

FLEMING (GEORGE), F.R.C S.—
ANIMAL PLAGUES : THEIR HISTORY, NATURE,
AND PREVENTION 8vo, cloth, 15s.
PRACTICAL HORSE-SHOEING. With 37 Illustrations.
Second Edition, enlarged. 8vo, sewed, 2s.
RABIES AND HYDROPHOBIA : THEIR HISTORY,
NATURE, CAUSES, SYMPTOMS, AND PREVENTION With 8 Illustra-
tions. 8vo, cloth, 15s.
A MANUAL OF VETERINARY SANITARY SCIENCE
AND POLICE. With 93 Illustrations. 2 vols. Demy 8vo, 36s.
FOR THEIR SAKES. By Various Authors.   Crown 8vo,
cloth, 2s 6d.

FORSTER (JOHN), M P for Berwick—
THE CHRONICLE OF JAMES I, KING OF ARAGON,
SURNAMED THE CONQUEROR Written by Himself Translated from
the Catalan by the late JOHN FORSTER, M.P for Berwick With an Historical
Introduction by DON PASCUAL DE GAYANGOS. 2 vols. Royal 8vo, 28s.

FORSTER (JOHN)—
THE LIFE OF CHARLES DICKENS. With Portraits
and other Illustrations. 15th Thousand. 3 vols 8vo, cloth, £2 2s.
THE LIFE OF CHARLES DICKENS Uniform with
the Illustrated Library Edition of Dickens's Works. 2 vols. Demy 8vo, £1 8s.
THE LIFE OF CHARLES DICKENS. Uniform with
the Library Edition Post 8vo, 10s
THE LIFE OF CHARLES DICKENS. Uniform with
the "C D" Edition. With Numerous Illustrations 2 vols 7s.

FORSTER (JOHN)—Continued—

THE LIFE OF CHARLES DICKENS. Uniform with
the Household Edition With Illustrations by F BARNARD Crown 4to, cloth, 5s.

WALTER SAVAGE LANDOR: a Biography, 1775–1864.
With Portrait A New and Revised Edition Demy 8vo, 12s.

FORTNIGHTLY REVIEW—

FORTNIGHTLY REVIEW.—First Series, May, 1865, to
Dec 1866 6 vols Cloth, 13s each.

New Series, 1867 to 1872. In Half-yearly Volumes. Cloth,
13s each

From January, 1873, to the present time, in Half-yearly
Volumes Cloth, 16s each

CONTENTS OF FORTNIGHTLY REVIEW. From
the commencement to end of 1878. Sewed, 2s.

FORTNUM (C. D E)—

A DESCRIPTIVE AND ILLUSTRATED CATALOGUE
OF THE BRONZES OF EUROPEAN ORIGIN in the SOUTH KEN
SINGTON MUSEUM, with an Introductory Notice Royal 8vo, half morocco,
£1 10s

A DESCRIPTIVE AND ILLUSTRATED CATALOGUE
OF MAIOLICA, HISPANO MORESCO, PERSIAN, DAMASCUS, AND
RHODIAN WARES in the SOUTH KENSINGTON MUSEUM Royal
8vo, half morocco, £2

MAIOLICA. With numerous Woodcuts. Large crown
8vo, cloth, 2s. 6d.

BRONZES. With numerous Woodcuts. Large crown
8vo, cloth, 2s 6d

FRANCATELLI (C. E)—

ROYAL CONFECTIONER: English and Foreign. A
Practical Treatise New and Cheap Edition With Illustrations. Crown 8vo, 5s.

FRANKS (A W)—

JAPANESE POTTERY. Being a Native Report. Numerous Illustrations and Marks Large crown 8vo, cloth, 2s 6d.

GALLENGA (ANTONIO)—

EPISODES OF MY SECOND LIFE. 2 vols. Demy 8vo
[In November

IBERIAN REMINISCENCES Fifteen Years' Travelling
Impressions of Spain and Portugal With a Map 2 vols. Demy 8vo, 32s

GORDON (GENERAL)—

LETTERS FROM THE CRIMEA, THE DANUBE,
AND ARMENIA By DEMETRIUS C BOULGER Crown 8vo, 2nd Edition, 5s

GORST (J E), Q.C, M P.—

An ELECTION MANUAL. Containing the Parliamentary
Elections (Corrupt and Illegal P actices) Act, 1883, with Notes. New Edition
Crown 8vo, 2s. 6d

GRIFFIN (SIR LEPEL HENRY) K C.S I —

THE GREAT REPUBLIC. New Edition Crown 8vo, 4s. 6d.

GRIFFITHS (MAJOR ARTHUR), H M Inspector of Prisons—

CHRONICLES OF NEWGATE. Illustrated. New
Edition Demy 8vo, 16s

MEMORIALS OF MILLBANK. With Illustrations. New
Edition. Demy 8vo, 12s.

HALL (SIDNLY)—
A TRAVELLING ATLAS OF THE EN\ H COUN-
TIES Fifty Maps, coloured New Edition, including : lways, correcte up to the present date Demy 8vo, in roan tuck, 10s 6d.

HARDY (LADY DUFFUS)—
DOWN SOUTH, Demy 8vo. 14s.
THROUGH C ES AND PRAIRIE LANDS. Sketches
of an American To emy 8vo, 14s

HATTON (JOSEPH) and HARVEY (REV. M)—
NEWFOUNDLAND. The Oldest British Colony. Its
History, Past and Present, and its Prospects in the Future. Illustrated from Photographs and Sketches specially made for this work. Demy 8vo, 18s.

TO-DAY IN AMERICA Studies for the Old World and
the New 2 vols Crown 8vo, 18s.

HAWKINS (FREDERICK)—
ANNALS OF THE FRENCH STAGE. 2 vols. Demy 8vo.
[*In November.*

HERBERT (AUBERON)—
A POLITICIAN IN TROUBLE ABOUT HIS SOUL.
Crown 8vo, 4s.

HILDEBRAND (HANS)—
INDUSTRIAL ARTS OF SCANDINAVIA IN THE
PAGAN TIME · Illustrated Large crown 8vo, 2s. 6d.

HILL (MISS G)—
THE PLEASURES AND PROFITS OF OUR LITTLE
POULTRY FARM Small crown 8vo, 3s.

HOLBEIN—
TWELVE HEADS AFTER HOLBEIN. Selected from
Drawings in Her Majesty's Collection at Windsor. Reproduced in Autotype, in portfolio. £1 16s.

HOLLINGSHEAD (JOHN)—
FOOTLIGHTS. Crown 8vo 7s. 6d.

HOVELACQUE (ABEL)—
THE SCIENCE OF LANGUAGE: LINGUISTICS,
PHILOLOGY, AND ETYMOLOGY With Maps Large crown 8vo, cloth, 5s.

HOW I BECAME A SPORTSMAN. By "Avon." Crown 8vo.

HUMPHRIS (H D)—
PRINCIPLES OF PERSPECTIVE. Illustrated in a
Series of Examples. Oblong folio, half-bound, and Text 8vo, cloth, £1 1s

HUNT-ROOM STORIES AND YACHTING YARNS By
"Wanderer," the Author of "Across Country" With Illustrations. Demy 8vo, 12s.

INTERNATIONAL POLICY By Frederic Harrison, Prof.
Beesley, Richard Congreve, and others New Edition. Crown 8vo, 2s 6d.

IRON (RALPH)—
THE STORY OF AN AFRICAN FARM. New Edition
Crown 8vo, 5s

JARRY (GENERAL)—
OUTPOST DUT I. Translated, with TREATISES ON
MILITARY RECONNAISSANCE AND ON ROAD MAKING. By Major-Gen W. C. E. Napier Third Edition. Crown 8vo, 5s.

JEANS (W T)—
CREATORS OF THE AGE OF STEEL. Memoirs of
Sir W Siemens, Sir H. Bessemer, Sir J. Whitworth, Sir J Brown, and other
Inventors Crown 8vo, 7s. 6d

JOHNSON (DR SAMUEL)—
LIFE AND CONVERSATIONS By A. Main. Crown
8vo, 10s. 6d

JONES (CAPTAIN DOUGLAS), R A —
NOTES ON MILITARY LAW. Crown 8vo, 4s.

JONES COLLECTION (HANDBOOK OF THE) IN THE SOUTH
KENSINGTON MUSEUM Illustrated Large crown 8vo, 2s 6d.

KEMPIS (THOMAS A)—
OF THE IMITATION OF CHRIST. Four Books.
Beautifully Illustrated Edition. Demy 8vo, 16s.

KENNARD (MRS EDWARD)—
TWILIGHT THOUGHTS. With Illustrations. Crown 8vo
[*In November.*

KENT (CHARLES)—
HUMOUR AND PATHOS OF CHARLES DICKENS,
WITH ILLUSTRATIONS OF HIS MASTERY OF THE TERRIBLE
AND PICTURESQUE Portrait Crown 8vo, 6s

KLACZKO (M JULIAN)—
TWO CHANCELLORS : PRINCE GORTCHAKOF AND
PRINCE BISMARCK Translated by Mrs Tait New and cheaper Edition, 6s

LACORDAIRE'S CONFERENCES. JESUS CHRIST, GOD,
AND GOD AND MAN New Edition in 1 vol. Crown 8vo, 6s.

LAVELEYE (EMILE DE)—
THE ELEMENTS OF POLITICAL ECONOMY.
Translated by W Pollard, B A., St. John's College, Oxford Crown 8vo, 6s

LECTURES ON AGRICULTURAL SCIENCE, AND OTHER
PROCEEDINGS OF THE INSTITUTE OF AGRICULTURE, SOUTH
KENSINGTON Crown 8vo, sewed, 2s.

LEFÈVRE (ANDRÉ)—
PHILOSOPHY, Historical and Critical Translated, with
an Introduction, by A. W Keane, B A. Large crown 8vo, 7s 6d

LETOURNEAU (DR CHARLES)—
SOCIOLOGY. Based upon Ethnology. Translated by
Henry M Trollope Large crown 8vo, 10s
BIOLOGY. Translated by William MacCall. With Illus-
trations Large crown 8vo, 6s

LILLY (W S)—
ANCIENT RELIGION AND MODERN THOUGHT.
New Edition   [*In the Press.*

LONG (JAMES)—
BRITISH DAIRY FARMING. With numerous Illus-
trations Crown 8vo   [*In December.*

LOW (C R)—
SOLDIERS OF THE VICTORIAN AGE. 2 vols. Demy
8vo, £1 10s.

LYTTON (ROBERT, EARL)—
POETICAL WORKS—
FABLES IN SONG 2 vols Fcap 8vo, 12s.
THE WANDERER Fcap 8vo, 6s.
POEMS, HISTORICAL AND CHARACTERISTIC. Fcap 6s.

MALLET (ROBERT)—

PRACTICAL MANUAL OF CHEMICAL ASSAYING,
as applied to the Manufacture of Iron By L L De Koninck and E Dietz Edited, with notes, by Robert Mallet. Post 8vo, cloth. 6s.

MASKELL (WILLIAM)—

A DESCRIPTION OF THE IVORIES, ANCIENT AND
MEDIÆVAL, in the SOUTH KENSINGTON MUSEUM, with a Preface. With numerous Photographs Woodcuts Royal 8vo, half morocco, £1 1s

IVORIES: ANCIENT AND MEDIÆVAL. With numerous Woodcuts. Large crown 8vo, cloth, 2s. 6d

HANDBOOK TO THE DYCE AND FORSTER COL-
LECTIONS With Illustrations. Large crown 8vo, cloth, 2s 6d

McCOAN (J. CARLILE)—

OUR NEW PROTECTORATE. TURKEY IN ASIA: ITS
GEOGRAPHY, RACES, RESOURCES, AND GOVERNMENT With Map 2 vols. Large crown 8vo, £1 4s.

MEREDITH (GEORGE) --

MODERN LOVE AND POEMS OF THE ENGLISH
ROADSIDE, WITH POEMS AND BALLADS. Fcap cloth, 6s

MERIVALE (HERMAN CHARLES)—

BINKO'S BLUES. A Tale for Children of all Growths.
Illustrated by Edgar Giberne Small crown 8vo, 5s

THE WHITE PILGRIM, and other Poems. Crown 8vo, 9s.

FAUCIT OF BALLIOL. Crown 8vo, 6s.

MILITARY BIOGRAPHIES—

FREDERICK THE GREAT By Col. C B Brackenbury;
containing Maps and Portrait Crown 8vo, 4s.

LOUDON. A Sketch of the Military Life of Gideon
Ernest, Freiherr von Loudon, sometime Generalissimo of the Austrian Forces. By Col. G B MALLESON, C S.I With Portrait and Maps. Large crown 8vo, 4s

TURENNE By Col. Hozier. Large crown 8vo, with
Maps. *[In the Press.*

MOLESWORTH (W NASSAU)—

HISTORY OF ENGLAND FROM THE YEAR 1830
TO THE RESIGNATION OF THE GLADSTONE MINISTRY, 1874 3 vols. Crown 8vo, 18s

ABRIDGED EDITION. Large crown, 7s. 6d.

MORLEY (HENRY)—

TABLES OF ENGLISH LITERATURE. Containing
20 Charts Second Edition, with Index. Royal 4to, cloth, 12s. In Three Parts Parts I and II, containing Three Charts, each 1s 6d. Part III , containing 14 Charts, 7s. Part III also kept in Sections, 1, 2, and 5. 1s 6d each, 3 and 4 together, 3s *.* The Charts sold separately.

MORLEY (JOHN)—

LIFE OF RICHARD COBDEN. With Portrait. Popular
Edition. 4to, sewed, 1s Bound in cloth, 2s.

LIFE AND CORRESPONDENCE OF RICHARD
COBDEN. Fourth Thousand. 2 vols. Demy 8vo, £1 12s.

DIDEROT AND THE ENCYCLOPÆDISTS. 2 vols.
Demy 8vo, £1 6s.

MORLEY (JOHN)—

NEW UNIFORM EDITION.

RICHARD COBDEN. With Portrait. Large crown
8vo, 7s 6d
VOLTAIRE. Large crown 8vo, 6s.
ROUSSEAU. Large crown 8vo, 9s.
DIDEROT AND THE ENCYCLOPÆDISTS. Large
crown 8vo, 12s
CRITICAL MISCELLANIES. First Series. Large crown
8vo, 6s
ON COMPROMISE. New Edition. Large crown 8vo, 3s. 6d
STRUGGLE FOR NATIONAL EDUCATION. Third
Edition Demy 8vo, cloth, 3s

MUNTZ (EUGÈNE), From the French of—
RAPHAEL : HIS LIFE, WORKS, AND TIMES.
Edited by W Armstrong Illustrated with 155 Wood Engravings and 41 Full-
page Plates. Imperial 8vo, 36s.

MURPHY (J. M)—
RAMBLE   NORTH - WEST AMERICA. With
Frontispiece ar   , 8vo, 16s.

MURRAY (ANDREW), F.L S—
ECONOMIC ENTOMOLOGY. Aptera. With numerous Illustrations Large crown 8vo, 7s. 6d.

NAPIER (MAJ -GEN. W C E.)—
TRANSLATION OF GEN. JARRY'S OUTPOST DUTY.
With TREATISES ON MILITARY RECONNAISSANCE AND ON
ROAD-MAKING Third Edition. Crown 8vo, 5s

NAPOLEON. A Selection from the Letters and Despatches of
the First Napoleon With Explanatory Notes by Captain the Hon D Bingham.
3 vols. Demy 8vo, £2 2s

NECKER (MADAME)—
THE SALON OF MADAME NECKER. By Vicomte
d Haussonville. Translated by H M Trollope 2 vols Crown 8vo, 18s

NESBITT (ALEXANDER)—
GLASS Illustrated. Large crown 8vo, cloth, 2s. 6d.

NEVINSON (HENRY)—
A SKETCH OF HERDER AND HIS TIMES. With
a Portrait Demy 8vo, 14s

NEWTON (E TULLEY), F G S—
THE TYPICAL PARTS IN THE SKELETONS OF
A CAT, DUCK, AND CODFISH, being a Catalogue with Comparative
Description arranged in a Tabular form Demy 8vo, cloth, 3s

NORMAN (C B), late of the in Light infantry and Bengal Staff Corps—
TONKIN, OR, FRANCE IN THE FAR EAST. Demy
8vo, with Maps, 14s

OLIVER (PROFESSOR), F R S , &c —
ILLUSTRATIONS OF THE PRINCIPAL NATURAL
ORDERS OF THE VEGETABLE KINGDOM, PREPARED FOR THE
SCIENCE AND ART DEPARTMENT, SOUTH KENSINGTON. With
109 Plates Oblong 8vo, plain, 16s ; coloured, £1 6s

OXENHAM (REV. H N)—
SHORT STUDIES, ETHICAL AND RELIGIOUS.
Demy 8vo. [*In December*

SHORT STUDIES IN ECCLESIASTICAL HISTORY
AND BIOGRAPHY Demy 8vo, 12s.

PERROT (GEORGES) and CHIPIEZ (CHARLES)—
HISTORY OF ANCIENT ART IN PHŒNICIA,
CYPRUS, AND ASIA MINOR. Containing about 500 Illustrations
2 vols. Royal 8vo. [*In November*

CHALDÆA AND ASSYRIA, A HISTORY OF ART IN.
Translated by WALTER ARMSTRONG, B A Oxon With 452 Illustrations. 2 vols
Demy 8vo Uniform with "Ancient Egyptian Art" 42s

ANCIENT EGYPT, A HISTORY OF ART IN. Trans-
lated from the French by W ARMSTRONG With over 600 Illustrations. 2 vols
Imperial 8vo, 42s.

PIASSETSKY (P.)—
RUSSIAN TRAVELLERS IN MONGOLIA AND
CHINA. Translated by JANE GORDON-CUMMING With 75 Illustrations
2 vols Crown 8vo, 24s

PITT-TAYLOR (FRANK)—
THE CANTERBURY TALES Being Selections from
the Tales of GEOFFREY CHAUCER rendered into Modern English, with close
adherence to the language of the Poet With Frontispiece Crown 8vo, 6s

POLLEN (J H)—
ANCIENT AND MODERN FURNITURE AND
WOODWORK IN THE SOUTH KENSINGTON MUSEUM With an
Introduction, and Illustrated with numerous Coloured Photographs and Woodcuts.
Royal 8vo, half-morocco, £1 1s

GOLD AND SILVER SMITH'S WORK With nume-
rous Woodcuts. Large crown 8vo, cloth, 2s 6d

ANCIENT AND MODERN FURNITURE AND
WOODWORK. With numerous Woodcuts Large crown 8vo, cloth, 2s 6d.

POYNTER (E J), R A —
TEN LECTURES ON ART. Second Edition. Large
crown 8vo, 9s

PRAED (MRS CAMPBELL)—
ZERO. A Story of Monte Carlo. Cheap Edition Crown
8vo. [*In November*
AN AUSTRALIAN HEROINE. Cheap Edition Crown
8vo, 6s.
NADINE. Cheap Edition. Crown 8vo, 5s
MOLOCH. Cheap Edition. Crown 8vo, 6s.

PRINSEP (VAL), A R A —
IMPERIAL INDIA Containing numerous Illustrations
and Maps. Second Edition Demy 8vo, £1 1s.

RAMSDEN (LADY GWENDOLEN)—
A BIRTHDAY BOOK. Illustrated. Containing 46 Illustra-
tions from Original Drawings, and numerous other Illustrations. Royal 8vo, 21s.

REDGRAVE (GILBERT)—
OUTLINES OF HISTORIC ORNAMENT. Translated
from the German and edited by. With numerous Illustrations. Crown 8vo, 4s.

REDGRAVE (GILBERT R.)—
MANUAL OF DESIGN, compiled from the Writings and
Address of RICHARD REDGRAVE, R.A. With Woodcuts Large crown 8vo, cloth,
2s. 6d

REDGRAVE (RICHARD)—
MANUAL AND CATECHISM ON COLOUR. 24mo,
cloth, 9d

REDGRAVE (SAMUEL)—
A DESCRIPTIVE CATALOGUE OF THE HIS
TORICAL COLLECTION OF WATER COLOUR PAINTINGS IN THE
SOUTH KENSINGTON MUSEUM. With numerous Chromo-lithographs and
other Illustrations Royal 8vo, £1 1s

RENAN (ERNEST)—
RECOLLECTIONS OF MY YOUTH. Translated from
the original French, and revised by MADAME RENAN Crown 8vo, 8s

RIANO (JUAN F.)—
THE INDUSTRIAL ARTS IN SPAIN. Illustrated. Large
crown 8vo, cloth, 4s

ROBINSON (JAMES F.)—
BRITISH BEE FARMING. Its Profits and Pleasures.
Large crown 8vo, 5s.

ROBINSON (J. C.)—
ITALIAN SCULPTURE OF THE MIDDLE AGES
AND PERIOD OF THE REVIVAL OF ART With 20 Engravings Royal
8vo, cloth, 7s 6d

ROBSON (GEORGE)—
ELEMENTARY BUILDING CONSTRUCTION Illus-
trated by a Design for an Entrance Lodge and Gate. 15 Plates Oblong fol o,
sewed, 8s.

ROBSON (REV. J. H.), M.A., ELM.—
AN ELEMENTARY TREATISE ON ALGEBRA
Post 8vo, 6s

ROCK (THE VERY REV. CANON), D.D.—
ON TEXTILE FABRICS A Descriptive and Illustrated
Catalogue of the Collection of Church Vestments, Dresses, Silk Stuffs, Needlework,
and Tapestries in the South Kensington Museum Royal 8vo, half morocco,
£1 11s. 6d

TEXTILE FABRICS. With numerous Woodcuts. Large
crown 8vo, cloth, 2s 6d.

ROLAND (ARTHUR)—
FARMING FOR PLEASURE AND PROFIT. Edited
by WILLIAM ABLETT 8 vols. Large crown 8vo, 5s. each
DAIRY-FARMING, MANAGEMENT OF COWS, &c.
POULTRY-KEEPING
TREE-PLANTING, FOR ORNAMENTATION OR PROFIT.
STOCK-KEEPING AND CATTLE-REARING
DRAINAGE OF LAND, IRRIGATION, MANURES, &c.
ROOT-GROWING, HOPS, &c.
MANAGEMENT OF GRASS LANDS.
MARKET GARDENING

RUSDEN (G. W.), for many years Clerk of the Parliament in Victoria—
A HISTORY OF AUSTRALIA. With a Coloured Map.
3 vols. Demy 8vo, 50s.

A HISTORY OF NEW ZEALAND. 3 vols. Demy 8vo.
with Maps, 50s.

SCOTT (A DE C., MAJOR-GENERAL, late Royal Engineers)—
LONDON WATER. a Review of the Present Condition and Suggested Improvements of the Metropolitan Water Supply. Crown 8vo, sewed, 3s.

SCOTT-STEVENSON (MRS.)—
ON SUMMER SEAS. Including the Mediterranean, the Ægean, the Ionian, and the Euxine, and a voyage down the Danube. With a Map. Demy 8vo, 16s.

OUR HOME IN CYPRUS. With a Map and Illustrations. Third Edition. Demy 8vo, 14s.

OUR RIDE THROUGH ASIA MINOR. With Map. Demy 8vo, 18s.

SHEPHERD (MAJOR), R.E.—
PRAIRIE EXPERIENCES IN HANDLING CATTLE AND SHEEP. With Illustrations and Map. Demy 8vo, 10s.

SHIRREFF (MISS)—
HOME EDUCATION IN RELATION TO THE KINDERGARTEN. Two Lectures. Crown 8vo, 1s. 6d

SIMMONDS (T. L.)—
ANIMAL PRODUCTS: their Preparation, Commercial Uses, and Value. With numerous Illustrations. Large crown 8vo, 7s. 6d

SMITH (MAJOR R MURDOCK), R E.—
PERSIAN ART. Second Edition, with additional Illustrations. Large crown 8vo, 2s.

SNOAD (MRS FRANK)—
ECHOES OF LIFE. Including 2nd Edition (revised) of "Clare Peyce's Diary," and "As Life Itself" Crown 8vo, 6s.

STORY (W W)—
ROBA DI ROMA. Seventh Edition, with Additions and Portrait. Crown 8vo, cloth, 10s 6d.

CASTLE ST. ANGELO. With Illustrations. Crown 8vo, 10s 6d.

SUTCLIFFE (JOHN)—
THE SCULPTOR AND ART STUDENT'S GUIDE to the Proportions of the Human Form, with Measurements in feet and inches of Full Grown Figures of Both Sexes and of Various Ages. By Dr G Schadow, Member of the Academies, Stockholm, Dresden, Rome, &c. &c. Translated by J. J Wright Plates reproduced by J. Sutcliffe. Oblong folio, 31s. 6d.

TANNER (PROFESSOR), F C S.—
HOLT CASTLE; or, Threefold Interest in Land. Crown 8vo, 4s. 6d.

JACK'S EDUCATION; OR, HOW HE LEARNT FARMING. Second Edition. Crown 8vo, 3s. 6d.

TOPINARD (DR PAUL)—
ANTHROPOLOGY. With a Preface by Professor Paul Broca. With numerous Illustrations. Large crown 8vo, 7s. 6d.

TRAILL (H D)—
THE NEW LUCIAN. Being a Series of Dialogues of the Dead. Demy 8vo, 10s.

TROLLOPE (ANTHONY)—

AYALA'S ANGEL. Crown 8vo. 6s.

LIFE OF CICERO. 2 vols. 8vo. £1 4s.

THE CHRONICLES OF BARSETSHIRE A Uniform Edition, in 8 vols., large crown 8vo, handsomely printed, each vol. containing Frontispiece. 6s each.

THE WARDEN and BAR-CHESTER TOWERS 2 vols	THE SMALL HOUSE AT ALLINGTON. 2 vols
DR. THORNE.	LAST CHRONICLE OF
FRAMLEY PARSONAGE.	BARSET 2 vols.

UNIVERSAL—

UNIVERSAL CATALOGUE OF BOOKS ON ART. Compiled for the use of the National Art Library, and the Schools of Art in the United Kingdom In 2 vols Crown 4to, half-morocco, £2 2s.

Supplemental Volume to Ditto.

VERON (EUGENE)—

ÆSTHETICS Translated by W. H. ARMSTRONG. Large crown 8vo, 7s. 6d.

WALE (REV HENRY JOHN), M.A.—

MY GRANDFATHER'S POCKET BOOK, from 1701 to 1796 Author of "Sword and Surplice" Demy 8vo, 12s.

WATSON (ALFRED E. T.)

SKETCHES IN THE HUNTING FIELD. Illustrated by JOHN STURGESS. Cheap Edition. Crown 8vo, 6s.

WESTWOOD (J O), M.A., F L S., &c —

CATALOGUE OF THE FICTILE IVORIES IN THE SOUTH KENSINGTON MUSEUM With an Account of the Continental Collections of Classical and Mediæval Ivories. Royal 8vo, half morocco, £1 4s

WHIST—

THE HANDS AT WHIST. By AQUARIUS. 32mo, cloth gilt, 1s

EASY WHIST. 32mo, cloth gilt, 1s.

ADVANCED WHIST. 32mo, cloth gilt, 1s.

WHITE (WALTER)—

HOLIDAYS IN TYROL: Kufstein, Klobenstein, and Paneveggio Large crown 8vo, 14s.

A MONTH IN YORKSHIRE. Post 8vo. With a Map. Fifth Edition 4s.

A LONDONER'S WALK TO THE LAND'S END, AND A TRIP TO THE SCILLY ISLES Post 8vo With 4 Maps. Third Edition 4s.

WILL-O'-THE-WISPS, THE. Translated from the German of Mane Petersen by CHARLOTTE J. HART. With Illustrations. Crown 8vo, 7s. 6d

WORNUM (R N.)—

ANALYSIS OF ORNAMENT: THE CHARACTER-ISTICS OF STYLES. With many Illustrations. Ninth Edition Royal 8vo, cloth, 8s.

WORSAAE (J J. A)—

INDUSTRIAL ARTS OF DENMARK, FROM THE EARLIEST TIMES TO THE DANISH CONQUEST OF ENGLAND. With Maps and Illustrations. Crown 8vo, 3s. 6d.

WYLDE (ATHERTON)—

MY CHIEF AND I, OR, SIX MONTHS IN NATAL AFTER THE LANGALIBALELE OUTBREAK. With Portrait of Colonel Durnford, and Illustrations. Demy 8vo, 14s.

YEO (DR. J. BURNEY)—

HEALTH RESORTS AND THEIR USES: BEING *Vari us Studies in various Health Resorts. New Edition.* [In the Press.

YOUNGE (C. D.)—

PARALLEL LIVES OF ANCIENT AND MODERN HEROES. New Edition. 12mo, cloth, 4s. 6d.

SOUTH KENSINGTON MUSEUM DESCRIPTIVE AND ILLUSTRATED CATALOGUES.

Royal 8vo, half-bound.

BRONZES OF EUROPEAN ORIGIN. By C. D. E. Fortnum. £1 10s.

DYCE'S COLLECTION OF PRINTED BOOKS AND MANUSCRIPTS. 2 vols. 14s.

DYCE'S COLLECTION OF PAINTINGS, ENGRAVINGS, &c. 6s. 6d.

FURNITURE AND WOODWORK, ANCIENT AND MODERN. By J. H. Pollen. £1 1s.

GLASS VESSELS. By A. Nesbitt. 18s.

GOLD AND SILVER SMITH'S WORK. By J. G. Pollen. £1 6s.

IVORIES, ANCIENT AND MEDIÆVAL. By W. Maskell. 21s.

IVORIES, FICTILE. By J. O. Westwood. £1 4s.

MAIOLICA, HISPANO-MORESCO, PERSIAN, DAMAS-CUS AND RHODIAN WARES. By C. D. E. Fortnum. £2.

MUSICAL INSTRUMENTS. By C. Engel. 12s.

SCULPTURE, ITALIAN SCULPTURE OF THE MIDDLE AGES. By J. C. Robinson. Cloth, 7s. 6d.

SWISS COINS. By R. S. Poole. £2 10s.

TEXTILE FABRICS. By Rev. D. Rock. £1 11s. 6d.

WATER-COLOUR PAINTING. By S. Redgrave. £1 1s.

UNIVERSAL CATALOGUE OF BOOKS ON ART. 2 vols. Small 4to, £1 1s. each.

UNIVERSAL CATALOGUE OF BOOKS ON ART. Supplementary vol. 8s. nett.

B

SOUTH KENSINGTON MUSEUM SCIENCE AND ART HANDBOOKS.

Handsomely printed in large crown 8vo.

Published for the Committee of the Council on Education.

RUSSIAN ART AND ART OBJECTS IN RUSSIA. A
Handbook to the Reproductions of Goldsmiths' Work, and other Art Treasures
from that Country, in the South Kensington Museum. By ALFRED MASKELL
With Illustrations Crown 8vo, 4s 6d.

FRENCH POTTERY By PAUL GASNAULT and EDOUARD
GARNIER. With Illustrations and marks. Crown 8vo, 3s

ENGLISH EARTHENWARE: A Handbook to the Wares
made in England during the 17th and 18th Centuries, as illustrated by Specimens
in the National Collections By PROF. CHURCH. With Illustrations

INDUSTRIAL ARTS OF DENMARK. From the Earliest
Times to the Danish Conquest of England By J J A WORSAAE, Hon F S A.,
M R.I.A., &c. &c. With Map and Illustrations. 3s. 6d

INDUSTRIAL ARTS OF SCANDINAVIA IN THE PAGAN
TIME By HANS HILDEBRAND, Royal Antiquary of Sweden With Illustrations.
2s 6d

PRECIOUS STONES By PROFESSOR CHURCH. With Illustrations. 2s. 6d

INDUSTRIAL ARTS OF INDIA. By Sir GEORGE C. M.
BIRDWOOD, C.S I With Map and Illustrations Demy 8vo, 14s

HANDBOOK TO THE DYCE AND FORSTER COLLEC-
TIONS By W. MASKELL. With Illustrations Large crown 8vo, 2s 6d

INDUSTRIAL ARTS IN SPAIN. By JUAN F. RIANO.
With Illustrations. Large crown 8vo, 4s

GLASS. By ALEXANDER NESBITT. With Illustrations Large
crown 8vo, 2s. 6d

GOLD AND SILVER SMITH'S WORK By JOHN HUNGER-
FORD POLLEN With Illustrations. Large crown 8vo, 2s 6d

TAPESTRY. By ALFRED CHAMPEAUX. With Illustrations. 2s 6d.

BRONZES. By C DRURY E. FORTNUM, F.S.A With Illustrations.
Large crown 8vo, 2s. 6d

PLAIN WORDS ABOUT WATER. By A H CHURCH, M.A.,
Oxon With Illustrations. Large crown 8vo, sewed, 6d.

ANIMAL PRODUCTS: their Preparation, Commercial Uses,
and Value. By T. L SIMMONDS With Illustrations Large crown 8vo, 7s 6d

FOOD : A Short Account of the Sources, Constituents, and Uses
of Food; intended chiefly as a Guide to the Food Collection in the Bethnal Green
Museum By A. H CHURCH, M A., Oxon. Large crown 8vo, 3s

ECONOMIC ENTOMOLOGY By ANDREW MURRAY, F L.S.
APTERA. With Illustrations Large crown 8vo, 7s 6d.

JAPANESE POTTERY. Being a Native Report. Edited by
A. W. FRANKS With Illustrations and Marks. Large crown 8vo, 2s. 6d.

SOUTH KENSINGTON MUSEUM SCIENCE & ART HANDBOOKS—*Continued*

HANDBOOK TO THE SPECIAL LOAN COLLECTION
of Scientific Apparatus   Large crown 8vo, 3s.

INDUSTRIAL ARTS · Historical Sketches   With Illustrations.   Large crown 8vo, 3s.

TEXTILE FABRICS.   By the Very Rev DANIEL ROCK, D D.
With Illustrations.   Large crown 8vo, 2s. 6d.

JONES COLLECTION IN THE SOUTH KENSINGTON
MUSEUM.   With Portrait and Illustrations.   Large crown 8vo, 2s 6d

COLLEGE AND CORPORATION PLATE.   By WILFRED
CRIPPS   With Illustrations   Large crown 8vo, cloth, 2s 6d.

IVORIES. ANCIENT AND MEDIÆVAL.   By WILLIAM
MASKELL   With Illustrations   Large crown 8vo, 2s 6d

ANCIENT AND MODERN FURNITURE AND WOOD-
WORK.   By JOHN HUNGERFORD POLLEN   With Illustrations.   Large crown 8vo, 2s. 6d

MAIOLICA.   By C DRURY E. FORTNUM, F S.A   With Illustrations.   Large crown 8vo, 2s. 6d

THE CHEMISTRY OF FOODS.   With Microscopic Illustrations   By JAMES BELL, Principal of the Somerset House Laboratory
Part I.—Tea, Coffee, Cocoa, Sugar, &c.   Large crown 8vo, 2s. 6d
Part II.—Milk, Butter, Cereals, Prepared Starches, &c.   Large crown 8vo, 3s.

MUSICAL INSTRUMENTS   By CARL ENGEL.   With Illustrations.   Large crown 8vo, 2s 6d.

MANUAL OF DESIGN, compiled from the Writings and
Addresses of RICHARD REDGRAVE, R.A   By GILBERT R. REDGRAVE.   With Illustrations.   Large crown 8vo, 2s 6d

PERSIAN ART   By MAJOR R. MURDOCK SMITH, R.E   Second
Edition, with additional Illustrations   Large crown 8vo, 2s

CARLYLE'S (THOMAS) WORKS.

CHEAP AND UNIFORM EDITION.

In 23 vols, Crown 8vo, cloth, £7 5s.

THE FRENCH REVOLUTION.
A History. 2 vols, 12s.

OLIVER CROMWELL'S LET-
TERS AND SPEECHES, with Eluci-
dations, &c   3 vols, 18s

LIVES OF SCHILLER AND
JOHN STERLING   1 vol, 6s.

CRITICAL AND MISCELLA-
NEOUS ESSAYS   4 vols., £1 4s

SARTOR RESARTUS AND
LECTURES ON HEROES 1 vol, 6s.

LATTER-DAY PAMPHLETS
1 vol, 6s

CHARTISM AND PAST AND
PRESENT   1 vol, 6s

TRANSLATIONS FROM THE
GERMAN OF MUSÆUS, TIECK,
AND RICHTER.   1 vol, 6s.

WILHELM MEISTER, by Goethe.
A Translation   2 vols, 12s.

HISTORY OF FRIEDRICH THE
SECOND, called Frederick the Great.
7 vols., £3 9s

CARLYLE'S (THOMAS) WORKS.

SIXPENNY EDITION.

4to, sewed.

SARTOR RESARTUS Eightieth Thousand.

HEROES AND HERO WORSHIP.

ESSAYS: Burns, Johnson, Scott, The Diamond Necklace.

The above are also to be had in 1 vol., in cloth, 2s. 6d.

LIBRARY EDITION COMPLETE.

Handsomely printed in 34 vols., demy 8vo, cloth, £18 8s.

SARTOR RESARTUS The Life and Opinions of Herr Teufelsdröckh. With a Portrait, 7s. 6d

THE FRENCH REVOLUTION. A History. 3 vols., each 9s.

LIFE OF FREDERICK SCHILLER AND EXAMINATION OF HIS WORKS. With Supplement of 1872 Portrait and Plates, 9s.

CRITICAL AND MISCELLANEOUS ESSAYS. With Portrait. 6 vols , each 9s

ON HEROES, HERO WORSHIP, AND THE HEROIC IN HISTORY 7s 6d

PAST AND PRESENT. 9s.

OLIVER CROMWELL'S LETTERS AND SPEECHES. With Portraits. 5 vols , each 9s

LATTER-DAY PAMPHLETS 9s.

LIFE OF JOHN STERLING. With Portrait, 9s.

HISTORY OF FREDERICK THE SECOND. 10 vols., each 9s.

TRANSLATIONS FROM THE GERMAN. 3 vols , each 9s.

EARLY KINGS OF NORWAY, ESSAY ON THE PORTRAITS OF JOHN KNOX, AND GENERAL INDEX. With Portrait Illustrations. 8vo, cloth, 9s.

CARLYLE'S (THOMAS) WORKS.

PEOPLE'S EDITION.

In 37 vols., small crown 8vo. Price 2s. each vol., bound in cloth; or in sets of 37 vols. in 19, cloth gilt, for £3 14s.

SARTOR RESARTUS.

FRENCH REVOLUTION. 3 vols.

LIFE OF JOHN STERLING.

OLIVER CROMWELL'S LETTERS AND SPEECHES. 5 vols.

ON HEROES AND HERO WORSHIP

PAST AND PRESENT.

CRITICAL AND MISCELLANEOUS ESSAYS. 7 vols.

LATTER-DAY PAMPHLETS.

LIFE OF SCHILLER.

FREDERICK THE GREAT. 10 vols.

WILHELM MEISTER. 3 vols.

TRANSLATIONS FROM MUSÆUS, TIECK, AND RICHTER. 2 vols.

THE EARLY KINGS OF NORWAY, Essay on the Portraits of Knox; and General Index

---

DICKENS'S (CHARLES) WORKS.

ORIGINAL EDITIONS.

In demy 8vo.

THE MYSTERY OF EDWIN DROOD. With Illustrations by S. L. Fildes, and a Portrait engraved by Baker. Cloth, 7s. 6d.

OUR MUTUAL FRIEND. With Forty Illustrations by Marcus Stone. Cloth, £1 1s.

THE PICKWICK PAPERS. With Forty-three Illustrations by Seymour and Phiz. Cloth, £1 1s.

NICHOLAS NICKLEBY. With Forty Illustrations by Phiz. Cloth, £1 1s

SKETCHES BY "BOZ' With Forty Illustrations by George Cruikshank. Cloth, £1 1s

MARTIN CHUZZLEWIT With Forty Illustrations by Phiz. Cloth, £1 1s.

DOMBEY AND SON. With Forty Illustrations by Phiz. Cloth, £1 1s

DAVID COPPERFIELD. With Forty Illustrations by Phiz. Cloth, £1 1s.

BLEAK HOUSE. With Forty Illustrations by Phiz. Cloth, £1 1s.

LITTLE DORRIT. With Forty Illustrations by Phiz. Cloth, £1 1s.

DICKENS'S (CHARLES) WORKS

THE OLD CURIOSITY SHOP. With Seventy-five Illustrations by George Cattermole and H. K. Browne. A New Edition. Uniform with the other volumes, £1 1s.

BARNABY RUDGE: a Tale of the Riots of 'Eighty. With Seventy-eight Illustrations by George Cattermole and H. K. Browne. Uniform with the other volumes, £1 1s.

CHRISTMAS BOOKS: Containing—The Christmas Carol, The Cricket on the Hearth; The Chimes, The Battle of Life; The Haunted House. With all the original Illustrations. Cloth, 12s.

OLIVER TWIST and TALE OF TWO CITIES. In one volume. Cloth, £1 1s.

OLIVER TWIST. Separately. With Twenty-four Illustrations by George Cruikshank. Cloth, 11s.

A TALE OF TWO CITIES. Separately. With Sixteen Illustrations by Phiz. Cloth, 9s.

*** *The remainder of Dickens's Works were not originally printed in demy 8vo.*

LIBRARY EDITION.

In post 8vo. With the Original Illustrations, 30 vols., cloth, £12.

						s	d
PICKWICK PAPERS	..	...	..	.. 43 Illustrns.,	2 vols.	16	0
NICHOLAS NICKLEBY	...	..	...	.. 39	,, 2 vols.	16	0
MARTIN CHUZZLEWIT		.	..	. 40	,, 2 vols.	16	0
OLD CURIOSITY SHOP & REPRINTED PIECES			36	,, 2 vols.	16	0
BARNABY RUDGE and HARD TIMES	..		.. 36	,, 2 vols.	16	0
BLEAK HOUSE	.	..	.	. 40	,, 2 vols.	16	0
LITTLE DORRIT	...	..	..	 40	,, 2 vols.	16	0
DOMBEY AND SON	.		...	... 38	,, 2 vols.	16	0
DAVID COPPERFIELD	.	.		38	,, 2 vols.	16	0
OUR MUTUAL FRIEND	...	..		40	,, 2 vol.	16	0
SKETCHES BY "BOZ"		...		... 39	,, 1 vol.	8	0
OLIVER TWIST	.	..	...	. .. 24	,, 1 vol	8	0
CHRISTMAS BOOKS		..		... 17	,, 1 vol	8	0
A TALE OF TWO CITIES	..	.	.	. 16	,, 1 vol	8	0
GREAT EXPECTATIONS			.	. 8	,, 1 vol.	8	0
PICTURES FROM ITALY & AMERICAN NOTES				8	,, 1 vol	8	0
UNCOMMERCIAL TRAVELLER	.	..	. 8	,, 1 vol.	8	0
CHILD'S HISTORY OF ENGLAND		...	. 8	,, 1 vol	8	0
EDWIN DROOD and MISCELLANIES			12	,, 1 vol	8	0
CHRISTMAS STORIES from "Household Words," &c		14	,, 1 vol	8	0

THE LIFE OF CHARLES DICKENS. By JOHN FORSTER. With Illustrations. Uniform with this Edition 1 vol. 10s 6d.

A New Edition of above, with the Original Illustrations, in crown 8vo, 30 vols. in sets only.

DICKENS (CHARLES) WORKS

THE 'CHARLES DICKENS' EDITION.

In Crown 8vo. In 21 vols., cloth, with Illustrations, £3 16s.

		s.	d.
PICKWICK PAPERS	8 Illustrations	4	0
MARTIN CHUZZLEWIT	8 "	4	0
DOMBEY AND SON	8 "	4	0
NICHOLAS NICKLEBY	8 "	4	0
DAVID COPPERFIELD	8 "	4	0
BLEAK HOUSE	8 "	4	0
LITTLE DORRIT	8 "	4	0
OUR MUTUAL FRIEND	8 "	4	0
BARNABY RUDGE	8 "	3	6
OLD CURIOSITY SHOP	8 "	3	6
A CHILD'S HISTORY OF ENGLAND	4 "	3	6
EDWIN DROOD and OTHER STORIES	8 "	3	6
CHRISTMAS STORIES, from "Household Words"	8 "	3	6
SKETCHES BY "BOZ"	8 "	3	6
AMERICAN NOTES and REPRINTED PIECES	8 "	3	6
CHRISTMAS BOOKS	8 "	3	6
OLIVER TWIST	8 "	3	6
GREAT EXPECTATIONS	8 "	3	6
TALE OF TWO CITIES	8 "	3	0
HARD TIMES and PICTURES FROM ITALY	8 "	3	0
UNCOMMERCIAL TRAVELLER	4 "	3	0
THE LIFE OF CHARLES DICKENS Numerous Illustrations.	2 vols.	7	0
THE LETTERS OF CHARLES DICKENS	2 vols.	8	0

THE ILLUSTRATED LIBRARY EDITION.

Complete in 30 Volumes. Demy 8vo, 10s. each, or set, £15

This Edition is printed on a finer paper and in a larger type than has been employed in any previous edition. The type has been cast especially for it, and the page is of a size to admit of the introduction of all the original illustrations.

No such attractive issue has been made of the writings of Mr. Dickens, which, various as have been the forms of publication adapted to the demands of an ever widely-increasing popularity, have never yet been worthily presented in a really handsome library form.

The collection comprises all the minor writings it was Mr. Dickens's wish to preserve.

SKETCHES BY "BOZ." With 40 Illustrations by George Cruikshank.

PICKWICK PAPERS. 2 vols. With 42 Illustrations by Phiz.

OLIVER TWIST. With 24 Illustrations by Cruikshank.

NICHOLAS NICKLEBY. 2 vols. With 40 Illustrations by Phiz.

OLD CURIOSITY SHOP and REPRINTED PIECES. 2 vols. With Illustrations by Cattermole, &c.

DICKENS'S (CHARLES) WORKS

BARNABY RUDGE and HARD TIMES. 2 vols. With Illustrations by Cattermole, &c

MARTIN CHUZZLEWIT. 2 vols. With 40 Illustrations by Phiz.

AMERICAN NOTES and PICTURES FROM ITALY. 1 vol. With 8 Illustrations.

DOMBEY AND SON. 2 vols. With 40 Illustrations by Phiz.

DAVID COPPERFIELD. 2 vols. With 40 Illustrations by Phiz.

BLEAK HOUSE. 2 vols. With 40 Illustrations by Phiz.

LITTLE DORRIT. 2 vols. With 40 Illustrations by Phiz.

A TALE OF TWO CITIES. With 16 Illustrations by Phiz.

THE UNCOMMERCIAL TRAVELLER. With 8 Illustrations by Marcus Stone.

GREAT EXPECTATIONS. With 8 Illustrations by Marcus Stone

OUR MUTUAL FRIEND. 2 vols. With 40 Illustrations by Marcus Stone.

CHRISTMAS BOOKS. With 17 Illustrations by Sir Edwin Landseer, R A, Maclise, R A, &c. &c

HISTORY OF ENGLAND. With 8 Illustrations by Marcus Stone.

CHRISTMAS STORIES. (From "Household Words" and "All the Year Round") With 14 Illustrations

EDWIN DROOD AND OTHER STORIES. With 12 Illustrations by S L. Fildes.

HOUSEHOLD EDITION.

Complete in 22 Volumes. Crown 4to, cloth, £4 8s 6d.

MARTIN CHUZZLEWIT, with 59 Illustrations, cloth, 5s

DAVID COPPERFIELD, with 60 Illustrations and a Portrait, cloth, 5s

BLEAK HOUSE, with 61 Illustrations, cloth, 5s

LITTLE DORRIT, with 58 Illustrations, cloth, 5s

PICKWICK PAPERS, with 56 Illustrations, cloth, 5s

OUR MUTUAL FRIEND, with 58 Illustrations, cloth, 5s.

NICHOLAS NICKLEBY, with 59 Illustrations, cloth, 5s

DOMBEY AND SON with 61 Illustrations, cloth, 5s.

EDWIN DROOD; REPRINTED PIECES, and other Stories, with 30 Illustrations, cloth, 5s

THE LIFE OF DICKENS By JOHN FORSTER With 40 Illustrations. Cloth, 5s

BARNABY RUDGE, with 46 Illustrations, cloth, 4s.

OLD CURIOSITY SHOP, with 32 Illustrations, cloth, 4s

CHRISTMAS STORIES, with 23 Illustrations, cloth, 4s

OLIVER TWIST, with 28 Illustrations, cloth, 3s.

GREAT EXPECTATIONS, with 26 Illustrations, cloth, 3s.

SKETCHES BY "BOZ," with 36 Illustrations, cloth, 3s.

UNCOMMERCIAL TRAVELLER, with 26 Illustrations, cloth, 3s

CHRISTMAS BOOKS, with 28 Illustrations, cloth, 3s

DICKENS'S (CHARLES) WORKS

THE HISTORY OF ENGLAND, with 15 Illustrations, cloth, 3s

AMERICAN NOTES and PICTURES FROM ITALY, with 18 Illustrations, cloth, 3s.

A TALE OF TWO CITIES, with 25 Illustrations, cloth, 3s.

HARD TIMES, with 20 Illustrations, cloth, 2s 6d

MR. DICKENS'S READINGS.

Fcap. 8vo, sewed.

CHRISTMAS CAROL IN PROSE. 1s

CRICKET ON THE HEARTH. 1s

CHIMES. A GOBLIN STORY. 1s.

STORY OF LITTLE DOMBEY. 1s.

POOR TRAVELLER, BOOTS AT THE HOLLY-TREE INN, and MRS. GAMP. 1s.

A CHRISTMAS CAROL, with the Original Coloured Plates, being a reprint of the Original Edition. Small 8vo, red cloth, gilt edges, 5s.

THE POPULAR LIBRARY EDITION
OF THE WORKS OF
CHARLES DICKENS,

In 30 Vols., large crown 8vo, price £6; separate Vols. 4s. each.

An Edition printed on good paper, containing Illustrations selected from the Household Edition, on Plate Paper. Each Volume has about 450 pages and 16 full-page Illustrations.

SKETCHES BY "BOZ."

PICKWICK. 2 vols.

OLIVER TWIST.

NICHOLAS NICKLEBY. 2 vols.

MARTIN CHUZZLEWIT. 2 vols.

DOMBEY AND SON. 2 vols.

DAVID COPPERFIELD. 2 vols.

CHRISTMAS BOOKS.

OUR MUTUAL FRIEND. 2 vols.

CHRISTMAS STORIES.

BLEAK HOUSE. 2 vols.

LITTLE DORRIT. 2 vols.

OLD CURIOSITY SHOP AND REPRINTED PIECES 2 vols

BARNABY RUDGE. 2 vols.

UNCOMMERCIAL TRAVELLER

GREAT EXPECTATIONS.

TALE OF TWO CITIES.

CHILD'S HISTORY OF ENGLAND.

EDWIN DROOD AND MISCELLANIES.

PICTURES FROM ITALY AND AMERICAN NOTES.

DICKENS'S (CHARLES) WORKS

The Cheapest and Handiest Edition of

THE WORKS OF CHARLES DICKENS.

The Pocket-Volume Edition of Charles Dickens's Works.

In 30 Vols small fcap 8vo, £2 5s

New and Cheap Issue of

THE WORKS OF CHARLES DICKENS.

In pocket volumes.

PICKWICK PAPERS, with 8 Illustrations, cloth, 2s.
NICHOLAS NICKLEBY, with 8 Illustrations, cloth, 2s.
OLIVER TWIST, with 8 Illustrations, cloth, 1s.
SKETCHES BY "BOZ," with 8 Illustrations, cloth, 1s.
OLD CURIOSITY SHOP, with 8 Illustrations, cloth, 2s.
BARNABY RUDGE, with 16 Illustrations, cloth, 2s.
AMERICAN NOTES AND PICTURES FROM ITALY, with 8 Illustrations, cloth, 1s.6d.
CHRISTMAS BOOKS, with 8 Illustrations, cloth, 1s. 6d

SIXPENNY REPRINTS.

(I)

A CHRISTMAS CAROL AND THE HAUNTED MAN.

By CHARLES DICKENS. Illustrated.

(II.)

READINGS FROM THE WORKS OF CHARLES DICKENS.

As selected and read by himself and now published for the first time. Illustrated.

(III.)

THE CHIMES: A GOBLIN STORY, AND THE CRICKET ON THE HEARTH.

Illustrated.

(IV)

THE BATTLE OF LIFE; A LOVE STORY, HUNTED DOWN, AND A HOLIDAY ROMANCE. Illustrated.

List of Books, Drawing Examples, Diagrams, Models, Instruments, etc.,

INCLUDING

THOSE ISSUED UNDER THE AUTHORITY OF THE SCIENCE AND ART DEPARTMENT, SOUTH KENSINGTON, FOR THE USE OF SCHOOLS AND ART AND SCIENCE CLASSES.

CATALOGUE OF MODERN WORKS ON SCIENCE AND TECHNOLOGY. 8vo, sewed, 1s.

BENSON (W.)—
PRINCIPLES OF THE SCIENCE OF COLOUR. Small 4to, 15s.

MANUAL OF THE SCIENCE OF COLOUR. Coloured Frontispiece and Illustrations. 12mo, 2s. 6d.

BRADLEY (THOMAS), of the Royal Military Academy, Woolwich—
ELEMENTS OF GEOMETRICAL DRAWING. In Two Parts, with 60 Plates. Oblong folio, half-bound, each part 16s.
Selections (from the above) of 20 Plates, for the use of the Royal Military Academy, Woolwich. Oblong folio, half-bound, 16s.

BURCHETT—
LINEAR PERSPECTIVE. With Illustrations. Post 8vo, 7s.

PRACTICAL GEOMETRY. Post 8vo, 5s.

DEFINITIONS OF GEOMETRY. Third Edition 24mo, sewed, 5d.

CARROLL (JOHN)—
FREEHAND DRAWING LESSONS FOR THE BLACK BOARD. 6s

CUBLEY (W. H.)—
A SYSTEM OF ELEMENTARY DRAWING. With Illustrations and Examples. Imperial 4to, sewed, 3s. 6d.

DAVISON (ELLIS A.)—
DRAWING FOR ELEMENTARY SCHOOLS. Post 8vo, 3s.

MODEL DRAWING. 12mo, 3s.

DELAMOTTE (P. H.)—
PROGRESSIVE DRAWING-BOOK FOR BEGINNERS. 12mo, 3s. 6d

DYCE—
DRAWING-BOOK OF THE GOVERNMENT SCHOOL OF DESIGN ELEMENTARY OUTLINES OF ORNAMENT. 50 Plates. Small folio, sewed, 5s., mounted, 18s.

INTRODUCTION TO DITTO. Fcap. 8vo, 6d.

FOSTER (VERE)—
DRAWING-BOOKS :
Forty-six Numbers, at 3d each
DRAWING-CARDS
Freehand Drawing First Grade, Sets I , II , III , 1s each,
Second Grade, Set I , 2s

HENSLOW (PROFESSOR)—
ILLUSTRATIONS TO BE EMPLOYED IN THE
PRACTICAL LESSONS ON BOTANY. Post 8vo, sewed, 6d

JACOBSTHAL (E)—
GRAMMATIK DER ORNAMENTE, in 7 Parts of 20
Plates each. Unmounted, £3 13s 6d , mounted on cardboard, £11 4s The
Parts can be had separately

JEWITT—
HANDBOOK OF PRACTICAL PERSPECTIVE. 18mo,
1s. 6d

LINDLEY (JOHN)—
SYMMETRY OF VEGETATION Principles to be
Observed in the Delineation of Plants. 12mo, sewed, 1s

MARSHALL—
HUMAN BODY. Text and Plates reduced from the large
Diagrams 2 vols , £2 1s

NEWTON (E TULLEY), F G S.—
THE TYPICAL PARTS IN THE SKELETONS OF A
CAT, DUCK, AND CODFISH, being a Catalogue with Comparative De-
scriptions arranged in a Tabular Form. Demy 8vo, 3s

OLIVER (PROFESSOR)—
ILLUSTRATIONS OF THE VEGETABLE KINGDOM.
109 Plates. Oblong 8vo Plain, 16s., coloured, £1 6s

POYNTER (E J), R.A , issued under the superintendence of—
THE SOUTH KENSINGTON DRAWING SERIES.
FREEHAND—ELEMENTARY ORNAMENT· books 6d., cards,
9d. each.
FREEHAND—FIRST GRADE · books 6d , cards 1s. each
FREEHAND—SECOND GRADE books 1s., cards 1s. 6d each.
FREEHAND—PLANTS FROM NATURE . books 6d., cards,
1s. each
FREEHAND—HUMAN FIGURE, ELEMENTARY: books 6d.
FREEHAND—HUMAN FIGURE, ADVANCED books 2s.
each
FREEHAND—FIGURES FROM THE CARTOONS OF
RAPHAEL four books, 2s. each.
FREEHAND—ELEMENTARY PERSPECTIVE DRAWING
By S. J. Cartlidge, F.R.Hist S. Books 1s. each; or one
volume, cloth, 5s.

REDGRAVE—
MANUAL AND CATECHISM ON COLOUR Fifth
Edition. 24mo, sewed, 9d.

ROBSON (GEORGE)—
ELEMENTARY BUILDING CONSTRUCTION. Oblong
folio, sewed, 8s.

WALLIS (GEORGE)—
    DRAWING-BOOK. Oblong, sewed, 3s. 6d., mounted, 8s.

WORNUM (R N)—
    THE CHARACTERISTICS OF STYLES · An Introduction to the Study of the History of Ornamental Art   Royal 8vo, 8s.

ELEMENTARY DRAWING COPY-BOOKS, for the Use of Children from four years old and upwards, in Schools and Families. Compiled by a Student certificated by the Science and Art Department as an Art Teacher. Seven Books in 4to, sewed.

Book I. Letters, 8d	Book IV Objects, 8d
„ II Ditto, 8d	„ V Leaves, 8d
„ III. Geometrical and Ornamental Forms, 8d.	„ VI Birds, Animals, &c , 8d
	„ VII. Leaves, Flowers, and Sprays 8d

. Or in Sets of Seven Books, 4s 6d

ENGINEER AND MACHINIST DRAWING-BOOK, 16 Parts, 71 Plates Folio, £1 12s., mounted, £3 4s

PRINCIPLES OF DECORATIVE ART. Folio, sewed, 1s

DIAGRAM OF THE COLOURS OF THE SPECTRUM, with Explanatory Letterpress, on roller, 10s 6d.

COPIES FOR OUTLINE DRAWING.
    LARGE FREEHAND EXAMPLES FOR CLASS TEACHING   Specially prepared under the authority of the Science and Art Department   Six Sheets Size 60 by 40. 9s
    DYCE'S ELEMENTARY OUTLINES OF ORNAMENT, 50 Selected Plates, mounted back and front, 18s., unmounted, sewed, 5s
    WEITBRICHT'S OUTLINES OF ORNAMENT, reproduced by Herman, 12 Plates, mounted back and front, 8s. 6d , unmounted, 2s.
    MORGHEN'S OUTLINES OF THE HUMAN FIGURE, reproduced by Herman, 20 Plates, mounted back and front, 15s , unmounted, 3s 4d
    TARSIA, from Gruner, Four Plates, mounted, 3s 6d , unmounted, 7d
    ALBERTOLLI'S FOLIAGE, Four Plates, mounted, 3s 6d , unmounted, 5d.
    OUTLINE OF TRAJAN FRIEZE, mounted, 1s
    WALLIS'S DRAWING-BOOK, mounted, 8s., unmounted, 3s. 6d
    OUTLINE DRAWINGS OF FLOWERS, Eight Plates, mounted, 3s 6d , unmounted, &c

COPIES FOR SHADED DRAWING ·
    COURSE OF DESIGN   By Ch Bargue (French), 20 Sheets, £2 9s
    ARCHITECTURAL STUDIES. By J B Tripon   10 Plates, £1
    MECHANICAL STUDIES   By J B Tripon   15s per dozen.
    FOLIATED SCROLL FROM THE VATICAN, unmounted, 5d., mounted, 1s. 3d.
    TWELVE HEADS after Holbein, selected from his Drawings in Her Majesty's Collection at Windsor   Reproduced in Autotype. Half imperial, £1 16s
    LESSONS IN SEPIA, 9s. per dozen

COLOURED EXAMPLES ·
    A SMALL DIAGRAM OF COLOUR, mounted, 1s. 6d ; unmounted, 9d
    COTMAN'S PENCIL LANDSCAPES (set of 9), mounted, 15s.
        „   SEPIA DRAWINGS (set of 5), mounted, £1.
    ALLONGE'S LANDSCAPES IN CHARCOAL (Six), at 4s. each, or the set, £1 4s.

SOLID MODELS, &c. :
    *Box of Models, £1 4s
    A Stand with a universal joint, to show the solid models, &c., £1 18s.
    *One Wire Quad-angle, with a circle and cross within it, and one straight wire. One solid cube. One Skeleton Wire Cube. One Sphere   One Cone. One Cylinder, One Hexagonal Prism. £2 2s

SOLID MODELS, &c.—*Continued.*

Skeleton Cube in wood, 3s 6d

18-inch Skeleton Cube in wood, 12s

*Three objects of *form* in Pottery

Indian Jar,   ⎫
Celadon Jar,   ⎬ 18s. 6d
Bottle,   ⎭

*Five selected Vases in Majolica Ware, £2 11s

*Three selected Vases in Earthenware, 18s

Imperial Deal Frames, glazed, without sunk rings, 10s. each.

*Davidson's Smaller Solid Models, in Box, £2, containing—

2 Square Slabs	Octagon Prism	Triangular Prism
9 Oblong Blocks (steps)	Cylinder	Pyramid, Equilateral
2 Cubes	Cone.	Pyramid, Isosceles
Square Blocks.	Jointed Cross	Square Block.

*Davidson's Advanced Drawing Models, £9.—The following is a brief description of the Models.—An Obelisk—composed of 2 Octagonal Slabs, 26 and 20 inches across, and each 3 inches high, 1 Cube, 12 inches edge, 1 Monolith (forming the body of the obelisk) 3 feet high, 1 Pyramid, 6 inches base, the complete object is thus nearly 5 feet high. A Market Cross—composed of 3 Slabs, 24, 18, and 12 inches across, and each 3 inches high, 1 Upright, 3 feet high, 2 Cross Arms, united by mortise and tenon joints, complete height, 3 feet 9 inches. A Step Ladder, 23 inches high. A Kitchen Table, 14½ inches high. A Chair to correspond. A Four-legged Stool, with projecting top and cross rails, height 14 inches. A Tub, with handles and projecting hoops, and the divisions between the staves plainly marked. A strong Trestle, 28 inches high. A Hollow Cylinder, 9 inches in diameter, and 12 inches long, divided lengthwise. A Hollow Sphere, 9 inches in diameter, divided into semi spheres, one of which is again divided into quarters, the semi sphere, when placed on the cylinder, gives the form and principles of shading a dome, whilst one of the quarters placed on half the cylinder forms a niche

*Davidson's Apparatus for Teaching Practical Geometry (22 models), £5

*Binn's Models for Illustrating the Elementary Principles of Orthographic Projection as applied to Mechanical Drawing, in box, £1 10s

Miller's Class Drawing Models.—These Models are particularly adapted for teaching large classes, the stand is very strong, and the universal joint will hold the Models in any position. *Wood Models* Square Prism, 12 inches side, 18 inches high. Hexagonal Prism, 14 inches side, 18 inches high; Cube, 14 inches side. Cylinder, 13 inches diameter, 16 inches high. Hexagon Pyramid, 14 inches diameter, 22½ inches side. Square Pyramid, 14 inches side, 22½ inches side. Cone, 13 inches diameter, 22½ inches side. Skeleton Cube, 19 inches solid wood 1¾ inch square. Intersecting Circles, 19 inches solid wood 2¼ by 1½ inches. *Wire Models* Triangular Prism, 17 inches side, 22 inches high. Square Prism, 14 inches side, 20 inches high. Hexagonal Prism, 16 inches diameter, 21 inches high. Cylinder, 14 inches diameter, 21 inches high. Hexagon Pyramid, 18 inches diameter, 24 inches high. Square Pyramid, 17 inches side, 24 inches high. Cone, 17 inches side, 24 inches high. Skeleton Cube, 19 inches side. Intersecting Circles, 19 inches side. Plain Circle, 19 inches side. Plain Square, 19 inches side. Table, 27 inches by 21½ inches. Stand. The set complete, £14 13s.

Vulcanite Set Square, 5s

Large Compasses, with chalk holder, 5s.

*Slip, two set squares and **T** square, 5s

*Parkes's Case of Instruments, containing 6 inch compasses with pen and pencil leg, 5s.

*Prize Instrument Case, with 6 inch compasses pen and pencil leg, 2 small compasses, pen and scale, 18s

6 inch Compasses, with shifting pen and point, 4s 6d

* Models, &c., entered as sets, can only be supplied in sets

LARGE DIAGRAMS.

ASTRONOMICAL :

TWELVE SHEETS   By JOHN DREW, Ph. Dr., F.R.S A.   Sheets, £2 8s, on rollers and varnished, £4 4s

BOTANICAL

NINE SHEETS Illustrating a Practical Method of Teaching Botany By Professor Henslow, F.L S £2, on rollers and varnished, £3 3s

CLASS	DIVISION	SECTION	DIAGRAM
Dicotyledon	Angiospermous	Thalamifloral .	1
		Calycifloral	2 & 3
		Corollifloral .	4
		Incomplete	5
	Gymrospermous		6
Monocotyledons	Petaloid	Superior	7
		Inferior .	8
	Glumaceous		9

* Models, &c., entered as sets, can only be supplied in sets.

BUILDING CONSTRUCTION:

TEN SHEETS By William J Glenny In sets, £1 1s

LAXTON'S EXAMPLES OF BUILDING CONSTRUCTION, containing 32 Imperial Plates, £1

BUSBRIDGE S DRAWING OF BUILDING CONSTRUCTION. 36 Sheets 9s Mounted on cardboard, 18s

GEOLOGICAL:

DIAGRAM OF BRITISH STRATA. By H W. Bristow, F R S, F G S A Sheet, 4s.; on roller and varnished, 7s 6d

MECHANICAL:

DIAGRAMS OF THE MECHANICAL POWERS, AND THEIR APPLICATIONS IN MACHINERY AND THE ARTS GENERALLY By Dr John Anderson 8 Diagrams, highly coloured, on stout paper, 3 feet 6 inches by 2 feet 6 inches Sheets £1, mounted on rollers, £2.

DIAGRAMS OF THE STEAM ENGINE By Prof Goodeve and Prof Shelley Stout paper, 40 inches by 27 inches, highly coloured. 41 Diagrams (52½ Sheets), £6 6s.; varnished and mounted on rollers, £11 11s.

MACHINE DETAILS. By Prof Unwin. 16 Coloured Diagrams. Sheets, £2 2s, mounted on rollers and varnished, £3 14s.

SELECTED EXAMPLES OF MACHINES, OF IRON AND WOOD (French) By Stanislas Pettit 60 Sheets, £3 5s, 13s. per dozen

BUSBRIDGE'S DRAWINGS OF MACHINE CONSTRUCTION. 50 Sheets, 12s 6d. Mounted, £1 5s

PHYSIOLOGICAL:

ELEVEN SHEETS Illustrating Human Physiology, Life Size and Coloured from Nature Prepared under the direction of John Marshall, F R S, F R C S, &c Each Sheet, 12s 6d. On canvas and rollers, varnished, £1 1s.

1 THE SKELETON AND LIGAMENTS

2 THE MUSCLES, JOINTS, AND ANIMAL MECHANICS.

3 THE VISCERA IN POSITION —THE STRUCTURE OF THE LUNGS

4 THE ORGANS OF CIRCULATION

5 THE LYMPHATICS OR ABSORBENTS

6 THE ORGANS OF DIGESTION.

7 THE BRAIN AND NERVES —THE ORGANS OF THE VOICE.

8 & 9 THE ORGANS OF THE SENSES

10 & 11 THE MICROSCOPIC STRUCTURE OF THE TEXTURES AND ORGANS

HUMAN BODY, LIFE SIZE By John Marshall, F R S, F R C S Each Sheet, 12s. 6d , on canvas and rollers, varnished, £1 1s Explanatory Key, 1s

1, 2, 3 THE SKELETON, Front Back, and Side View

5, 6, 7 THE MUSCLES, Front, Back, and Side View.

ZOOLOGICAL

TEN SHEETS. Illustrating the Classification of Animals. By Robert Patterson. £2, on canvas and rollers, varnished, £3 10s.

PHYSIOLOGY AND ANATOMY OF THE HONEY BEE.

Two Diagrams 7s. 6d

THE FORTNIGHTLY REVIEW.

Edited by T. H. S. ESCOTT.

THE FORTNIGHTLY REVIEW is published on the 1st of every month, and a Volume is completed every Six Months

The following are among the Contributors :—

SIR RUTHERFORD ALCOCK.
MATHEW ARNOLD
PROFESSOR BAIN
SIR SAMUEL BAKER
PROFESSOR BEESLY
PAUL BERT
BARON GEORGETON BUNSEN
DR. BRIDGES
HON. GEORGE C. BRODRICK
JAMES BRYCE, M P
THOMAS BURT, M P
SIR GEORGE CAMPBELL, M.P.
THE EARL OF CARNARVON
EMILIO CASTELAR
RT HON J CHAMBERLAIN, M.P.
PROFESSOR SIDNEY COLVIN
MONTAGUE COOKSON, Q C.
L. H COURTNEY, M P
G H. DARWIN
SIR GEORGE W. DASENT.
PROFESSOR A. V. DICEY
RIGHT HON H FAWCETT, M.P
EDWARD A FREEMAN
SIR BARTLE FRERE, Bart
J A FROUDE
MRS GARRET-ANDERSON.
J W L. GLAISHER, F R S
M E. GRANT DUFF, M P
THOMAS HARE
F HARRISON.
LORD HOUGHTON
PROFESSOR HUXLEY
PROFESSOR R C JEBB.
PROFESSOR JEVONS
ANDREW LANG
ÉMILE DE LAVELEYE.

T E CLIFFE LESLIE
SIR JOHN LUBBOCK, M P.
THE EARL LYTTON.
SIR H S. MAINE
DR MAUDSLEY.
PROFESSOR MAX MULLER.
G OSBORNE MORGAN, Q C , M P
PROFESSOR HENRY MORLEY
WILLIAM MORRIS.
PROFESSOR H. N. MOSELEY
F W H MYERS
F W NEWMAN
PROFESSOR JOHN NICHOL
W G. PALGRAVE
WALTER H. PATER.
RT HON LYON PLAYFAIR, M P.
DANTE GABRIEL ROSSETTI
LORD SHERBROOKE.
HERBERT SPENCER.
HON E L STANLEY.
SIR J FITZJAMES STEPHEN, Q C.
LESLIE STEPHEN
J HUTCHISON STIRLING
A C SWINBURNE.
DR VON SYBEL.
J A. SYMONDS.
THE REV EDWARD F TALBOT
(WARDEN OF KEBLE COLLEGE).
SIR RICHARD TEMPLE, Bart
W T. THORNTON
HON LIONEL A. TOLLEMACHE.
H. D TRAILL.
ANTHONY TROLLOPE
PROFESSOR TYNDALL.
A J WILSON
THE EDITOR

&c. &c &c.

THE FORTNIGHTLY REVIEW *is published at 2s. 6d.*

CHAPMAN & HALL, LIMITED, 11, HENRIETTA STREET, COVENT GARDEN, W C.

CHARLES DICKENS AND EVANS,]   [CRYSTAL PALACE PRESS

CPSIA information can be obtained at www.ICGtesting.com
Printed in the USA
LVOW111654060313

323028LV00006B/269/P